OPENLY BOB

OPENLY *BOB*

Bob Smith

ROB WEISBACH BOOKS

William Morrow and Company, Inc. New York

Published by Rob Weisbach Books
An Imprint of William Morrow and Company, Inc.
1350 Avenue of the Americas, New York, N.Y. 10019

It is the policy of William Morrow and Company, Inc., and
its imprints and affiliates, recognizing the importance of pre-
serving what has been written, to print the books we publish
on acid-free paper, and we exert our best efforts to that end.

Library of Congress Cataloging-in-Publication Data
has been applied for.

ISBN 0-688-15120-5

Printed in the United States of America

First Edition

1 2 3 4 5 6 7 8 9 10

BOOK DESIGN BY RICHARD ORIOLO

For Tom

Contents

Nostradamus Said There'd Be Days Like This

THE PLANE is going to land in Buffalo in ten minutes. I feel Tom tense up when the flight attendant makes the announcement. Tom took half a Xanax, but tranquilizers don't alleviate his anxiety about flying, they only make it more casual. Instead of brooding about doom and destruction, he relaxes and mentions possible crash scenarios with the breeziness of a businessman trying to pick a good restaurant. I sometimes think that I'm able to relax *only* on airplanes: It's as if the Universe said, "You'll fret about every other area in your life, but at thirty thousand feet, that's where you'll really be able to kick back." I like that air travel is an opportunity to shirk all your responsibilities and put your life completely in someone else's hands. Riding in an airplane can be compared to taking a car trip with

your parents when you were a kid. You know your destination but have no idea how to get there, you have about the same amount of leg room that you did when you sat with your brothers in the backseat, and you're still expected to sit quietly and amuse yourself without bothering the other passengers. Unfortunately, now it's *really* not acceptable to cause a commotion by deliberately poking someone with a pencil.

I'm glad that we're visiting my parents for Thanksgiving because I prefer it to Christmas. It involves shopping at only one store, a supermarket, and you never have to save the receipts to return something, even if you discover that the turkey you bought is too big. Thanksgiving is also the perfect holiday for families to come together because it's based on the great American tradition of people who could just as easily kill one another trying to ignore their differences over a heavy meal.

As we walk off the plane, I start to feel a vague anxiety that makes me feel right at home because our favorite holiday traditions are emotional discomfort and unfocused guilt. They've been in the family for generations. My parents are standing at the gate and my first thought is that they look so old. It then occurs to me that my parents might be thinking the same thing about me. I suspect this because my mother, after saying hello, looks closely and says with a note of concern in her voice, "Bob, you look tired." Which as an unwelcome greeting ranks right up there with "You're under arrest. You have the right to remain silent. . . ." Why would anyone feel compelled to inform someone about their rested status? There's nothing restorative about the observation. Is the idea that lowering another person's self-esteem slows down the metabolism and allows rejuvenation to occur? Like most creative types in Manhattan, I take pride in the dark circles under my eyes, the halos of artistic sainthood. Tom proceeds to firmly grasp my father's hand

because he's been warned that my father judges people by the quality of their handshakes—an odd method of determining character by a man who doesn't always have a solid grip on reality. He once told me, "Bob, I like your friends because all the men have very solid handshakes, and come to think of it, all the women do too." We then proceed to the three traditional ice-breaking questions asked at every airport reunion:

1. Your dad asks, "Can I carry something?"

2. Your mom asks, "Did you eat?"

3. You ask, "Were you waiting long?"

In the parking lot I have to decide whether to accept my mother's offer to sit up front with my father or sit in the back with Tom. Every time I visit my parents I change time zones—I have to set my watch back to my childhood. Tom and I ride in the backseat, which does inexplicably make everything momentarily seem smaller, and even though it's only ten A.M., I have a sudden urge to stop for an ice cream. As the car passes several fast-food restaurants, my mother warns, "Are you sure you don't want to get something to eat now?" She's concerned because we're not going to be able to eat again for another fifteen or twenty minutes. Since my father has retired from the state police, food has become the major focal point of my parents' lives. This has actually made my visits home more enjoyable, because after a certain age eating and drinking are the only activities that most parents and children still honestly enjoy doing together. As we drive to their house, my parents' only comments are capsule reviews of passing restaurants.

"We should go to Chi-Chi's while you're here. They have really good margaritas."

"There's Damon's. They have really good ribs but we like the one near us better."

"We tried The Olive Garden. I wasn't too crazy about it. Remember that Italian bakery you took me to in New York? What was its name?"

"Veniero's."

"That was really good."

I'm afraid that at some point when we visit, instead of bringing me up to date on our family, my mother will start giving us progress reports on some of the waiters they know at their favorite restaurants: *Do you remember Sally at The Ground Round? She's thinking of quitting because the manager there wants her to work Thursdays and she's told him that's the night of her wood-refinishing class.*

One of the first announcements my mother makes after one of her children has returned for a visit is that she went grocery shopping before we arrived. She plans every possible meal and snack that could be needed during our visit with the thoroughness of a hospital dietitian. The refrigerator is so overstuffed that you can practically see the eggs pressing through the door. It's as if she's terrified that one of her children will have a sudden craving for a food that can't be procured immediately. Whatever happened to the mother who didn't want her children to eat too much junk because it would spoil their appetites? My mother has become the Anti-Mom, tempting her children with sinfully rich foods of never less than 666 calories.

"Bob, while you're here I want you to have your favorite meal."

It's sweet of my mother to say that. She always makes this offer when I come home. Out of respect for her feelings, I don't mention that my favorite meal now is having dinner with friends in New York, not eating her meatloaf while listening to her yell at my father for eating cashews before dinner—*when he should know better with his diverticulitis.*

"Boy, it's really cold today."

Tom says this in an attempt to make conversation. This is a big mistake. In most places, it's considered good advice to never talk about religion and politics if you want to avoid an argument. Buffalo is the only city where talking about the weather is also considered to be a risky subject. If you mention the weather in Buffalo, you will start a blizzard of anecdotes about the worst winter survived, foggy predictions about whether it's going to be a bad or good winter ranging from Nostradamus to *The Farmer's Almanac,* heated discussions about the windchill factor, and dry explanations about the Lake Effect, which is when the Arctic air of Canada blows over the warmer Lake Erie, thereby creating mass quantities of snow.

"Tom, it's not cold today. Last winter, it got so cold that you could get frostbite going from the house to the garage."

"No, that was the winter before."

"All right, Sue."

At this point I start to worry that the car will skid on the ice forming between my parents. My memories of Buffalo are separated by the seasons of summer and winter. They're almost like episodes from the television series that I liked to watch growing up during the 1960s. Some of my memories, like some of the episodes of *Bewitched* and *Lost in Space,* are in black and white and some are in color, but they all have the same cast and settings. It's difficult to appreciate Buffalo at this time of year because even though it's still early in the winter, all the cars and street signs are already covered in a gray mixture of soot and road salt. It's as if the highway department is determined to prove that with the right amount of seasoning, asphalt can be quite palatable.

"It's too bad no one else could get home now."

I say this because it suddenly strikes me that Tom and I are going to be the complete center of attention for this entire visit.

My father says, "Yeah, Ted has to work. Carol and Mark are going to his parents, and John and his new girlfriend are going skiing in Colorado."

My mother adds, "They're all going to try to come home at Christmas. And you'll be at Tom's parents down in Florida. I bet they'll be glad to see you."

While we're driving in the car my mother discusses several possible people we should visit. Of course, she says, she's just making some suggestions—we should do what we want to do. I don't understand why she wants me to see relatives whom I avoided when I still lived at home. It's as if she needs to reconfirm that I still don't enjoy their company. "Mom, we'll see if there's time to visit Aunt Lorraine," I lie. My mother isn't even particularly fond of Aunt Lorraine because my mother is more judgmental than Jehovah in the Old Testament. Whenever she mentions Aunt Lorraine it's usually with a slow, disapproving shaking of her head, "The last time I went over there—at two in the afternoon—she was still in her housecoat, the sink was full of dishes. . . . I couldn't live like that."

We stop at Anderson's, a landmark fast-food restaurant that has attracted droves of Buffalonians for decades. Their specialties are huge roast beef sandwiches and custard ice cream. The portions are stupendous. There's enough meat in each sandwich to reassemble the cow. I've traveled to many of America's cities and Buffalo does have the best junk food in the country. If Chicago is the City of Broad Shoulders, then Buffalo should be the City of Wide Asses. After all, this is where Buffalo-Style Chicken Wings were invented. Leave it to a Buffalonian to take an inedible piece of meat, fry it in grease, slather it with excruciating hot sauce, and then, in a moment of culinary genius, dunk it in chunky blue cheese dressing.

When we reach my parents' house, our dog Smitty

welcomes us with a little howl of recognition and so much tail-wagging enthusiasm that she starts to pee all over the floor. A dog's unconditional love can really deform your standards of human affection. When I was in therapy, I should've realized that one of my problems is that after years of being welcomed by Smitty, I now question the sincerity of anyone who greets me without wetting themselves. My parents still live in the house I grew up in on Palmer Avenue. We bring our luggage upstairs to my old bedroom and while we're going upstairs my mother calls out, "There's extra blankets if you get cold up there." After she says this I recall that when I brought Tom home for the first time, I wondered if my mother was going to talk about the sleeping arrangements. It was a relief when she dealt with the situation by completely ignoring it—which just goes to show that there are times when having an uncommunicative, repressed family can be a real benefit. It still seems a little weird to be sleeping with Tom in this room. When I was a teenager fantasizing about different guys, it never occurred to me that someday I'd be bringing one home.

After we unpack we go downstairs and continue to stretch out that initial awkward moment to a full four days. Tom is much more comfortable now that he's been through several visits to my parents'. When I first brought him home, I made the mistake of trying to brief him on all the strange things my parents do, in the naive belief that my family was really peculiar and that all other families were somehow more "normal." But what I forgot to consider was that the weirdest things your parents do, they've been doing for your entire life and they've warped your standards of normalcy. After our first night at my parents', I was caught by surprise when Tom asked, "Does your mother always wear that blue foam-rubber helmet when she goes to bed?" I was shocked. It had never occurred to me that my mother has always been overprotective about her hair.

That first night we went out to dinner with my parents to one of their favorite restaurants. We had wine, which made the meal much more pleasant. It's a shame that alcohol isn't customarily served to children in America. I've read that in France children are served wine mixed with water from an early age, whereas here that would probably be considered a form of abuse. But I believe that having a glass of wine with dinner might have improved some of the more stressful meals that we had while growing up. It certainly would've been much easier to show your dad a bad report card after everyone had a couple glasses of chardonnay. At the end of the meal, Tom and I offer to pick up the check, which is a ritual that we always go through. We offer; my father insists on paying. He still reserves the father's prerogative to be the family bread winner even if that now involves nothing more strenuous than asking a waitress for more rolls at a restaurant.

Watching television with my parents is a big part of most of my visits home. What could be more sentimental than sitting in the living room and after watching an hour of sit-coms to have your mom say, "There's ice cream in the freezer if you guys want a snack later." I worry that my parents watch too much television. I've noticed that after my father retired, their viewing habits changed. They now watch morning programs because they have the time for leisurely breakfasts. They've become too media savvy. It's disconcerting to hear your mother say when Kevin Costner appears on television, "He needs a hit." Tom and I are always interested in my mother's opinions about celebrities because she has a gift for mispronouncing their names. She once called Liza Minnelli "Lisa," and after her and my father's first trip to Las Vegas she referred to Siegfried and Roy as "Sigmund and Freud." Tom and I now share a fantasy of "Lisa" Minnelli being Liza's drab, nonperforming alter ego. My parents have also become avid movie view-

ers since my brother John gave them a VCR last Christmas. They rent movies for a dollar at the supermarket and their reviews are better than most professional film critics.

My father will start, "We watched that movie *Good Son, Bad Son.*"

Then my mother will gently correct him, "*The Good Son* with Macaulay Culkin."

"Yeah. But we didn't watch the whole thing. It was too violent. They threw a kid off a bridge!"

"Matt, it was a dummy," she'll say with exasperation.

"I don't care."

And my mother has better commercial instincts than half the producers in Hollywood.

"I saw an ad for that movie *Nell.* I don't want to see it. Jodie Foster plays a backwoods girl with perfect teeth."

Every night we have to negotiate which programs to watch. My mother does all the negotiating because I think my father believes that having a preference for any television show is somehow unmanly. There are a few shows that we all enjoy, but the difficult thing is asking your parents to watch a show that you know that they'll have no interest in. I try to convince myself that my parents might enjoy watching *The X-Files.* But however capable we are of continuing to grow intellectually as we age, it seems unduly optimistic to expect sixty-three-year-olds to suddenly develop an interest in extra-terrestrials and mutants at this point in their lives.

As the night progresses, I'm hoping that my parents decide to go to bed before the local news at 11. The reason why I harbor this strange desire is because it seems that the local news always runs at least one story that makes me feel uncomfortable to watch with my parents. Is it just a coincidence or do they always apprehend a psychotic homosexual killer whenever Tom and I visit? I know on a rational level that I shouldn't feel responsible for the behavior of every gay man, but

having been raised Roman Catholic, I'm capable of producing guilt from nothing. It's like the miracle of the loaves and fishes.

"Tom, do you want a pillow for your head? Bob, hand Tom a pillow."

Tom's lying on the floor watching television and he thanks my mother for her concern and then thanks me as I hand him one. My mother now treats Tom better than she treats her own children. This is quite a change from when I first insisted on bringing him home. At that time, she warned that it would be too stressful for my father to meet Tom, which really meant that it was going to be too stressful for her. But we came anyway and, of course, she liked Tom immediately. My sister, Carol, has told me that now my mother holds Tom up as an example to her own children. Let me explain that the communication system in our family is that my mother talks about her children to the other children who then report back to the object of discussion on what my mother's been saying about them. It's my mother's version of the Internet. Anyway, after that first Christmas, my mother called my sister and said, "I've been reading that gays are very involved with fashion and then I remembered that Tom gave me the nicest Christmas gift of any of you. I returned all yours. You gave me a Rancho Cucamonga T-shirt for Christ's sake." This Christmas, all of her children have decided to chip in and buy my mother a display case for her prized collection of small misunderstandings and resentments.

After my parents go to bed, Tom and I have an opportunity to review and discuss the events of the day. One of the most desirable benefits of being in a relationship is that it gives one the opportunity to talk about people behind their backs without the social stigma of being considered a gossip. There's a profound difference between sharing your thoughts and opinions with the person who you share your life with and sharing the

same disparaging remarks with a stranger at a cocktail party.

While Tom and I lie in bed the next morning, we can already smell the turkey roasting. During our first cup of coffee, my mother announces that we'll just have something light for lunch because we're going to have an early dinner. For my parents, Thanksgiving is almost like going on a diet because they normally overeat so much every day that Thanksgiving is an opportunity for them to cut down by just consuming one huge meal.

It hasn't been properly acknowledged that Thanksgiving and Christmas are incredibly boring holidays. Families are cooped up in the house all day and the only recreational activities are watching television and eating. And since these two days are just about the only time most modern families spend entirely together it sends out a negative reinforcement that time spent with your family is dull. Instead of bringing families closer together, the holidays probably push them apart. During the morning, we watch part of the Macy's Thanksgiving Day Parade and then my father watches football. Later on, Tom and I read the newspaper and all the back issues of *Reader's Digest*. My mother must be a little bored, too, because at one point she says to me, "Bob, don't tell me you *still* bite your nails?"

Sometimes I don't understand why we're not the most psychologically well-adjusted family in America because we're not in denial about anything. We never get a chance to be because my mother never stops reminding her children of their various faults.

"Carol, do you really need that cookie?"

"John, how many drinks is that?"

"Ted, you'll never meet anyone if you keep that attitude."

During the day, my brothers and my sister call from various parts of the country. It's interesting watching my parents when they carry on a telephone conversation. My

mother or father will be talking to one of their children while the other simultaneously corrects and/or comments. I think that when the last child leaves the house, all parents should be required to buy speaker phones. It's surprising that the telephone companies haven't picked up on this marketing opportunity. A speaker phone would allow parents to bicker with ease while talking to their children.

Around five o'clock we sit down for dinner. There are only four of us, but my mother has made enough food for nine people on the principle that any absent family members should have physical proof of what they're missing. We have a lot to be thankful for this year. I try to concentrate on our health, love, material blessings, but the thoughts flash through my mind like a spiritual music video and I always feel that if I leave something out of my Thanksgiving inventory, God will decide that I don't care about that one thing and make trouble. No wonder I become depressed during the holidays. My mother soon makes her annual comment on how moist the turkey is this year. We all murmur agreement thereby closing the subject of poultry humidity until next Thanksgiving. I have two huge helpings of mashed potatoes and gravy and then wait patiently for my body to be stunned by the saturated fats and carbohydrates. At the end of the meal, my mother always suggests waiting for the food to settle before having dessert. She makes it sound like we're washing machines and she's waiting before adding the fabric softener.

Before going to bed, Tom and I decide that the next day we want to go shopping downtown. We announce this to my parents over pumpkin pie, and my father generously insists that we take his car, which is a vintage 1974 Caprice convertible. But I'm not falling for his phony generosity. That car is my father's favorite possession and he knows that I won't borrow it. My father raced stock cars as a young man and has always considered working on cars a form of recreation. His love of

the automobile is an affection that I don't share because I consider automobiles to be just very large expensive appliances with a wider range of colors. Borrowing his car would be like being the first unrelated baby-sitter for first-time parents. There would be more repeated warnings and cautionary advice than there are in an entire carton of cigarettes. The stress of worrying about his car would be the certain cause of an accident. Instead, we will take my mother's car because I know that she will only worry about the possible dangers of our being downtown. My mother suffers from a suburban version of agoraphobia in which she's afraid of going out in public in big cities. We go to bed early that night, exhausted from an entire day devoted to doing nothing.

"Bob! Bob!"

"What?"

I look at the clock. It's 5:26 A.M. Why is my mother waking us up at this hour?

"Bob, you have to get dressed and drive your father to the hospital. He doesn't feel well."

I get up and pull on a pair of pants and step outside. My mother's dressed and my father is sitting in his chair in the living room.

"What's wrong?"

My father's had two heart attacks and I'm wondering if this is number three.

"Your father's having chest pains. He's not sure what's wrong but he thinks he should go to the hospital."

This makes me feel queasy because I know that my father would only seek medical attention if something was really wrong.

I say, "Let me get dressed and we can go."

I go back in the bedroom and Tom is pulling on a pair of pants.

"I'll come with you."

When we're ready to go my mother attempts a smile and says, "I'm sorry to get you up so early, Tom. We'll

have to get breakfast later. I'm sure the hospital has something to eat."

This is really serious. My mother's letting us leave the house on an empty stomach, which she considers as dangerous and socially unacceptable as drunk driving.

"Hey, Tom. Sorry to get you up so early."

"That's okay, Mr. Smith."

"Take your father's car, there's more room."

My mother hands me the keys.

I'm nervous as I start the car. Tom pats my leg as I pull out of the garage and then hops out to open the door to the backseat to help my parents get in. The hospital is only five minutes away, and as I drive I can see my father sitting uncomfortably in the backseat.

"Bob, turn your head when you change lanes because the mirror has a blind spot. That's how you get in an accident."

How is it that my father decides to give me driving lessons while having a possible heart attack? Do they ever stop being dads? I imagine my father telling the driver of an ambulance, *"Listen, don't gun the engine after you turn the key. You're gonna burn out the starter that way."*

My father is admitted right away while my mother goes through the entire process of filling out forms and answering the nurse's questions as Tom and I sit in the waiting room. After forty-five minutes my mother comes out and tells us that the doctor examining my father doesn't think it's a heart attack but he won't be sure until they've done some more tests. She then adds that the doctor is "young, but he seems very knowledgeable." My mother is very serious in hospitals and has the matronly manner of a head nurse. She suggests that we go down to the cafeteria and eat something as if she's prescribing medicine. "Have a cup of coffee and some eggs. You have to eat."

We're relieved to discover later that my father is having some sort of stomach problem, which surprisingly

I can't blame on overeating because my father ate less than the rest of us at Thanksgiving. They release him after a couple of hours and by then Tom and I don't feel like going downtown. Instead we head out to the local mall and do some half-hearted shopping.

The next day our plane leaves at 11 A.M. My father insists on driving us to the airport even though Tom and I insist that he stay home and rest. I suggest to my parents that they should visit us in New York. My father will never do this because his attitude has always been that real Americans don't visit cities on a vacation. Before we leave the house, my mother asks us to double-check and make sure that we didn't forget anything because she can never forget that five years ago I left my contact lenses and she had to spend twelve dollars sending them by overnight delivery. I look around my bedroom one last time and think, *Did I forget anything?* No. But if I did—it's nothing that can't be recovered with a few years of therapy.

A Few Notes on
Sex Education

THERE EXISTS a widespread folk myth that humans should learn about sex from their parents. The reticence most parents have about discussing sex with their children almost ensures confusion. Although it's possible parents may not be shirking their responsibility in refraining from teaching sexual education, it may be a genetically programmed strategy to allow children and parents to survive adolescence. For example, my relationship with my father nearly ended when he tried to teach me how to drive. I can't imagine our relationship having survived his instructing me how to operate my penis. Imagine the stress of a first date, as you clumsily explore intimacy, your father in the backseat coaching: *Just put your arm around her! No, no, like this—here, lemme show you how.*

While talking about sex with your parents is difficult for straight teenagers, it's even more trying for gay teenagers. It takes considerable maturity, when your parents are attempting to tell you the facts of life, to interrupt and inform them of the facts of *your* life. Since our society regards producing a gay child as an event rarer than being abducted by extraterrestrials, it's not surprising that most parents of gay children are unprepared to give them guidance. Instead of giving their gay children the benefit of their own experience, they unintentionally make the mistake of giving advice based upon a heterosexual model of same-sex relationships. The results can be disastrous. Heterosexual men frequently keep their male friends happy for years by golfing with them once a week and then buying them a few beers afterward— behavior that may not be enough to sustain a relationship with the principal dancer of the Miami City Ballet. Of course, a gay son could ask his mother about keeping a man happy, but it's doubtful whether even the most ardent gay activists would—or should—feel comfortable talking about oral sex with Mom.

Lesbian daughters find themselves in a similar predicament. Their mothers may suggest that the best way to sustain a relationship with another woman is to "stay in touch," a turn of phrase that can mean something completely different to a woman who has the hots for a lanky blond lawyer named Jean. It's also not advisable for a lesbian daughter to try to use her father's method of keeping a woman happy: Agree to whatever she says and then do what you want anyway.

Since most parents are reluctant to talk about sex, schools have tried to fill the gap. In America, when we decide to ignore a subject, our favorite form of denial is to teach it incompetently. Familiarity without true understanding is not only the basis of our families but of our educational system as well. When it comes to sex, Americans have been reluctant to spell it out since the time of *The Scarlet Letter.*

Our schools teach only the most basic principles of human reproduction: naming and identifying the sexual organs and a simple explanation of how the sperm fertilizes the ovum. If mathematics was taught in the same cursory manner as human sexuality, when children learned to count they would be considered masters of the subject. The teaching of human sexuality in our schools can also be compared to how they teach music— most students of the oboe become proficient enough to use the equipment, but they never develop the ability to give anyone else pleasure. Part of the problem is the reserved textbooks used to teach human sexuality. Due to the puritanical nature of our school boards and a fear of offending conservatives, most textbooks on sexual education are simultaneously explicit and vague—a writing style most frequently employed by daily horoscopes.

Our educational programs are only explicit when they try to scare teenagers off sex, alcohol, and drugs by arousing their fear of death. As a means of dissuasion, it doesn't take into account that what most young people fear more than death is embarrassment because only a handful of people have returned from the other side to write New Age best-sellers about death, but we've all experienced embarrassment. Depending upon the circumstances, a film showing drunken relatives at a family gathering can actually be more horrifying than a film showing drunken cheerleaders killed in a car accident. Just as a five-hour film of nothing but a baby crying constantly on a nonstop flight between New York and Los Angeles would be a major deterrent to teenage pregnancy.

The opponents of sex education believe that if we keep our teenagers ignorant about a topic, then they won't become interested; a theory that has proven itself by the lack of interest shown by teenagers in other subjects missing from the curriculum, such as playing loud music, eating French fries, and the use of pimple creams.

In many school systems, the teaching of safe sex has

even been a source of controversy. Schools should obviously give extensive and explicit information about safe sex and the transmission of AIDS, but right-wing extremists have suggested that homosexuals want to teach about safe sex because they're trying to recruit children into the "homosexual lifestyle." If anyone is trying to recruit, it's the militant conservatives who are trying to draw children into their own unnatural lifestyle in which people who are different are evil, and creating fear is considered a form of affection.

If the goal of conservatives is to discourage young people from having sex, they should change their strategy and push to make comprehensive sexual education compulsory. Our educational system has proved that if a subject is taught in a boring enough manner, Americans will make every effort to avoid it for the rest of their lives. If homosexuality was taught in the same manner as trigonometry, even most gay people would have no use for it after graduation.

There are many proven educational techniques that could be used to make Sex Ed unpopular. Dissecting the sex lives of most Americans could become as repugnant a classroom experience as dissecting a frog. Children could be drilled relentlessly in the spelling of sexual vocabulary, such as orgasm, cunnilingus, fellatio, clitoris. Teachers could encourage science fair projects in human sexuality, therefore making any kids interested in sex seem like total geeks. Boredom could be induced by dismal graphs of orgasms per capita and pie charts illustrating the conflicting percentages of the population who are straight, gay, bisexual, and transgender. Furthermore, textbooks on human reproduction could be made voluminously heavy—ensuring that they would only leave the lockers of aspiring shot putters.

Second only to AIDS, our educational system needs to address the subject of another frequently incurable sexually transmitted disease: Bitterness, the Glib Reaper.

Bitterness has reached epidemic proportions among gay and straight alike. Optimism alone won't guard you against this scourge of modern life because it takes only one sharp remark to tear a hole in your protection. What are the symptoms of Bitterness? A burning sensation occurs whenever you think of your ex's name. If you start uncontrollably dripping with sarcasm, seek help immediately.

The test for Bitterness is simple, quick, and accurate. The doctor merely asks, "Are you seeing anyone?" and then waits for your response. The difference between being tested for HIV and for being tested for Bitterness is that with HIV, if you're negative, it's good news. With Bitterness, if you're negative—you're infected.

American teenagers urgently need a program to show them the horrifying consequences of Bitterness. One way to do this would be to bring the bitter into classrooms to give a presentation which would then be followed by a short question-and-answer period. Invite a single woman in her late thirties, give her three wine spritzers, and then get her started on her last boyfriend. Pair her testimony with a twenty-six-year-old straight man with a comb-over, smiling to express every emotion but happiness, talking as an expert on the nature of women, his expertise based upon two brief, failed relationships. Follow him with a gay man, a cigarette dangling from his hand like a smoldering piece of jewelry, exuding acrimony as if it were a designer cologne. End the program with a dejected lesbian who "is working through" her rage about breaking up with her last girlfriend with a series of chiropractic adjustments. Ninety relentless minutes of despair, broken promises, and crushed hopes should be enough to turn most young people off sex for years.

Another subject that isn't being adequately addressed by our schools is whether or not to have sex on the first date. From my experience, it's usually better to wait. Sex on the first date is like dinner on the first date—years

later you can never remember what you had. To help teenagers make informed decisions, we need to provide them with good reasons not to have sex on a first date:

Number One: If you need immediate gratification on a first date, order dessert. Always remember: It's easier to not finish a piece of cake than it is to not finish a blow job. If you feel guilty after eating a piece of mud pie, you can always work it off on the StairMaster—which is much cheaper and easier than trying to burn off your sexual guilt with your therapist, the StareMaster.

Number Two: Before sleeping with someone, consider trying to find out if you're sexually compatible by thinking about them while masturbating. Remember: If you can't make a relationship work in a fantasy, then it will never work in reality.

The purpose of sex education should be to prepare us for real-life problems. For example, I've often heard well-meaning people say that "too many of our young people feel pressured to have sex for the wrong reasons," presupposing a utopian world where all adult sexual activity occurs without vacillation or doubt. What must be made clear to young people is the desirability of waiting until they establish a loving relationship and *then* having sex for the wrong reasons.

From my experience of being in a relationship for eight years, I think it would be healthy to admit that everyone will, at some point in their lives, have sex for the wrong reasons. There will come a time, with even the most devoted couples, when one partner will initiate sex and the other partner will think, *Oh, I just want to go to sleep. Well, I'd better do IT—it's been a while— and if we don't he'll be in such a bad mood tomorrow.* What educators need to address and thoroughly explain are the differences among consenting sex: consenting to have sex for an inadequate reason, consenting to have

sex for a reason that's reasonable but unappealing, and the much rarer and more desirable instances of consenting to sex when the person, time, and place are right.

What it comes down to is this. There are just two things that every student of human sexuality should always remember: Most people don't know sex from a hole in the ground, and the more you know, the better off you'll get.

Mysterious Kitchens

Performances, assortments, résumés—
Up Times Square to Columbus Circle lights
Channel the congresses, nightly sessions,
Refractions of the thousand theatres, faces—
Mysterious kitchens . . . You shall search them all.

—Hart Crane, *The Tunnel VII*

 Y PREPARATION for becoming a New Yorker was entirely intellectual. Growing up in Kenmore, a suburb of Buffalo, I had never once eaten Chinese food, but after reading Susan Sontag's over-enthusiastic review in *The New York Review of Books*, I had gone to see Hans-Jürgen Syberberg's interminable seven-hour film *Our Hitler*. It was only after moving to New York that I learned that knowing something about General Tso's Chicken was probably more valuable than having seen General Rommel portrayed by a puppet.

I was especially unprepared for life in New York. Before moving, I had visited the city only once before, having spent seven hours at the friend of a friend's apartment after I missed a connecting flight at Newark Airport. It's not like I was some hick, though by virtue of

being born in Buffalo I was technically a *Western* New Yorker. Having read *The Village Voice* and *The New Yorker*, I somehow felt that I was savvy because I knew where to buy cheap futons below 14th Street and that the porn film currently playing at the Adonis Theater was Rock Bottom's latest, *Splendor in the Ass.* Trying to prepare yourself for life in New York by reading about it is like preparing yourself for the view from the top of the Empire State Building by climbing a ladder.

For a year after graduating from the University of Buffalo, I used my degree in Creative Writing to pen dinner orders at the Tralfamadore Cafe. I felt rather smug because I was the only waiter on staff who had read *Slaughterhouse Five*, from which the restaurant's name was taken.

The Tralfamadore Cafe was a small jazz club that on Tuesday nights featured stand-up comedy. Five years before, after reading a small notice in the newspaper that said that they were looking for comedians, I wrote some jokes, arranged to get a spot, performed, got some laughs, and was added to the small roster of comedians. I felt pretty cool for an eighteen-year-old because immediately after that first performance I was offered a part in a North Tonawanda dinner theater's production of a Neil Simon play.

I had wanted to be a stand-up comic after reading Lenny Bruce's autobiography, *How to Talk Dirty and Influence People*. In homage to him, every time I performed, I always wore a white button-down shirt, faded blue jeans, and a skinny black leather tie, signaling that I was also a cutting-edge performer. (Although I don't believe that Lenny Bruce needed to ask his mother to drive him to and from his gigs.)

The Tralf, as it was nicknamed, was extremely successful and eventually moved to a much larger location farther downtown. Since the new club had more seats to fill, the management began to bring in "name" stand-ups from New York. After performing steadily for years,

my opportunity to perform now dwindled to once every six months when I was allowed five minutes as the opening act.

At twenty-three, I still lived at home and had reached the age when that admission is not a statement of address but of arrested development. The problem was that I had no idea of what I wanted to do with my life. Maybe I would apply to graduate school—a respectable alternative to making a decision. But more reading assignments wasn't what I needed. My life was already a book that I had started awhile ago, but I never got beyond the first couple of chapters and I seemed to have lost my place. I wasn't confused about my sexuality, I just didn't know what to do about it.

Then, during my last year of college, I came out: I took a bus downtown to a gay bar. Taking a bus to declare your sexuality only proclaims that you're a loser. One of the reasons it took me until the end of college to come out was that I tend to procrastinate about everything. In the ninth grade, I realized and had easily accepted that I was gay but, like getting my driver's license, I had never, until college, done anything about it.

The bar was called Mean Alice's, a terrible name that sounded as if it should be cackled. It was possibly the worst name for a gay bar in history, only to be superseded years later, when I performed at a bar called Feathers. I knew where Mean Alice's was located because my sister Carol had recently mentioned being taken there by her friend Rick, who had just come out to her. Knowing the location made my life easier because I was too scared to ask anyone for directions to a gay bar. For a while, I thought that I might have to use the one failproof method a timid person has of finding a gay bar in an unfamiliar city—feel every building and find the one that's thumping.

I had prepared myself for my coming out by reading about being gay. My mentors were Walt Whitman, Oscar Wilde, E. M. Forster, Ronald Firbank, Evelyn

Waugh, Christopher Isherwood, and Joe Orton. With this impractical preparation, I was ready to meet and fall in love with a handsome, aristocratic Oxford student from the 1920s, or even a muscular working-class youth from prewar Berlin. I wasn't fussy. I just hoped that he had his driver's license.

I arrived at Mean Alice's at nine-thirty in the evening because at midnight I needed to catch the last bus back to Kenmore. When I walked in the door, my heart was pounding louder than the music, but as soon as my eyes adjusted to the room's dim light, my disappointment was immeasurable. There was no one else in the bar. It hadn't occurred to me that since the bars in New York State can stay open until four A.M. that the bar wouldn't become crowded until after eleven o'clock. I had come out of the closet to an empty room. If Cinderella was a gay man, she would have never met her prince as he wouldn't have gone out before midnight. Don't get me wrong. I like being gay but I hate the long hours. Frustrated, I sat at the bar and ordered a beer.

I had plenty of time to admire my surroundings. The place looked as if someone had decided to remodel their basement into a gay bar. From floor to ceiling, the bar was upholstered in red carpeting, making me wonder if the local decorator misunderstood the term "wall to wall." Across from where I sat, there was a small raised dance floor. The dance floor's light system was state of the art, circa 1978. First, beams of colored light swayed unsteadily in small circles. When they stopped, a spinning mirrored disco ball sprayed shafts of light over the dance floor. Then the spinning stopped and a strobe light would begin to flash. It was as if the light system was trying to give a visual equivalent to intoxication—feeling tipsy, being drunk, and having a hangover. Several times during the evening, a fog machine would, at unpredictable intervals, emit a malodorous vapor. This added a sense of atmosphere to the room evocative of living next to an oil refinery. When the noxious fumes

poured out, I felt like I was dancing in an enclosed garage with the car engine running. The purpose of the fog machine eluded me. Why would anyone in Buffalo want bad weather indoors too?

After eleven, the bar finally started to fill up with men, giving me just thirty minutes of gaiety before I had to leave to catch my bus. I didn't speak to anyone during that half hour, but I still felt like I was having a great time.

A month later, I had my driver's license and I started going to Mean Alice's every Saturday night, even though I felt awkward going out to a bar by myself. If you saw me then, you might have mistaken my motionless figure for the bar's cigarette machine. All night, I would stand in the same spot, glowing with anticipation, waiting for someone else to make the first move. Imagine my chagrin, when over the course of the evening, the cigarette machine was approached more than I was.

I wanted the man of my dreams to come and interrupt what had become an interminable conversation with my own virginity. Couldn't anyone tell that we had nothing more to say to each other?

After my second visit to Mean Alice's, I decided to change my appearance. During the 1970s and early '80s, the Gold-Tone Age of Ugly Eyewear, I had progressed from a pair of cumbersome frames that brutally mocked tortoiseshell and contained more plastic polymer than a goalie mask to a pair of "antiqued pewter," aviator-style frames, which instead of making me look daring made me seem reckless in appearance.

To add insult to impairment, I had grown more nearsighted yearly and the thickness of my lenses steadily approached the heft of glass bricks. So I bought my first pair of tiny, expensive, incredibly uncomfortable hard contact lenses. Taking down the storm windows of my soul had an immediate positive influence on my outlook. When I gazed in the mirror, I didn't only see glass anymore.

* * *

On September 15, 1984, I arrived in New York on a fifty-nine-dollar one-way People Express flight. I had picked the day at random, well over a year before, in an attempt to make a date with destiny. I needed more than a year to prepare for my Big Date because I had to save up enough money to pay for it. What still surprises me is that I had finally worked up the nerve to actually ask Destiny out and that I didn't try to cancel at the last minute.

After landing in Newark, I took the shuttle bus to Port Authority. As I piled my luggage in the backseat of a cab, I felt like a gay emigrant to Manheaven. It occurred to me that there should be a hunky male companion to the Statue of Liberty, standing in his designer underwear, facing New Jersey with a come-hither look— he would welcome new arrivals from the rest of United States: accountants who want to be a number; drag queens who think the streets are paved with gold lamé; art historians who know Michelangelo's *David* and now desperately want to meet his *Bill*, *Rick*, or *Henry*. We had left the cast of *Our Town* to audition for the cast of *Wonderful Town*.

I had to find a job, an apartment, a boyfriend, and a life. Fortunately, New York is a city where there are classified listings for all four. I soon realized that the ad descriptions were not always accurate. The apartments were usually much smaller than their description while the boyfriends' problems were usually much bigger. I had no idea what I wanted to do in New York. Did I want to be a stand-up comic or did I want a real job? I was a Wannamaybe.

The only person I knew in the city was my friend Mark, who had moved there himself six months before to work for a bank. Mark offered to let me stay with him, but he made it clear, it had to be only for two weeks. On my first night he introduced me to a friend

of his named Steven, a Cordon Bleu chef who had just started a catering company called Taste Alliance.

During dinner, Steven asked if I would like to start work the following week as a waiter for their first big event. He also asked if I owned a tuxedo. Unfortunately, I didn't—I presumed that I would only be attending my senior prom once. The next day, I bought one. Since my father was a state trooper and my grandfather had worked on a railroad, I believe that I was the first member of my family to own a tuxedo. My pride was held in check by the realization that unlike Fred Astaire, I was only going to clear the dance floor with a broom.

Steven told me to show up at three o'clock the following Wednesday at the service entrance to the Metropolitan Museum of Art. Working as a cater-waiter made me think of Jesus' statement that a rich man has as much of a chance of entering the gates of heaven as a camel does through the eye of a needle. It would be poetic justice if the reason why the rich can't enter through the gates is because they have to use the service entrance.

A museum guard directed me to where the party was to be held. When I entered the gallery, I saw two spectacular sights—the reconstructed Egyptian Temple of Dendur, displayed in a huge sparse gallery with windows overlooking Central Park, and fifty handsome muscular men milling about in tank tops and shorts. I found Steven and he introduced me to Pam, one of the two captains in charge of all the waiters. Pam was a struggling artist who made everyone's life difficult. She only wore black and after becoming acquainted with her I couldn't decide if this was a deliberate fashion choice or whether it was physically impossible for any color to escape from the gravitational pull of her dark and bitter personality.

It soon became clear that the only *Joy* in Pam's life was the bottle of dishwashing liquid in her kitchen. One

of the reasons Pam was so miserable was that she was a martyr to art and catering. A self-canonized Saint Sebastian impaled by paintbrushes and swizzle sticks and bleeding Cadmium #3.

Pam had ideas for artistic projects of such grandiosity that she made Christo seem like a miniaturist. Her current plan was to videotape the creation of an artificial coral reef by sinking two thousand empty oil drums off the coast of New Jersey. The resulting three-hour "video document" would be her artistic statement. Pam found it incomprehensible that the wealthy people we catered for wouldn't just give her the two hundred thousand dollars she required to create this desperately needed addition to our cultural canon.

Since we frequently worked in apartments filled with wonderful art, I naively thought Pam would appreciate my attempts to discuss some of the works we had a chance to view. One night we were working in an apartment filled with a spectacular collection of American modernists: Georgia O'Keeffe, Edward Hopper, Marsden Hartley, and Arthur Dove. I said to Pam, "Aren't the Georgia O'Keeffes in the living room great?"

"Do you really think so?" she asked in a tone that would have intimidated Rembrandt.

"Yes, her work is beautiful."

"Bob, if something is pretty, it doesn't mean that it's a work of art. Art should engage the viewer and question the underlying values of society, not just reinforce them."

For Pam the word "engage" was a euphemism for "assault."

"Well, didn't O'Keeffe change the way we look at bones and skulls and the landscape of New Mexico?"

"No. What's the difference between how she uses the land and how a strip miner uses the land? They both exploit it for their own purposes."

"Well, painting's a lot quieter than strip-mining."

"Why don't you pass the tray of shrimp again," she said dismissively.

Over the next few months, I learned that Pam wasn't unique. Every cater-waiter in New York was only working this job until they became established in their *real* careers. Only artists suffer from this vocational schizophrenia. One rarely meets a Department of Motor Vehicles clerk who is only renewing driver's licenses until he can break into his real love, selling auto insurance. Cater-waitering is the perfect job for all the actor-painter-playwright-novelist-dancer-performance artists—or those yet unable to determine their vast untapped talents. For one thing, it's freelance—the caterers ask your availability for a certain date and one has the option of working that party or refusing—and it pays really well for a job that only requires the minimal skills of knowing how to open a bottle of champagne without the cork wounding a guest and being able to say with feigned enthusiasm to hundreds of repeated inquiries while passing hors d'oeuvres, "It's sundried tomatoes and smoked mozzarella in a polenta corn cup with a touch of basil-infused extra virgin olive oil."

After meeting Pam, I was introduced by Steven to the other captain, Tim Gordon. When I addressed him by his first name, he immediately told me that he preferred to be called by his last name, Gordon. Meeting Gordon was my first introduction to an idea that took me many years to understand. It's simple for a relatively attractive man in his early twenties to get a job as a cater-waiter. However, what I didn't know then was how difficult it is, in your late thirties or forties, to stop being a cater-waiter.

Many of the captains in catering were aging actor-waiters who should have long ago given up any hopes of ever making it. Gordon was in his late forties and he seemed to be waiting for a callback for the original cast of *Hair*. In an attempt to avoid acknowledging his age,

Gordon used a headshot that was badly out of date. He could probably earn more money selling his headshots as vintage photographs than he would ever earn as an actor. At his age, his first big break would have been a hip injury.

A former Marine who had served in Vietnam, Gordon was the most macho cater-waiter in New York. He was a catering commando in the social jungle of Manhattan. The major difference between 'Nam and Gotham being that in the social jungle the most effective form of camouflage is a pair of oversized sunglasses and an Hermès scarf. Every party he captained always felt as if we were landing on the beaches of the Hamptons, wading ashore in our tuxedos to take drink orders or die trying. Any time Gordon captained a job, his waiters always felt confident that he would take care of them. Just when I began to feel tired or hungry, he would tap me on the shoulder and tell me to go take a break and eat something. Gordon insisted that all the waiters under his command eat before he did. No matter how long and dull the party, as Gordon opened and poured magnums of Veuve Clicquot and liters of San Pellegrino, he never suffered from bottle fatigue. Gordon was the hardest-working man in catering, but the gleam in his eye wasn't from the reflection of the Baccarat crystal. Sometimes I felt that the only thing holding him together was his cummerbund and bow tie. There were nights when I was afraid that the sound of champagne corks popping might trigger a flashback—causing him to smear his face with guacamole and try to fight his way out of the foyer with a fish knife.

One night I gingerly asked Gordon about his experiences during the war. He said that he had joined the Marines when he was seventeen by lying about his age. His unit was involved in some of the most intense fighting of the war. Evading detail, he said, "I'm sorry. It was the worst fucking year of my life. Thank god for marijuana." After his discharge, he admitted that he

needed to spend two years chilling out. He spent that
time in the Bahamas, where he taught meditation. It
was difficult to imagine this restless man teaching med-
itation. His mantra was probably *Moveit Moveit Moveit
Moveit....* Despite the gung-ho with which he ap-
proached every job, Gordon also talked frequently about
his desire to get out of catering. He'd occasionally men-
tion that "a buddy of mine's opening a restaurant and
he said that if I want to bartend—the job's mine" or
else he'd say "I'm thinking of moving to California.
That's where the acting work is." But Gordon never did
quit. He was a P.O.W.—Prisoner of Waitering.

That first job was a seductive introduction to the city.
As I circulated through the crowd with my silver tray
of skewered chicken saté, I fantasized that the exhibition
of a pagan temple in the middle of a modern American
city would have appealed to that master of overwrought
horror H. P. Lovecraft. I could imagine him writing an
eldritch tale called *The Dunwich's Horrible Party*. It
would be the story of a waiter at a reception, discovering,
to his increasing terror, that society women in Manhat-
tan retain their look "of a certain age" by sacrificing
waiters in large chafing dishes to the fierce Egyptian
goddess of hospitality, Thankuforcummun.

In addition to my tuxedo, I wore a fez that night
because the party, which was being held by a depart-
ment store to welcome the then-hot new fashion de-
signer Jean-Paul Gaultier, had a Moroccan theme. It was
a major concession when I agreed to wear the fez be-
cause I was violating my vow of never working any job
that requires a hat not worn as protection. But it wasn't
to be the last time. Over the years, for different catering
jobs, I would find myself sometimes wearing other cos-
tumes: a cowboy hat and a bandanna tied around my
neck for a children's birthday party; a djellaba for an-
other Moroccan feast; a Santa hat for a Christmas party;
a black turtleneck and black jeans for an art gallery

opening and for the showing of his spring collections, an Armani-designed waiter's outfit that looked like a cross between a Nehru jacket and a bellhop's uniform. I felt like an employee of a theme park called The Big Apple where I was a cartoon character in the fantasy lands of Broadway, Wall Street, and Seventh Avenue.

Right after that first job at the museum, Steven began regularly booking me as a waiter, making it unnecessary for me to find other work. But I needed to find an apartment as my two weeks' staying as Mark's houseguest were coming to an end. I estimated the amount of money that I could afford to pay for rent and started looking. The first ad that I answered was for a place located in the East Village on Avenue B. Judging from the neighborhood, I assumed the rest of the street's name had been stolen. As I walked to the apartment I thought, *This is a really bad neighborhood.* I grinned when I realized that living in a bad neighborhood was a classic set-up for jokes: *My neighborhood's really bad. The zip code is 911. I look through the peep-hole before I open the refrigerator....*

From the outside the building looked all right. Once inside, I wanted to leave immediately. The hallway smelled like a Last Meal. The walls were painted *Jaundice* and a fluorescent light coughed occasionally as it expired from consumption. But before I had a chance to retreat, the landlord called from the top of the stairs on the fourth floor. After I trudged up, he showed me the features of the apartment. Many of the apartments listed in my price range were described in their ads as "recently renovated," which meant that the apartment had gone from uninhabitable to unpleasant. The apartment was a studio with a newly exposed brick wall, a refinished hardwood floor that sloped noticeably, and a woman across the hall who was insane. During my look-see, she screamed, "Bastards. Whores. Pukes. Fuckers," as if she was reading aloud from a thesaurus of expletives. "She loud. I evic' her," the Chinese landlord told

me. "She only noisy during day. At night, she quiet."
That was a relief; she was insane but she wasn't incon-
siderate. "I take fifty bucks off rent until she move out."
I thanked him for showing me the place and told him
that I was going to keep looking. If I had signed the
lease I would have been crazier than her.

After a week spent unsuccessfully looking for an
apartment, Mark suggested that I meet Philip, a friend
in his late thirties who wanted a roommate. He was an
interior decorator who lived in a tiny one-bedroom
apartment on the corner of 35th and Lexington. Philip
said that I could have the bedroom for four hundred
dollars a month and that he would sleep on the couch.
At the time, it seemed like a good deal because my law-
yers were Young & Stupid, the legal representatives for
everyone under twenty-five. I reluctantly moved in with
Philip because I didn't know where else to go.

Philip's apartment was a bonsai of a more spacious
Park Avenue apartment. The walls of the nine-by-twelve
main room were lacquered a dark red and hung with
oversized reproductions of eighteenth-century portraits
of English spaniels and blue-and-white porcelain plat-
ters. The chair and sofa were fringed and the floor was
covered with a needlepoint carpet. It's a style that
should be called "Big Queen Anne." The walls of the
tiny bedroom and bathroom were covered with grass
cloth and furnished with bamboo furniture. The tropical
motif made me worry that someday the apartment's nu-
merous cockroaches would be joined by scorpions and
tarantulas.

On our first Saturday night together, Philip revealed
that he liked to dress in head-to-toe leather and hang
out at a bar called The Spike. Somehow dressed in chaps,
he seemed even more like a decorator. I could imagine
him furnishing a dungeon but I could never imagine
him being the master of one. He might as well have
worn a navy blue three-piece pin-striped suit to The
Spike and carried a sample book of various leathers.

As soon as I moved in with Philip, I regretted my decision. He drank too much and when I would come home from a catering job, he would ramble on about the latest person who had ruined his day. After listening to his tired orations, I decided that since Philip was into S&M, he must have been extremely masochistic—he was anti-Semitic and racist and yet he had chosen to live in New York City. For Philip, the world was literally white and off-white. I immediately started looking for someplace else to live.

One of Steven's catering accounts was *House & Garden* magazine, and he had become friendly with an editor, Anita, who owned and lived in a brownstone in the South Bronx. She told him that she wanted to rent an apartment in her building but that she wanted a tenant who wouldn't be any trouble. I fit her description. I still felt nervous about introducing myself to a stranger over the telephone. Anita and I agreed to meet at her house at four o'clock. When I reached the Alexander Avenue stop at 135th Street, I followed Anita's directions and exited by the large police precinct station that was only seven houses away from Anita's brownstone.

Anita informed me that she and her ex-husband had bought the building for ten thousand dollars as part of an urban homesteading program and had then remodeled the entire place. The studio apartment that I eventually took was on the ground floor and went from the front of the house to the back. It was clean and modern, with a microwave, dishwasher, and even a trash compactor. I didn't like that there were metal bars on all of the windows and the front door. In Buffalo, the only building with barred windows was the mental hospital. As Anita showed me around, she added enticingly that I would be able to use the washer and dryer in the basement. When I decided to take it, I thought that it would do for a short time, until I found something better—a thought that most forty-year tenants in crappy

apartments had probably consoled themselves with at one point.

Explaining to my parents that finding a cheap, clean apartment in the South Bronx was good news was beyond my powers of suburban translation. It was like bragging to them that I got a great deal on some heroin. I explained to them that where I lived on Alexander Avenue was part of a small landmarked historic district called Mott Haven. On her envelopes, Anita used Mott Haven because "Mott Haven, New York" sounds like a lovely hamlet on Long Island or in Westchester, instead of being what was reported to be one of the worst areas of New York.

Six months after I moved to the South Bronx, I finally told my parents that I was gay. Looking back on it, I should have announced my sexual orientation and my new address at the same time. Having my parents get over two major worries about my safety would have been just as easy as having them get over one. For the next four years, I lived in the South Bronx and the only serious problem that I ever had was more rural than urban—a raccoon kept breaking into my garbage.

While I was looking for an apartment, I also continued to look for a boyfriend. During my first months in New York, I tried venturing out to gay bars in the mystical belief that an environment where I felt awkward and uncomfortable was the perfect place for someone to find me attractive. On Saturday nights, after eleven o'clock—I knew better now—I would go to a video bar called Uncle Charlie's in Greenwich Village. After ordering a light beer, I would stand and watch one of the numerous monitors showing music videos and clips from old movies and television shows. I don't know what I was thinking. In over twenty years of watching television, I had never met anyone before—I don't know why I now thought that doing it in public would suddenly improve my chances. In retrospect, I think that like

many single people I couldn't decide if I was there to pick someone up or to be picked up. It's the indecision that is off-putting.

I told my friend Sean about my inability to meet anyone, and he seriously suggested that the secret of allure is: Relax your lower lip. Sean claimed that if you do that, your entire body follows suit and you immediately become more attractive. Out of desperation, the next time I went to Uncle Charlie's, I tried out Sean's advice and concentrated on relaxing my lower lip. I succeeded but the rest of my body was racked with tension. What I didn't consider was that Sean was a strikingly handsome, dark-haired, muscular man who had moved to New York to pursue modeling. With the wisdom of maturity, I know that instead of consciously trying to relax my lip, I should've just smiled.

After a few weeks in New York, I realized that for a skinny gay man, the pickings are slim. So I joined a gym in an attempt to undergo mesomorphosis. In gay bars, I had the uncanny sense that my life had come full circle but I was still being asked to jump through the same hoop. I was back in gym class—only now I was worried that I was going to be the last one picked for a date.

Of course there were times when even I understood that someone was interested in me. But, like everyone else in the bars, I quickly learned to push down the stares of anyone I didn't find attractive. My strategy to meet men was different in the bars of New York than the bar in Buffalo. Instead of standing in the same spot for the entire night, every twenty-five minutes or so I would change the position of where I stood, as if the reflection of a different television monitor might make me appear in a new light. I would slowly move around the bar like a figure in a medieval clock mechanism, at each appointed spot raising my beer to my lips. When two o'clock struck, my circuit complete, I took a cab home.

* * *

My second big purchase in New York, after buying a tuxedo, was an answering machine. An indispensable device to New Yorkers because being able to screen your calls is the telephone equivalent of looking through the peephole in the door of your apartment. The messages on my machine sometimes sounded as though the caterers were trying to entice me to work by serving up celebrities:

"Hi, Bob. It's Bill Carroll. Do you want to work at three-thirty A.M. on Saturday? It's a Christmas party for all of New York City's go-go boys."

"Hi, Bob. It's Steven. I want to know if you're available on the eighteenth for a cocktail party. The guest of honor is Shelley Winters. Call me."

"Hello, Bob! It's Edward Darbin. Mrs. Darbin and I are giving a dinner party for the Ambassador of Switzerland on December third and would like to know if you're available. Thank you."

It was as if they assumed that my incentive to work wasn't paying the rent but having the opportunity to witness an aging character actress demand her chicken broiled and without sauce. It was quite a disappointment when I checked my schedule and discovered that I was unavailable for the Rated X-mas party. It would have been fascinating to observe the holiday traditions of go-go boys. Do they unwrap their presents *really* slowly? When decorating a Christmas tree, do they only hang one artfully placed ornament, or do they cover their ornaments with a G-string? And it must be a challenge to try to pick out a suitable gift for a go-go boy. What do you get for the man who has everything and shows it for a living? I was also curious about what go-go boys do when they've had too much to drink. Do they lose all self-control and start putting on extra layers of clothing? If the caterers had really wanted to tempt me, they

should have left messages on my answering machine about what they were serving for dinner:

"Hi, Bob. It's Steven. I need you at the New School dinner on the twelfth. We're having Ginger-Carrot Soup, Filet of Beef with a Morel Sauce, Potatoes au Gruyère, Haricots Verts, and Chocolate and Coconut Sorbets with Biscotti for dessert."

One of the fringe benefits of being a cater-waiter is that, unlike restaurant waiters, you're fed the exact same dinner as the guests. The foods were a revelation to someone whose only knowledge of foreign cuisine was Canadian. For the first time, I tried sundried tomatoes, radicchio, caviar, risotto, and chocolate truffles. I realized quite quickly that it's possible for starving artists to eat extremely well.

During my first year in New York I felt that the world was my oyster: It was either going to give me pearls or hepatitis. And I was more adventurous with food than I was with men. I was willing to experiment with *fromage* but I was afraid of bondage. My attitude toward unfamiliar foods was the same as unfamiliar sex. There were some things that I knew beforehand that I wasn't going to like—no matter how much I was told that I would. But there were other things that I tried that I learned to love. I was careful either way. I always asked a lot of questions before putting something in my mouth.

When I first started catering, all the parties fascinated me, but after a short time I understood why the slang term for wealth and inebriation is the same. In New York, when you describe someone as being "loaded," it's usually true in both senses of the word. As my interest in the parties waned, my interest in the other waiters grew.

During a catering job, there was always time for intense conversations with the other waiters about every-

thing, from the novels of Wallace Stegner, to President Reagan's despicable environmental policies, to the night life of Katmandu. There were times when I felt like inviting the guests into the kitchen because our party was much more interesting than theirs.

From my experiences, New York's criminals treat waiters better than the so-called "high society." Members of the Mafia, ruthless real estate developers, and drug dealers have been some of the nicest people, and certainly the most generous tippers, that I worked for.

My most lucrative catering job was working once or twice a month at the Darbins' apartment on Central Park West in the Dakota. Mr. Darbin was a ruthless real estate developer who had recently paid a two-million-dollar fine for illegally demolishing an inconvenient building. In his favor though, he remembered every waiter's name, was genuinely friendly, and, after each party, tipped everyone fifty bucks. Waiters tend to develop a Manichaean waitercentric outlook. The universe is seen as a battleground between the good and the cheap. If a waiter wrote history, Abraham Lincoln's leadership might be passed over quickly to vilify him for being a notoriously poor tipper. "And say what you will about Stalin, he always left twenty-five percent."

Don Shea captained all of the Darbins' parties. Don was a heavyset Cabernet-faced man in his late forties whose personality was breezy enough to sail a schooner. During a party, no disaster could disturb his composure. If a waiter ran into the kitchen and announced that a guest at the dinner table had burst into flames, he would answer without a moment's hesitation and without even a flicker of surprise, "Thank you, sweetheart. Okay, let's extinguish the flames as unobtrusively as possible with this extra tablecloth and then bring the guest in the kitchen for emergency treatment—I think I saw some saline and an IV in the pantry—and then offer more wine to everyone and check their water glasses."

Don referred to everyone as "sweetheart" with the

exception of the hostess, whom he always referred to as "Madam." He would start most parties with a cocktail, although he never appeared drunk at any time. "Sweetheart, get me a vodka and orange juice from the bar, will you? I worked the most dreadful party last night. Bootsie Biddle had a little get-together celebrating her divorce and got a little carried away during cocktails and tripped over the Giacometti. We had to hold dinner for half an hour while she composed herself in the powder room. I don't know, I think she may be hypoglycemic." What I found fascinating was how Don maintained a carefully balanced relationship with our employers. It was a unique combination of familiarity and formality. At one moment, he might say, "Mr. Darbin, the next time you and Mrs. Darbin are in Rome, you must try a restaurant called Vespa. It only seats fifteen but the food and service are superb." Then later he would say to our twenty-eight-year-old hostess without the slightest hint of irony, "Now, would Madam like us to announce dinner at eight o'clock?" After observing Don's behavior, I decided that he was bisexual, since he seemed to experience a form of heterosexual passion kissing the asses of wealthy women.

When Don called to book me for catering jobs, he would leave messages that caused the red light on my answering machine to blink with more alarm than usual.

> "Sweetheart, it's Don Shea. I hope that you're screening this call because you're getting fucked. So don't bother getting up. Listen, I'm captaining a party for the Darbins on March twenty-fifth and I'd love it if you're available. Call me."

Since I was new to New York, Don felt that it was his duty to help with my unsentimental education. Unfortunately, the knowledge Don imparted was not particularly useful beyond certain milieus. He knew the best places in New York to buy prosciutto and male prosti-

tutes, neither of which I was in the meat market for—
but my vocabulary profited from my association with
him. The first time I worked at the Darbins', he told
me, "Sweetheart, bring a glass of champagne to Mrs.
Darbin."

"Um, Don. Which one is Mrs. Darbin?"

"Sweetheart, the one in the cerise dress."

"Um, Don. . . . What's cerise?"

"The red one, sweetheart."

Don passed on the Queen-lore of aging homosexuals
using a Socratic method of increasingly embarrassing
questions. He would inquire about the sexual orientation
and practices of each waiter with the tone of an ex-
tremely gracious and considerate dirty old man. Don of-
ten startled me by asking questions of such a graphic
nature that the glasses of white wine on my tray would
blush. In the manner of Miss Jean Brodie talking to her
pupils, Don used his life as an example to be emulated.

"Sweetheart, do you have a dildo?"

"No!"

"You really should consider one. If you get one—
and you must—get one with a suction cup. You just stick
it on the ceramic tile in the shower. It's better than
Valium and cleanup's a breeze."

I had never met anyone before who considered talk-
ing about his sex life to be a casual conversation.

"Can you believe it? I had a wet dream last Saturday.
I haven't had one since I was eighteen. And have you
seen the new Meryl Streep film? It's delightful. I really
recommend it."

Sometimes, while we changed into our tuxedos, Don
offered unsolicited advice: "Sweetheart, you should really
consider having nude photos taken of yourself. Jim and
I had it done years ago and we're really glad that we
did. And you must do it *now*—before it's too late."

Since the Darbins entertained frequently, I became
friendly with their housekeeper, Lily, an eccentric Ar-
menian immigrant who hated the woman she worked

for with an intensity normally only encountered in men nicknamed "The Jackal." Lily and Mrs. Darbin communicated through memos left on the kitchen counter, which Lily insisted on reading aloud to us. Their correspondence was more threatening than the messages sent between Kennedy and Khrushchev during the Cuban Missile Crisis. When I arrived at the Darbins', Lily would often be muttering as she did the laundry. I would try to be cheerful, "Hi, Lily. How are you?"

"Hello, Bop. Te*rrr*ible." She rolled her *r*'s with an Old World sense of tragedy that evoked thousands of years of lousy days.

"Oh, that's too bad. What's wrong, Lily?"

"Id's dat bidch! Mrs. Darbin!"

Mrs. Darbin's name passed Lily's lips with the same ease as a kidney stone.

"She issso dirdy! Look at dis!"

Lily waved a pair of soiled panties in the air like a banner in the ongoing battle between her and Mrs. Darbin. It was a shock to realize that the idea of someone airing your dirty laundry wasn't just a metaphorical conceit.

Lily's only source of pleasure in the Darbin household was a small black-and-white television with a tiny four-inch screen that she kept in the kitchen. She never missed the local news report. Tales of other people's misery often seemed to be the only thing that could cheer her up. One evening, while we were assembling hors d'oeuvres and Lily was ironing dinner napkins, we heard the news anchorman say, "Two teenage boys in Secaucus were today accused of raping and sodomizing a teenage girl."

Lily said to herself, "Oh my Got. Thad's te*rrr*ible. Raping is bat enough bud sotomy—eading da flesh."

Don then looked up from cutting limes into wedges and said, "What, Lily?"

Lily repeated, "Sotomy. Eading the flesh."

Then to my utter disbelief Don said, "Sweetheart, that's not sodomy. That's cannibalism."

"Den whad is sotomy?"

I was eager to hear his explanation.

Don briefly thought for a moment and said, "Sweetheart, it's when they . . . how can I put this? Take her from behind."

"Oh my Got! Dat's worse. If dat wass my sson I'd keel him."

I sympathized with Lily about Mrs. Darbin. She could be difficult. It was in her company that I learned that quiet good taste is only achieved by people who scream at their personal assistants. Even though her father had operated a lathe in Milwaukee, Mrs. Darbin acted as if she knew the difference between sevruga and beluga at the same age when most children are figuring out the difference between chunky and smooth. When I first met her, Mrs. Darbin introduced me to her two standard poodles by saying, "This is Picasso and this is Gorky—*the painter, not the writer.*" She made the distinction as if the dog had insisted upon the clarification. One time she asked Don, "Do we really need to cut up so many lemons and limes?" She also liked to impress her husband with her frugality by making her own ice cubes for their many parties each year. Of course, Lily did the actual filling and refilling of the ice cube trays. Mrs. Darbin seemed to rationalize that the money saved from buying one hundred dollars' worth of ice each winter would therefore more than justify the expense of spending two months every summer in Provence and Tuscany.

Mrs. Darbin also was extremely particular about how the Limoges dinner plates were washed. If one was chipped or broken, she would become extremely angry with Lily, who was the only person allowed to handle them. Lily and I bonded after one accident when I suggested that the next time she broke a dish, she should

glue it to the Julian Schnabel painting in their living room that was covered with broken dinner plates. She laughed and said, "Bop, you're te*rrr*ible. I like dat. Here, ead one of my coogies. Dey are Armenian."

The Darbins' art collection included a Jeff Koons sculpture of a basketball floating in an aquarium. After the sculpture arrived, Mrs. Darbin often complained that it needed to be refilled when the water evaporated. When Mrs. Darbin was out of earshot, I would make Lily smile by pretending to be angry and saying, "*Lily, I told you to water the art!*"

I soon realized that I didn't want to be a cater-waiter for the rest of my life. I didn't want to be like Pam, Gordon, or Don and stay too long at the party. The allure of New York had dimmed. During the 1980s living in New York sometimes felt like being a guest at a bad party. It was too crowded. It was too smoky. There wasn't enough food. People got sick. Things got broken. Nobody knew the host. But I would've hated not to have been invited.

As I approached the age of thirty, I was also no longer as responsive to my self-inflicted queer pressure. On Saturday nights I stopped going out to Uncle Charlie's. I decided that trying to meet eligible gay men at a crowded bar was ridiculous when most nights I was serving drinks with the same eligible gay men. At least, when I worked cater-waitering, I earned fifteen dollars an hour. Then, like in a realistic romance novel, when I least expected it and after two years of therapy, I met someone. While serving canapés at Radio City Music Hall, I met and later started dating an actor named Tom.

I became increasingly aware that it might not be wise to take a lifetime to decide what to do with your life, especially since the span of a lifetime could vary considerably. I also kept saying or writing down ideas for jokes. So two years after moving to New York, I

started performing stand-up again at a club in SoHo, but this time I talked about being gay. Once I decided to pursue stand-up, I knew that I needed to figure out a way to make a living that left me my nights free to perform. I needed a day job.

One night, I invited a group of my friends to come see me perform in the East Village at a tiny club improvised from a storefront called Cafe Bustelo. Don Shea brought his boyfriend, Fred, Gordon came with his boyfriend, Gary, and to my surprise and pleasure even Lily showed up. Pam also came with her new boyfriend, an equally morose artist named Gunther. They were perfectly suited for each other, like Angst and Ennui.

After the show, Don said, "Sweetheart, you were delightful and so cute. When you were on stage, I almost forgot myself and wanted to stuff a dollar in your pants." Gordon was gung-ho even in his congratulations, "Fuck, man, it takes guts to do stand-up." Lily grabbed my hand and said, "Bop, you was ver*rry* good. But dat one comick wassso dirdy." Pam thanked me for the invitation without showing any sign of levity and then proceeded to ask me who Gunther should talk to about having some of his paintings displayed in the club.

I continued to work as a cater-waiter until one day when I was working another party at the Metropolitan Museum, Don and I found ourselves talking, as we had both arrived early. I casually mentioned that I wanted to do less catering and find a day job. Don listened intently and then said, "Well, sweetheart, we'll have to take care of that right now. Come with me." When I hesitated, Don said commandingly, "Sweetheart, please, we don't have much time before the other waiters arrive." He led me upstairs to the museum restaurant where he knocked on the office door of the restaurant manager. After we heard a gruff "Come on in!" we entered and I was introduced. Then Don said, "Excuse me, Bill. The other day you mentioned that you needed a

waiter for the Staff Dining Room and I can't think of anyone more qualified than Bob. I've worked with him for years and he'd be perfect for the job."

Before I had a chance to think about it, I was hired to work lunches five days a week. It was the perfect job for me. My hours were from eleven to three and even though I only worked twenty-three hours a week, I also received benefits, like health insurance and a paid vacation. As we walked downstairs, I thanked Don, but he brushed aside my gratitude and said, "Now, sweetheart, I couldn't let you work as cater-waiter forever as much as I love working with you. You have other things to do. Now let's hurry, I'd hate to miss seeing the other waiters change into their tuxedos."

Natural Born Collectors

IT'S SO annoying: At flea markets, Tom has to examine absolutely everything. Now he's inspecting an old Barbie carrying case and the dealer's giving him a strange look. I try to move Tom along, joking that we're going to be gay bashed if he keeps stopping to appraise collectibles that all too clearly reveal his sexual orientation. After all, we are antiquing in a redneck section of Florida near the retirement community where Tom's parents have settled. As we finally move on, Tom teasingly accuses me of paranoia and of having internalized homophobia. It's not that, I explain. It's just that I don't feel like fighting for your right to come out of the closet of Barbie's Dream House. For Tom, Lord Alfred Douglas was wrong: The Love that dare not speak its name was for his cousin's Barbie.

Occasionally while antiquing, I like to imagine that at some point in the 1970s North America sank like Atlantis, and every table at a flea market is an island where the flotsam of our culture has washed ashore. Every collectible is an artifact from a lost civilization, even if that civilization was as recent as the strange and mysterious Ford administration. At the next dealer's booth a plaster bust of Michael Jackson is sitting on top of a dishwasher with a missing door. Further along, Tom picks up a copy of the 1953 edition of *Europe on Five Dollars a Day*. This odd juxtaposition of junk somehow makes a profound, almost unsettling statement about American life, one that I couldn't have articulated better myself (even if I don't know what it means).

Tom points out a *Waltons* lunchbox. We share a moment of nostalgia, which is television's real gift to our generation. It's easier for us to be sentimental about the fictional households we grew up with than it is to be about our own families. Yet, its homespun decoration makes me wonder: What kind of child carried a *Waltons* lunchbox to school? Who would want to be eating a sandwich and a Ho-Ho and be reminded of Appalachian poverty? Less literal-minded than I, Tom wants to buy it, having come up with a fantasy of decorating the kitchen of our country house with lunchboxes from old TV series with rural themes, such as *Green Acres, The Beverly Hillbillies,* and *The Andy Griffith Show.* I tell him to save the twenty-five bucks—first we need to buy the country house.

We move on to the next dealer. I take pride in my ability to scan a table, spot the one piece of Russell Wright American Modern dinnerware hidden among the piles of undistinguished Fifties' knockoffs, snatch it up, immediately notice the chip on its edge, reject it, and move on. Like most flea-market regulars, I have an uncanny ability to focus precisely on what I collect: Russell Wright (in chutney, gray, or the scorned and therefore available chartreuse); Roseville Pinecone Pottery (*only*

the brown); Fiestaware; and my latest obsession, the Happy Face cookie jars made by McCoy.

Tom, however, is less discriminating, and belongs to that promiscuous class of shoppers who leave no stoneware unturned. He has to make eye contact with each piece of junk and flirt with the possibility of taking it home for an intense, if brief, fling. I'm into longer-term relationships with my possessions. I never buy anything I can't imagine still owning when Tom and I are elderly men finally living in that country house. The place will be packed with the things we bought for pennies that are now worth a small fortune, and that our nieces and nephews can't wait to auction when we finally kick the bucket.

There are several components of the collecting urge. There's the obvious analogy of the hunt: The thrill is the same whether you're bagging a deer or shopping bagging a Rookwood vase. But for many gay men, what starts them collecting is a form of sympathy for the cast-off and rejected belongings of America. At one time, all of the trendy antiques of the twentieth century such as Stickley furniture, Tiffany lamps, Art Deco, Fifties, etcetera, were unappreciated, neglected, and inexpensive until they were rediscovered by discerning collectors. Another reason for the popularity of flea markets is that they combine the all-American virtues of being a democratic form of recreation, open to anyone with the ability to browse, and offering the possibility of making real money. The collector starts by appreciating something's value and also hoping that it appreciates in value. The financial security of Amish quilts and Navaho rugs can be quite comforting.

There is a common misconception about collecting. For most collectors, it's not a violation of the commandment: Thou shall not covet thy neighbor's goods. That's too simple an explanation for a more complicated emotional process. The real thrill is that you want your neighbor to covet *your* goods. This is one commandment

that right-wing fundamentalists don't use against gay men, because some gay men are so particular about their possessions that it's doubtful whether they'd desire any of their neighbors' furniture. My next-door neighbor is a sixty-four-year-old retired legal secretary, and after seeing her apartment I was certain that I didn't covet her goods. In fact, I had to resist the impulse to make some suggestions about a few things that she and everyone else on the planet could do without. As an armchair theologian, I've always wondered if God distinguishes among degrees of covetousness? What if you covet something that only five other people on the planet value? Would a beer-can collector have to roast in hell for lusting after a Rheingold empty holding nails in his neighbor's basement?

Tom picks up a cracked pink-and-gray 1950s ashtray marked AS IS. Although these pieces are labeled in the present tense, it's obvious to the serious buyer that their lives as collectibles have all but ended. There are times when I feel that if I see one more repaired Eva Zeisel saltshaker I'm going to snap. I have an idea for a screenplay called *Natural Born Collectors*. Two temperamental men on a cross-country shopping spree force dealers to throw out all their defective antiques. And if they refuse—then they'll wind up on a shelf in the city morgue with a toe tag proclaiming, AS WAS.

I feel fortunate that Tom and I have a mutual interest in antiquing, because it seems that one of the most typical problems with many couples is that they don't share any recreational activities. It's easy to spot the many straight men at flea markets who have been dragged there by their wives. They inevitably end up huddled around the dealer who's selling a van load of rusty antique tools, relieved that they can leave behind the vintage table lamps so garish that turning them on seems redundant, and pick their way through gas caps for cars that haven't been produced since 1936.

Not that there aren't gay men equally drawn to tools. Once, in a barn in upstate New York, I tried to talk Tom into letting me buy a two-handled Paul Bunyan–type saw, which, at that moment, I had a vision of hanging fetchingly on the wall of our apartment. Tom dryly asked if I was also going to start wearing wool plaid shirts and work boots, and then went on to point out that only a big queen would want to own a decorative tool of a job that he wouldn't dream of doing in the first place. I reluctantly passed on that purchase.

I have to admit Tom and I make a good shopping team. What Tom lacks in the ability to spot a good deal, he makes up for with his ability to *make* a good deal. He's perfected a look of grudging desultory interest, shading imperceptibly into disdain, which has duped dealers from Orlando to Buffalo. Of course, I wonder if his parents, who paid thousands of dollars for his acting training at a prestigious university, would consider the expenditure justified, given the $2.50 he just saved on an *Archie* jelly-jar glass. At flea markets, when I'm attracted to something, I can't hide my interest—a trait that once caused me to make a purchase that has forever sullied my reputation as a savvy collector. I'm willing to share my tale of shopping shame in the hope that other young collectors will avoid my mistake:

At a New Mexico flea market my eye was caught by a small table that looked like something the Joads might've tossed off the back of the truck on their way to California. A rickety piece of junk held together by numerous coats of peeling paint, it would have been described in New York by that decorating euphemism "distressed," but the table went far beyond that—all the way to "screaming for help." Nevertheless, my first sight of this unfortunate object was a moment of collecting rapture and I decided that—at any reasonable cost—I was going to buy it. The table's appeal to me was that it seemed to embody many of the values I most cherish.

It had a matter-of-fact honesty yet was capable of charm, it had a demonstrated knack for survival, and it was a deal.

As I began to ask its price, I reached for my wallet and saw Tom flinch. I realized then, with that gesture, I had forfeited any bargaining power. When the dealer told me twenty dollars, I knew that I could've gotten it for fifteen, maybe even ten. I lamely tried to recover my authority with a timidly ventured, "Can you do any better than that?" but the price was firm. I handed over a twenty-dollar bill and consoled myself by imagining what a piece with this patina might go for in SoHo.

But this story gets worse. When I discovered at the shipping company that it would cost forty-nine dollars to ship this bargain from Santa Fe to New York, my humiliation was complete. Tom offered to dismantle the table in order to bring it back on the airplane, but I proudly refused to mar a perfect example of Vintage Americana. Why, the table could've been built by a homesteading farmer out of scraps of wood from an old Conestoga wagon. I just wouldn't be able to have the same feeling toward it knowing that it had been reassembled by a man whose closest experience of living off the land is growing fresh basil in a window box in Hell's Kitchen. But all this happened years ago, and I can now take some comfort from the fact that I've seen similar tables in SoHo that sell for way more than what I paid, shipping included.

Eureka! From several tables away, I see the signature yellow and distinctive shape of a Happy Face planter. I resist the impulse to clap my hands and skip. Happy Face planters are much rarer than the Happy Face cookie jars or coffee mugs, and I only own one. I keep my enthusiasm in check. I pick up the piece, looking discreetly for flaws.

"That's McCoy," says the dealer.

"Oh?" I respond, with as much nonchalance as I can

muster. "Tom, look at this," I say casually. I'm behaving in the emotionally restrained manner I spent two years in therapy trying to overcome. Tom turns up his nose.

"How much?" Tom inquires.

"Eighteen," says the dealer.

Tom knows I'm inwardly shrieking, *Eighteen! They can go for as high as forty!* So he takes the lead. He gives me a look implying I'm out of my mind for having any interest in a Happy Face planter, sneers at it briefly, and then puts it back in my hands. Shrugging his shoulders as if to say, *Do what you want,* and then he turns to walk away, his role in the transaction complete. I can feel the dealer's eyes upon me. I resist the impulse to reach for my wallet. "It's really more than I wanted to spend," I say, with distracted disappointment. The dealer clearly enjoys haggling. He's missing teeth and I suspect that someone once offered him fifty cents a piece for them. And he probably thinks that he got the better of the deal because those teeth didn't cost him a dime.

"Well . . . it's McCoy," he says, "but I'll take sixteen."

Yes!

Now Tom and I live in Los Angeles, the city where all collections are at the mercy of tectonic plates. During the last earthquake, I witnessed the destruction firsthand in wrecked houses and trashed apartments.

It hasn't stopped us from hitting the flea markets, but something has changed: maybe it's just my imagination, but I sometimes feel that my Happy Faces now have a nervous smile because they know that at any moment, they could come to a tragic end.

Between the Lines: On Auditioning to Play Tom Cruise's Gay Brother and Other Roles

ONE BLOCK away from my apartment in Hollywood lives an actor named Dennis Woodruff. I know this because Dennis wears his heart on the hood of his car. A psychological stratagem that makes sense only in Los Angeles. Dennis is quite possibly the only actor who ever thought that the right vehicle to launch his career is a 1979 Impala. Hanging on the sides of his car are several large signs, written in glued glitter, that say: HIRE DENNIS WOODRUFF, ACTOR. He also shrewdly included something visual to capture the passing-lane interest of movie and television executives—the types who think nothing of asking their personal assistants to read the Stop signs for them and write up a short synopsis. Randomly epoxied to the surface of Dennis's car are nine bogus Academy Award statuettes

and an array of his headshots. This display is made all the more absurd by the fact that Dennis's headshot photo is too candid. Instead of presenting his appearance, the portrait startlingly reveals the intensity of his desperation. The photographer has captured brooding good looks incubating a psychosis. He deludes himself that his career is gaining momentum because his job application travels at sixty-five miles per hour. It's all too apparent that the only time his chosen pursuit moves forward is when he pulls into a parking space. Although, as someone who auditioned unsuccessfully for two years before being offered my first acting job, I understand his predicament.

Two years before I moved to Los Angeles from New York, my first audition for a movie role came about after I performed a seven-minute spot of my stand-up on a Tuesday night at a gay bar in West Hollywood called Surge. I was in Los Angeles for two weeks because I had a job in Palm Springs and because my manager had arranged for me to perform at an "industry showcase." Using the adjective "entertainment" before the word "industry" is superfluous in Los Angeles, a city where the inhabitants think the world is a corporate symbol for Universal Studios. My manager wanted me to practice my set as much as possible before the showcase. So, in addition to spots at comedy clubs, he arranged for me to perform at the weekly talent contest hosted by "The Ravishing Rita," a lumbering woman named Donna in an oversized red wig and a wedding dress who impersonated her own gender. I hadn't learned yet that in Hollywood, the paradox of someone completely without talent hosting a talent competition isn't ironic—it's nontraditional casting.

For seven years, Donna persisted in hosting the show because of her belief that The Ravishing Rita would eventually catch on. She was unable to grasp that sensible people would rather catch polio than her act. Her

character development consisted of taking the worst qualities of human nature and presenting them as entertainment. Throughout the talent contest, she sat on the stage smirking or rolling her eyes at the performers. Her facial expressions were priceless only in the sense that you couldn't pay me enough to see them again. She garnered laughs doing this, proving conclusively that it's only a stereotype that all gay men have good taste.

Fortunately, due to my status as a special guest and not as a contestant, Donna refrained from doing her shtick during my performance, and although I was well received by the crowd, I felt no satisfaction in my accomplishment. For a performer, the applause of an undiscriminating audience is being damned with fans' praise. Afterward, while I was standing at the bar talking to my manager, a man approached me. He offered his business card, told me that he was a casting agent, and said that he'd like me to audition for a small part in a movie he was casting. I was flabbergasted. This was the first time that I had ever been offered a part in a gay bar that wasn't a bodily appendage.

My acting experience was limited. The last role I'd performed was that of an explorer in a sketch I wrote in high school for the Junior Class Talent Show. I'd written a Tarzan parody because the captain of the football team had asked me to write a role for him. He had an incredible physique and since the only thing "out" about me in high school was my frustration, I took this opportunity to display his talents in a loincloth. I was well suited to play the explorer because I had already discovered that I was gay, even though I still hadn't planted my flag in anyone's territory.

My manager called the agent the next day and was faxed the "sides"—the pages of dialogue I needed to prepare for my audition for the part of Walter in a movie called *The Scout*. When I picked up the script at his office, he was excited about the possibility of my becoming a movie star. He said, "Bob, this could take

your career in a whole new direction." He also thought it was good luck that the agent had discovered me. In a way, it was logical. In the history of Hollywood, more movie stars have probably been discovered standing in gay bars than sitting in drug stores.

I have to admit that the thought had also occurred to me that maybe I would become a movie star. It's hard not to think of becoming a movie star when you're in Los Angeles because there's not much else to do. So far, compared to New York, I had found the museums mediocre and the theater a bunch of actors auditioning for their own television shows, and since I had already been to the big theme parks in Florida, I could have skipped their smaller, dirtier sister parks in California. During my stay, I was sleeping on my friend Patty's couch and spending an exorbitant amount of money on meals and a rental car—all for the purpose of "helping my career." I needed a dream in order to not become completely depressed.

I read over the pages of script immediately. The character I was auditioning for, Walter, was an "elegantly dressed man" who was waiting in his therapist's office. I felt confident that I could bring a certain authenticity to the role. This was an activity I had some experience doing. My manager informed me that he had been told that the character was a gay man, but that he wasn't meant to be played stereotypically. After reading the script, I pointed out to him that Walter's big moment in the scene is when he looks through some magazines and asks the therapist:

WALTER
What happened to all the perfume samples?

In my next scene as Walter, I make Al, the film's main character, uncomfortable as they sit together in the waiting room. Finally, Al asks Walter why he's staring at him. Walter reveals that Al looks familiar and then asks

if he ever played baseball. When Al admits that he played for the Yankees, Walter informs him that he recognizes him from the baseball cards that he collected as a boy.

AL

Well, don't give that card up. You know what that's worth today?

WALTER

Oh, I don't have those cards anymore. I hated it. I started collecting fish when I was thirteen.

I assumed that the audience was to gather that Walter was gay because he was elegantly dressed, hated baseball, and probably wore too much cologne—he was a priss-elegant queen. It sounded stereotypical to me. But what did I know? Maybe that's the definition of "good acting": Making a silk purse out of a sow's ear. On second thought, perhaps that's not the right metaphor. I needed to butch up this character. I needed to make a sow's ear out of a silk purse. I didn't know yet that this was an equally impossible task. I was still enthusiastic and thought that it was possible to take an undistinguished line of dialogue and bring my unique interpretation to it. Whenever this insidious thought occurs to an actor, he should, paraphrasing King Lear, always remember: That way badness lies.

Was I selling out? I decided that by just *going* to the audition I wasn't selling out—that would only occur when I got the job and cashed the check. I didn't know it yet, but after reading some more scripts, I'd realize that an actor with scruples is probably unemployable. At some point, I might come to a line of dialogue that I wouldn't cross. But first I wanted to see if I could even get an acting job.

That night I took a fluorescent highlighter and marked my lines. Clearly, I was still new to acting. Over

the next few years, I'd realize the futility of trying to find highlights in most scripts. I felt reasonably confident about my audition because I had recently started taking acting lessons, but I had no aspirations of Shakespearean grandeur. My goal was to master the advice Spencer Tracy reputedly gave to every actor: Know your lines and don't bump into the furniture. However, for the big queens I was going to be asked to play, better advice would have been: Know your furniture and don't bump into the lines.

My audition was at Warner Brothers in Burbank. Arriving at the gate of the studio, I told the guard my name and was directed to a remote parking area. The hierarchy of parking spaces is a recognized system of power in Los Angeles. Having your own conveniently located, reserved space on the studio lot is a coveted perk. What's surprising is that the system is still relatively egalitarian. While the locations may differ, all parking spaces are approximately the same size. In L.A., where the name of the city is the only thing ever abbreviated, the Bigger Is Better ethos of big money, big breasts, and big muscles hasn't yet affected parking. Someday, if just one superstar demands a bigger space for his Porsche, white lines and contracts will be redrawn across Southern California—having your own lot will become the ultimate in career and parking validation.

After I stepped off the elevator and looked down the hallway, I knew immediately where the casting office was located because several extraordinarily handsome men were pacing back and forth, muttering their lines. From a distance, they appeared to be Apollos praying to themselves. One particular actor drew my attention. As he walked, he recited his lines, charging every word, every punctuation mark, with meaning. His dialogue must have been written entirely in **BOLD**. It was uncomfortable to watch him rehearse. Even the pages of his script turned in embarrassment.

As I knocked on the door of the casting office, I was

aware of the other actors sizing me up. I suddenly felt self-conscious, a sensation that evaporates quickly in the climate of Los Angeles, where drawing undue attention to yourself is considered free publicity. From behind the door, someone said, "Come in." I entered and saw a young woman sitting at a desk. She had the perpetually disturbed look typical of personal assistants. (Being a personal assistant is the most thankless job since food tasting for the pharaohs. Only personal assistants are expected to give up their lives screening phone calls and visitors in an attempt to prevent deadly chaos from ever reaching their bosses. It's tragic that the people in both careers think that the job is going to be a stepping-stone and end up discovering it can be tombstone.) She was harried, which meant that for convenience she acted haughty. She had mastered one of the prerequisites for a career in show business: the ability to act lofty while standing on the bottom rung of the ladder of success. "Are you here for the lifeguard?" she snapped. So *that* explained all the beautiful men. "No," I told her, "I'm here for Walter." She abruptly asked me to sign in and then wait outside until my name was called.

In the hallway, I sat down in the only remaining empty seat. I noticed that all of the auditioning actors seemed to be cut from the same cloth—a skin-tight fabric that hugged their well-developed bodies in deserved self-congratulation. My acting teacher had suggested that it would help the audition if I dressed for the part of Walter. Since I'd neglected ever to buy a caftan or a red silk smoking jacket, I wore penny loafers, chinos, and an indigo button-down shirt. My Walter could be mistaken for a preppie college student.

While waiting to be called, I was interrupted from reading through my lines when a god spoke to me. I'd been chosen, and when he asked, I was willing to sacrifice my only pen. He was magnificent—his shadow was better looking than most people. He had a spectacular body that he knew how to display—if his tank top

had been any tighter it would have been subcutaneous. His tousled black hair made him appear to have just woken up—a look that most people find hard to maintain with consciousness. And his voice was so deep and incredibly sexy that I had to resist the impulse to grope for his words.

My encounter with divinity made me a changed man. I threw a bucket of cold water on my libido but that dousing only gave it another reason to strip off its clothing. My boyfriend, though, had nothing to worry about because the animal my lust most resembles is a 'fraidy cat. Conversation with a god is usually one-sided. It's a shame because only afterward do you realize that you've missed the opportunity to find the answers to questions that have always baffled humanity: What is the meaning of life? Why is there suffering? Are your eyes really that color?

At some point during our conversation, I realized that his snow-capped teeth were his brightest feature. When he asked me what part I was auditioning for, I told him Walter. He added unnecessarily that he was auditioning for the lifeguard. Then the god confessed that he was nervous because this was only his second audition. I wasn't nervous until he spoke to me.

After twenty minutes, my name was called. The casting agent was a woman in her early thirties who wore a pair of thick black eyeglasses that were so stylish they affected my vision more than hers. Her desk groaned under the piles of headshots and résumés, which was understandable—I'd complain too if I had to support that many lies. Following our handshake, she politely asked me if I was ready. "Sure." We read through the lines quickly. I surprised myself by remembering most of the dialogue. After we finished the scene, I watched her face, searching for a clue to how I did. She smiled broadly. "Bob, that was great. Thank you so much for coming in." Her smile was like a Samuel Beckett play— easy to read but difficult to interpret. So I left the au-

dition thinking that it went well but not knowing for certain. Acting wasn't remotely similar to stand-up comedy, where I always knew if I did well by the reaction of the audience.

The next day I flew to Rochester to perform at a comedy club. When I arrived at my hotel, there was a message from my manager asking me to call him immediately. He told me that I had received a callback, which meant that the following week I would audition for the director of the film. I was elated to hear this, but for the first time I also felt nervous about the audition. My anxiety turned out to be gratuitous. Two days later, my manager called again to inform me that Walter's scenes were going to be cut from the script. It was just as well, I needed more time to work on my character. If I were going to play a stereotypical queen, I'd need to be shameless.

My next round of auditions occurred on my next trip to Los Angeles. I had just come back from performing in Australia, and I was trying to prepare myself for the taping of my own half-hour comedy special in San Francisco. For a few days I had known that I needed a haircut. I finally reached that state of dissatisfaction with my appearance when getting a haircut became the most important and satisfying accomplishment of the entire day. No matter what their sexual orientation, when most men decide that they really need a haircut, they pursue a barber with the same single-minded desire that they pursue sex: We need to get our locks off.

I went to a barber on Sunset Boulevard who taught me an insightful lesson about the metropolitan differences between New York's In-Your-Face attitude and Los Angeles's In-Your-Face-Lift phoniness. In New York, if you tell a barber that you're a comedian he'll tell you a joke. In Los Angeles, if you tell a barber that you're a comedian he'll tell you the names of celebrities whose hair he once cut. That's the difference between the two

cities: In New York, everyone thinks that they're talented. In Los Angeles, everyone knows someone talented.

Since arriving in Los Angeles, I had been going out on auditions. I had recently auditioned for an underwear commercial in which the opening line of dialogue was, "Ladies, you do most of the shopping, and speaking for the guys, thanks. But please, don't buy us that low-end cheap underwear." It was reassuring to know that heterosexual men suffer from their own stereotypes.

My manager was trying to get me an audition for a part that he had recently read about in the "breakdowns," short character descriptions provided to agents and managers of upcoming parts in feature films and television programs. The show that he wanted me to audition for was an untitled pilot about a female television news reporter in Chicago. The character I would play was described as:

ANDREW HAWKINS: The show's makeup man. A flamboyant busybody. Andrew is married with two children. . . .

It was comforting that the character of Andrew Hawkins was fictional because then one could at least hope that he didn't exist. I highlighted my lines in Day-Glo pink, but somehow the color wasn't flamboyant enough for this character's screaming dialogue, a more appropriate hue would have been Mama Rose. As I highlighted, I couldn't quite believe what I saw.

ANDREW
Chaos! I'm seeing chaos! This is an elevator not a playpen, people!

*

ANDREW
Everyone knows who I am, missy.

*

ANDREW

I don't think I was talking to you, Mr. Smarty Pants.

*

ANDREW

My name is Andrew. I am the station's cosmetologist and coiffeur.

*

ANDREW

Can I give you one more little piece of advice?

TOM

Does she have a choice?

ANDREW

Your hair.

BONNIE

My hair.

ANDREW

Needs to be big. TV is big. Chicago is big. Your hair needs to be big. Big big big big big big big!

BONNIE

Let me see if I understand what you're saying: Big?

ANDREW

Snap-a-doodle-do! You come see me any time. I'm a Houdini with a hot comb!

From the dialogue, I assumed that in the show's next episode Andrew would try to get into Mr. Smarty's Pants. He's described as flamboyant and very effeminate, yet married with two children. It was gratifying to see that I wasn't being typecast; I was being considered to play a straight man who only appears to be a big fag. I couldn't imagine this character being able to reproduce children; I doubted whether he could reproduce a photocopy. I suppose the likelihood of his fathering two children was possible if he and his wife had used artificial

insemination, although my guess is that he would be more accustomed to being inseminated than his wife. Maybe I'm being cynical. There are many gay men who are fathers. There are also probably some extremely effeminate gay men who are fathers. But an extremely effeminate gay man who calls a woman "missy," uses the exclamatory phrase "Snap-a doodle-do!" *and* who is the father of two children strains the credulity of biology and dramaturgy.

Somewhere it is written in Hollywood that sassy black women, old people talking dirty, and flamboyant gay men are always funny. Straight queens are a recent addition to this cast of stock characters. They allow the writers to employ a broad stereotype, without suffering the stigma of being accused of perpetuating an old stereotype, by propagating a new stereotype. It's a brilliant strategy. It allows them to have their cocksucker and eat him too.

Why is the shorthand for a gay man still usually a limp wrist? There's nothing intrinsically wrong with portraying a gay man—or even a straight man—as a big queen. But the defining characteristic of being a big queen isn't effeminacy—some of the biggest queens I know are built like brick operahouses—the defining characteristic of a big queen is flamboyant *enthusiasm*. This enthusiasm can be for anything: musicals, muscles, or even for one emotion, such as bitterness. And it's quite possible for heterosexuals to be big queens. The overly enthusiastic heterosexual fans of Elvis Presley and *Star Trek* are definitely big queens in the exact same way as the over-enthusiastic homosexual fans of Judy Garland and *The Mary Tyler Moore Show*. It's even possible for women to be big queens. I've known lesbians who are as devoted to the stars of women's tennis as some gay men are to Sixties girl groups. As somewhat of a connoisseur of queens—a Queen queen—I would love to witness a Judy queen and an Elvis queen debating the respective demerits of each of their idols:

"Elvis had a drinking problem."
"Judy could drink Elvis under the table."
"Elvis gained more weight."
"Judy lost more weight."
"Elvis was addicted to painkillers."
"No pill could stop Judy's pain!"

Contrary to television situation comedies, being a Big Queen is an uncommon calling. For most people, whether straight or gay, it's sometimes difficult to have much enthusiasm for your own life, let alone the life of someone who died thirty years ago. The hallmarks of a big queen are ardor, verve, and vehemence bordering on the fanatic. Or to put it more crudely, a queen is a man who would rather have a paint job than a blow job. Big queens are aesthetic extremists who, unlike most extremists in the twentieth century, have so far eschewed violence. All it would take is one overly critical queen with a misguided love of the theater and a penchant for terrorism to give "bombing" on Broadway a terrifying new connotation.

I knew that I wasn't right for the part of Andrew Hawkins, but after I read the script, instead of just being honest and telling my manager how I felt, I pretended to be enthusiastic about the audition. No wonder I wasn't being cast in anything. I was devoting all of my energy to acting in my real life instead of at the auditions. It's not a good idea for an actor to spend more time protecting others' feelings rather than expressing his own. And it was unfair that I was auditioning only for characters who were such stereotypes. For the audition, not only did I have to give a good performance as the character, I also had to act like I would be happy playing such a character.

I sat down with the casting director for the audition, but before we started, she used her intercom to yell at her assistant, "Karen, I *really* don't understand why

we're out of diet Coke." I could tell that she was a sour-puss. Every time a smile crept across her face, it took one look and ran. As my heart sank, my confidence scrambled to find a lifeboat. I made a joke in an attempt to relax myself. Her lips curled slightly. I should have known better. There's nothing more difficult than trying to entertain people in the entertainment industry. The chips on their shoulders are like dandruff. If you knock one off, there's always another.

For this audition, I based my performance on a food processor in use: I was loud, irritating, and mincing. I deliberately overplayed the part. Imagine my dismay when later my manager was told by the casting director that I wasn't flamboyant enough. Later, when I gave her criticism some consideration, I blamed my upbring-ing for this setback. I don't consider myself to be espe-cially masculine, but I'm undemonstrative—which, in my family, is the definition of manliness. In my family, masculinity isn't about being macho because even act-ing macho requires the expression of some degree of emotion. The men in my family are taciturn and inhib-ited—hardly the qualities expected of a Hollywood sissy.

Almost a year passed before I had my next audition. I had to finish writing a book and it had been a relief to deal with an editor instead of casting directors. He at least told me when he liked or didn't like something. I was in Los Angeles to perform at a charity event when my manager called and told me that I was going to receive a fax at my hotel for an audition the next day. By now I was less enthusiastic. I asked him what "they" were looking for this time: gay, homo, or faggy? He laughed and said that he hadn't seen the script, which was being faxed to me directly.

On the top of the first page of the fax transmission was a note scribbled in heavy black ink:

IT'S ROY'S BIRTHDAY—HE'S INVITED HIS GAY SON
(R.J.) TO A PARTY ON THE ISLAND—R.J. BRINGS HIS
OBVIOUSLY GAY BUT <u>NOT</u> OVERDONE!! LOVER
LUKE.

Someone had felt the need to write additional stage
directions to clear up any confusion there might be as
to the desired level of queerness. I doubted whether the
same person would ever have written OBVIOUSLY
BLACK or OBVIOUSLY JEWISH BUT <u>NOT</u> OVER-
DONE!!

The script pages were for an episode of the television
sitcom *Wings*, for which I was to audition for the part
of Luke. I called my manager. "What exactly does 'Ob-
viously gay but *not* overdone!' mean? Camp without a
bonfire? Breezy but not swishy? Regal but not too
queeny? Dizzy but don't spin out of control? A fairy with
clipped wings? A pansy but not in full-bloom? Hit the
falsetto note but don't hold it too long?"

I took a look through the pages.

HELEN
How was your flight?

LUKE
(THIS IS SAID IN A GOOD-NATURED WAY NOT BITCHY)
Hideous. I don't do well in the air. If God intended people
to fly, we'd have all been born with wires in our backs like
Mary Martin in "Peter Pan."

*

LUKE
Have you guys thought about a bed and breakfast?

JOE
Nah, we can't afford to get away right now. Besides, I hate
sharing a bathroom with strangers.

LUKE
No, as an investment. I bought one five years ago just out-
side the city and it's really been profitable.

I went in to audition for the part of Luke at Paramount Studios. While sitting in the waiting area outside the casting director's office, I could hear the other actors' auditions through the door. One actor auditioning was overprojecting, the walls unable to muffle his unctuousness. Someone had once made the unforgivable mistake of complimenting his voice and consequently, when he spoke, it sounded like he patted each word on the back with his tongue before bidding it adieu. His voice would be impossible to live with—I imagined his uvula hanging by a noose. When he finished his audition, to my astonishment, out of the office came a rugged-looking man with a face like a snow tire, who wore a flannel shirt, blue jeans, and cowboy boots instead of a blue blazer and an ascot.

When I was asked in, I noticed that posters for several plays—*Pippin* at the Westbury Music Fair; *Little Me* at the Bucks County Playhouse—were hanging on the walls of the office. Theater memorabilia in a casting director's office is always an indication that he's a former actor. Now in his early forties, he probably thought of himself as having a nose for talent, although for years he'd been incapable of detecting that he stunk as an actor. Incapable of having his own career, he now had the power to crush other actors' hopes and dreams, proving that sometimes those who can't do, teach everyone a lesson.

After I sat down, the first thing I noticed was his clothes: Whatever money he made wasn't being spent on his appearance. He looked in need of a haircut, and though he may have called his rumpled clothing "vintage," it was merely out of date. We chatted for a few minutes before the audition, and when I mentioned living in Manhattan he offered the fact that he had once lived there. I waited for him to pour out his eagerness to return to New York if he could only build a split-level ranch house and carport in Central Park. I was mistaken: He was the other type of ex–New

Yorker, the kind who moved to Manhattan when they were twenty-two but then after six months fled in terror and have been complaining about it ever since. Instead of inducing my sympathy, they just go on and on about how hard it was to live there, while I'm thinking about how hard it is to listen to them whine. They fail to make the connection that the reason they found the city unfriendly is because most New Yorkers are too astute to become friends with a bore.

We read through the lines, twice, and it seemed to go okay but I never received a callback. I was beginning to think that Alfred Hitchcock's famous comment that actors are like cattle was inaccurate. He chose the wrong ruminant animal; actors are lambs who with every audition are led to slaughter.

At the end of 1995, Tom and I finally moved to Los Angeles. Over the previous two years, I made most of my income working in Los Angeles and it seemed ridiculous to keep flying out there from New York almost every month.

One morning, after our expensive move, I was talking to my manager when he off-handedly mentioned that I had been asked to audition for a sitcom pilot but that he knew I wasn't right for the part. He said that the character was offensively stereotypical. I asked him for more information. Since we had moved I had done nothing but spend money and I felt that I couldn't afford to turn down a possible job. He reluctantly arranged for me to do the audition. After reading the character description and script I understood why even my manager had misgivings. The character was:

Sheldon "Margarita" Horn: 33 years old, jovial and clearly effeminate, this effusive bartender works at Hals's Bar.

The character was entirely summed up when another character asked him:

HAL

Sheldon, why do you insist on calling yourself Margarita?

MARGARITA

Every bartender needs a name to hang his purse on. Bill down the street already claimed Shirley Temple. And Virgin Mary didn't seem to suit my life-style.

I was late for my audition for the part of Margarita. Since moving to Los Angeles I hadn't mastered the ability to determine the amount of time it takes to do an errand as I had in New York. In New York, most of the threats to my punctuality were easily visible or well-publicized beforehand: dogshit on sidewalks, bad weather, parades, Christmas shoppers, bomb threats. In Los Angeles, the obstacles to promptness are usually caused by unforeseeable disasters: car accidents, mud slides, earthquakes, jury verdicts, cult suicides, the premiere of a big-budget movie where the biggest special effect is inadvertent—the audience hated it.

I thought I could go to the bank and still have plenty of time to get to the studio by eleven. My bank is the AFTRA-SAG Credit Union, open only to members of the American Federation of Television and Radio Actors and the Screen Actors Guild. The credit union is located on the third floor of an office building located on Hollywood Boulevard directly across from Mann's Chinese Theater, where some former members of the credit union have their proof of identification inconveniently preserved in cement.

The AFTRA-SAG Credit Union is a unique financial institution if only for the portrait it presents of the acting profession. The chorus line of customers always looks like a casting call. Actresses whose overuse of makeup

indicates a willingness to go on stage at a moment's notice. Character types who, after years of struggling to make it, now look more unsavory than off-beat. Studly actors wearing T-shirts emblazoned with a picture of the young Marlon Brando in *The Wild Ones*, therefore making it that much easier for a possible movie director to notice the resemblance. Every time the tellers yell, "Next," I almost expect the customer at the front of the line to start a dramatic or comic monologue and have one song prepared. It's common knowledge though that most of the customers probably spend more time each year before the bank's security cameras than they do before a 35-millimeter Panaflex. Behind the row of bank tellers is a large window filled by the marquee of a nearby theater that taunts the aspirations of actors depositing paychecks from their day jobs. While standing in line, I always feel melancholy. Somehow we all seem to be waiting for a call that might never come. When I leave, I always notice the temp agency located conveniently near the elevator.

Well, after my stop at the bank, I became stuck in traffic on the Hollywood Freeway. As I crept toward my exit, I recalled that an actress I knew was in a serious car accident while she was on her way to an important audition. As the paramedics and police assisted her, she found herself saying, "I've got to call my agent. Please, I've got to call my agent." She was aware that she sounded like a ridiculously self-absorbed actress, but she was unable to stop herself. At that moment, she was frightened that her new agent would think that she was irresponsible and her biggest concern was that the accident would hurt her career.

I was fifteen minutes late but the casting director was extremely gracious about it. Because I was flustered, I was much more talkative than I normally would have been and started an impromptu conversation about the quality of the script. The casting director, Alice, in-

formed me that she had been told that "they" (she didn't mention whether she was referring to the writers or the producers) didn't want the role played stereotypically.

While saying this, her eyebrow lifted almost imperceptibly as if she were aware of the absurdity of the request but she was too professional to openly be disparaging. I fortunately was under no such constraints. "C'mon, Alice, the character's a man called Margarita. Dialogue like this probably *causes* homosexuality." She laughed and then asked me to stand when I performed the scene—she wanted me to try to make an entrance as Margarita. When we started reading, I stumbled on the first words because I wasn't used to speaking in imaginary heels. I soon found my balance but I was unsteady as I sashayed through the rest of the dialogue. When I didn't get the part, I wasn't surprised. I think I put my foot in my mouth when I told the casting director that doing this scene would be committing a heinous act.

I temporarily stopped going out for auditions when I was hired to write for what would turn out to be a short-lived television show. This was my first network writing job, and my initial enthusiasm was like that of most virgin television writers: It was unencumbered by considerations of anything but giving pleasure and making enough money to qualify for the Writers Guild health insurance. I really wanted to do well on this job and when my manager called to ask if I was interested in going out on an audition, I hesitated. The movie was *Jerry Maguire*, and the part was the gay brother of a character to be played by Tom Cruise. It was just one line, but my manager reminded me, "Bob, if you got the part, you'd get to meet Tom Cruise," a thought that had crossed my mind with enough force to leave a welt. I immediately asked him to fax me the part:

JERRY MAGUIRE

149 EXT. DOROTHY'S BACKYARD—DAY

Rod Tidwell sings Marvin Gaye's "What's Going On" at the wedding for assorted guests here in the backyard.
Contrary to his own belief, Rod is not a gifted singer.
In the wedding band, standing on a small stage in the corner are Chad and Dooler.

ON JERRY

Who stands watching, smile pasted on, with FATHER and well-dressed BROTHER. They are the stoic Maguires.

> BROTHER

Where are all your friends?

> JERRY
> (looking around)

In the band.

(CUT TO THE NEXT SCENE)

I couldn't claim that this character was stereotypical because even though he was well dressed, it wasn't due to his sexual orientation; he was after all a guest at a wedding. But here's why Cameron Crowe, who wrote the script, earned my deepest respect: If this character was gay, at least for once he was described as stoic. Stoic is my forte as an actor. What the casting directors don't understand is that my headshot is a perfect illustration of my ability to find one unvarying expression and to hold it.

I went into the audition in high spirits. There were two casting directors in the room almost as if the smallness of the part required the attention of two observers because one of them might blink and miss my talent. I shook hands with the casting directors and then settled in my chair, confident that I would get this part.

And then, I forgot the line. For some reason, I faltered when we started the scene and we had to do it again. My face flushed in humiliation, causing the room to tint pink. The casting directors averted their eyes from the glare. After the audition I tried to slip out of the room as unobtrusively as possible.

There are other gay characters that I've auditioned for. I auditioned for not one but two parts on a sitcom where one of the show's main characters opens the door of her apartment on New Year's Eve and finds two men who have accidentally rung the wrong doorbell.

<div align="center">

PARTYGOER

</div>

Oh, wait a minute. This is not Apartment 4.
(TO HIS BOYFRIEND) Honey?

<div align="center">

PARTYGOER'S BOYFRIEND

</div>

(TO HEATHER) We're sorry. Happy New Year.

Before the audition, all of the actors were asked by the casting director to pair off and audition as couples. When we were called in, each of us took turns playing both the partygoer and his boyfriend. It was discouraging to learn that some of these arranged relationships actually worked out but somehow even these couples still weren't right for the parts.

A few months ago, at the end of a gloomy day that I had spent in contemplation on the idea that hope springs eternal while despair sits comfortably, I received a telephone call from my manager announcing that I was going to be a writer and a performer on a new sketch comedy series. Eight months before we had submitted a package of sketches and a videotape, but I hadn't given it further thought since anyone who attempts a career in the arts learns quickly that most potential jobs remain in perpetual abeyance while we

continue to stick our résumés in bottles and throw them into the we'll-see.

My first question to my manager was "Don't I have to audition?" He replied, "No, the producer knows you and he loved the sketches." It was such good news that I was almost tempted to exclaim, "Snap-a-doodle-do!" I recognized that this show could be that legendary opportunity of a lifetime. The producer's premise for the program was for it to feature a "gay and lesbian sensibility," and since he's heterosexual, maybe he could finally define that illusive concept. It was exciting. I was going to be able to write my own parts without feeling compelled to make them obviously gay. But listen, Mary. Between you and me, girlfriend to girlfriend, I just hope that I don't suck and blow my big chance.

Ma Nature

DON'T RISE and shine. I rise and flicker, unsteadily, until I've had my coffee. It's six A.M. on a Monday in May and I'm going on a guided birdwalk in Central Park. Coffee in the morning is my religion. We true believers drink two cups to lead us not into temptation to go back to bed. I keep telling myself: I'm a morning person. I just wish the sun rose at noon. We're meeting at seven A.M. and I have to hurry to make it. Outside my building, I see my first birds of the day: two sparrows on the sidewalk pecking at a discarded half-eaten slice of pizza. In New York, even the birds love Italian food. I'm reminded of Lord Tennyson's line that Nature is red in tooth and claw, although it loses some of its poetic impact when the source of the color is tomato sauce.

Dawn in Manhattan is magical. The sunlight on the storefronts looks like an Edward Hopper—if someone installed ugly, graffiti-covered metal gates on the windows. When I reach the subway station and put my token in the slot, even the grudging turnstile seems reluctant to be pushed this early. I board the train and the grim faces of my fellow subway passengers make it clear that no one ever takes public transportation for a joyride. I soon arrive at the corner of 81st Street and Central Park West, where several birders have already arrived and are walking in small circles, looking remarkably like a group of pigeons. Our guide, Opal Lawton, is busy collecting the three-dollar fee for the birdwalk. A flamboyantly plain woman in her mid-forties, Opal's hair is mousy brown with highlights of gerbil and hamster. She wears prim, gold wire-rimmed eyeglasses and her pilled gray sweater is shedding stuffed animals while her unfashionably generic white running shoes seem to caution, "Slow down." Opal is a tote-bag lady. Tote-bag ladies can't be bothered with their appearance because they're too busy donating time and money to charities and public service organizations. Opal's tote bag features the logo of the New York City Audubon Society, the sponsor of our birdwalk.

I have to confess something: For years, I was a closeted bird-watcher. It was difficult for me to admit because there still seems to be a social stigma attached to being considered a nerd. There has been considerable speculation as to whether people choose to be bird-watchers or are just born that way. I'm not sure. I've always been interested in nature but there was no recruitment by other bird-watchers. There just came a time when I finally had to admit that my interest in birds wasn't a phase that I was going through. So I bought a pair of binoculars, a field guide, and started birding.

I nod hello to a few people while Opal announces the day's big news with the exact same intonation in

which she probably gave her speech as high school vale-dictorian. "I know that you've all probably heard on the Birding Hotline about the recent sighting of the Painted Bunting." A hubbub of anticipation arises from our group, and like an elementary school teacher taking her pupils on a field trip, Opal waits a moment for us to settle down before she continues: "The Bunting was spotted yesterday near the trees north of the Delacorte Theater and that's where we'll start today. I think everyone's here. Let's get going."

Roger Tory Peterson in his masterpiece *Birds of the Eastern United States* describes the Painted Bunting as "the most gaudily colored North American songbird." The male has a purple head, a red breast, and a bright green back. Imagine a House Sparrow impersonating a Macaw. I'm familiar with the Painted Bunting's appearance because I own the complete forty-two-volume set of the *Roger Tory Peterson Field Guides*. Each volume is devoted to a different aspect of Natural History, covering such topics as birds, beetles, mammals, plants, fish, reptiles, amphibians, and even rocks and minerals. What I admire is that each book is written by an expert who has devoted years to mastering one subject. Then, in an act of audacity that springs from a narrow-minded focus seemingly shared only by naturalists and the founders of religious cults, they spend years writing and illustrating a book, sharing their particular and possibly peculiar en-thusiasm. In theory, I now have the resources to identify every species of flora and fauna in North America, from arbor vitae to zebra mussels. My fantasy is that someday I'll be able to step outdoors and know the name of every plant and animal as I know the names of my relatives, but with the added bonus that I won't have to stop and ask how they're doing. Field guides fascinate me. Reading a field guide is like flipping through a lavish shopping catalog for The Planet Earth: *"Cuckoos come in your choice of Yellow Billed and Black Billed. I'm sorry, the California Towhee is not available east of the Mississippi*

and the Passenger Pigeon is out of stock. We're not going to re-order.

When I first started going on Opal's birdwalks I didn't feel particularly welcome. And it's really a blow to one's self-esteem when geeks give you attitude. But since then I've become friendly with many of Opal's regulars, and after observing the birders in our group, I now feel qualified to write a social field guide for identifying every species of wallflower. The weedy types who are always a mess and thrive anywhere. The rare orchids who only flourish under mysterious conditions and can't be transplanted from their natural habitat. The wild mushrooms who look scary but are really delightful and the thistles who make everyone uncomfortable.

"Hi, Bob."

I hear a deep male voice that sounds as if it's rising from the bottom of a large purse. It's Martin. We struck up a conversation during one of Opal's birdwalks and while the topic was birds there was something about Martin that made me suspect that he too was gay. What this Q-factor is I can't say. Devotees of Eastern religions might say that his inner eye winked at me. Of course, there are no field guides that teach us to identify members of our own species. We have to learn to look for the identifying marks in a gay man just as we would an unfamiliar bird. What makes identification sometimes difficult is that gay men have many confusing plumages, from odd birds in feather boas to bald eagles in leather. But the process of attribution is the same whether one is trying to determine a warbler's identity or whether a businessman has a boyfriend.

The problem is that some gay men are more difficult to identify than others. There are gay men who, like some birds, give away their identities as soon as they open their mouths. Everyone can spot the flamingos of our species, but most gay men are more like the confusing sparrows where the differences are more subtle. We have to look for the distinguishing field marks.

Check for the arched eyebrow. Is that a nipple ring?
What ruffles his feathers? But that isn't enough. Because
gay men often act and look exactly like their straight
counterparts, this means that instead of basing an iden-
tification upon appearance, one has to make close obser-
vations about behavior in the field. Choice of habitat,
flocking patterns, diet, and nest building can all give
one important clues in determining sexual orientation.
Using my powers of deduction in this manner makes me
feel like Sherlock Homo. Only the genre is not a who-
dunit, it's a whoyadunitwith, where the detective tries
to figure out what kind of bodies would be found in the
suspect's bed.

When I first met Martin, I immediately noticed that
he was in his midfifties and yet wore a tiny silver-and-
turquoise earring. In our enlightened era, it's perfectly
acceptable for straight men also to have a fondness for
accessories, but then I asked Martin what he did for a
living. "I teach bridge," he said. I had to suppress the
urge to melodramatically yell, "Aha!" His admission let
me make the call that Martin was gay because the odds
of a middle-aged heterosexual man wearing an earring
and teaching a card game for a living are so remote as
to be almost statistically impossible. Martin later verified
my attribution by mentioning the country house in New
Hope, Pennsylvania, which he shares with "Roger."

"Bob, you're not awake yet. Don't worry, this Painted
Bunting's a real eye-opener. We saw three of them last
year in Florida. They look like they're wearing golf out-
fits."

Jessica tells me this in a loud voice that causes heads
to turn in China. Martin recently introduced me to Jes-
sica and Herb, a heavyset couple in their early forties. I
can tell that they're serious birders by their Zeiss bin-
oculars and their canvas jackets, which are completely
covered with the patches of various birding organiza-
tions, making them look like two old suitcases.

In Manhattan, even the small talk is the biggest in

the world. During the first five minutes of our meeting, Jessica learned more about my private life than I had revealed to a therapist in the first month, and she told me everything about herself, including her opinion that right-wing conservatives want to destroy the environment because "those bastards think their property on Martha's Vineyard will increase in value if the rest of the planet's unlivable." I immediately liked her. Jessica's a voice teacher, which is somewhat surprising because her heavy New York accent dots every *i* with a bagel. I'm pleased that she's in our group because she should be able to flush out birds with a whisper. Herb and Jessica have birded all over the country, and from anecdotal evidence they seem to have fought for a parking space in all of our national parks and wildlife refuges. Herb told me, "Longneck Beach was the worst. They only had room for about forty cars and I'm sorry but I didn't know that family from Iowa was waiting. When the other car pulled out, I pulled in."

"Good morning, Miss Shoup."

"Good morning, Robert."

Miss Emma Shoup is English, and for some reason she always calls me Robert even though I was introduced to her as Bob. She makes me feel like we're characters in a Barbara Pym novel. Miss Shoup is the oldest birder in our group. I'm unsure of her exact age but it seems possible that she has birding memories of the Carolina Parakeet, which became extinct in 1914. Miss Shoup is a memorable sight in a city filled with people who covet notoriety. She birds with a pair of ancient field glasses of such an unwieldy size that it would be easier for her to hand-hold the Palomar Observatory. Her tweedy outfits are so coarsely woven that she seems to be thatched, and they're constructed with a sturdiness ordinarily seen only in dams and bridges. Ornithology is Miss Shoup's passion and she will frequently carry on a conversation without once making eye contact as she constantly scans the trees in search of birds. "Did you see the Nashville

Warbler?" she'll inquire, and before you can answer she'll walk away mumbling, "Its call is most distinctive. *Seebit, seebit, seebit, seebit, tititititititi.*"

"Opal, has anyone alerted the National Rare Bird Alert about the Painted Bunting?"

Jack Heatherly asked this question in the ominous tone of voice of a man used to getting things done by making people fear for their jobs. He is one of the several businessmen who bird the park early in the morning before heading down to Wall Street. Jack birds with such competitiveness that I wonder if he's using *The Wealth of Nations* as a field guide. He is extremely knowledgeable and authoritative about the attribution of a hard-to-identify bird. "No. That's *definitely* a Marsh Wren. *Look* at the white markings on its back," he'll say with the same arrogance that must cause secretaries to shudder.

"Hi, Rick."

"Hi, Bob. Have you seen a Blackburnian today?" asks Rick Lorber.

Rick always asks me about the Blackburnian Warbler—it's become a running joke between us that I still haven't seen one yet. The Blackburnian is one of the most spectacular Eastern warblers. It's a black-and-white bird with what every guide book describes as a fiery orange head and throat. They are regular migrants through the park each year, but they're always sighted on the day I don't bird, or even more maddening, I'm told that someone just spotted one five minutes ago. Rick's a very handsome African-American man who works as an editor for a comic-book company. Reading comic books has somehow made Rick assume all the attributes of a superhero. He has a massive bodybuilder's physique and his personality is as friendly and helpful as Clark Kent's. Even Miss Shoup makes eye contact and smiles when she speaks to Rick about a recently reported Red-headed Woodpecker.

As we walk, I discreetly note the other birders' bin-

oculars. A birder's level of interest in birding can be determined by how much money has been spent on binoculars. One of the most grueling aspects of birding is buying a pair of binoculars because you have to master complicated optical terminology such as depth of field and light-gathering abilities. The consensus among serious birders is that the best binoculars are manufactured in Germany. The binoculars manufactured there are so ruthlessly proficient that I'm grateful that the Germans don't dominate the manufacture of dental floss. After a year of neurotic comparison shopping, trying to comprehend laws of optics that eluded Galileo, I finally bought a pair of Leica Ultra 10x42 binoculars that cost enough to fly a migrating warbler first-class from Manhattan to Ecuador.

"Guess what? We have—" Martin pauses for dramatic effect and when there's no curtain call, continues, "—a family of Eastern bluebirds living in one of our birdhouses out in New Hope."

Martin says this with the same ecstatic pride that other gay men would have if a legendary movie actress or a notorious porno star had moved in next door. Martin and I have a tendency to swap birding anecdotes like gossiping teenagers:

"You're not going to believe what I saw yesterday . . . a Kentucky Warbler . . . in Strawberry Fields."

"Oh, I wish I had been there."

As we walk, I'm struck by how lovely the park is early in the morning, but I'm also never able to forget that there is nothing bucolic about Central Park. This is one piece of real estate that's been around the block. Central Park is not some unspoiled preserve like wholesome Bryce Canyon in Utah. (Mental note: Bryce Canyon would make an excellent stage name.) During the nineteenth century, almost every tree and rock in the park's 840 acres was carefully planted and placed by Frederick Law Olmsted and Calvert Vaux, the park's designers. Central Park's natural look is more contrived than that

of a forty-one-year-old actress who claims to be thirty-five.

More than 270 different species of birds have been recorded in Central Park and most people are surprised to learn that wildlife can thrive in the middle of a large city. I once was watching a Great Blue Heron stalking fish in a lily pond in San Francisco's Golden Gate Park when a woman passing by stopped to ask me if the heron was "real." She had to reassure herself because the heron was motionless and we were able to view it from a distance of only three feet. Finding truly wild birds in a big city is almost as disconcerting as finding performance artists in Yosemite. Although most people would find Red Tailed Hawks nesting on Fifth Avenue preferable to a depressing one-man show in a grove of Sequoias.

I find it comforting to think of Mother Nature as a native New Yorker. The source of all of our environmental problems is that people mistakenly think of Mother Nature as a sweet Mom instead of who she really is: a tough cookie, Ma Nature. Picture her with a cigarette dangling from her lips as she threatens, "What the fuck's your problem? You put a hole in my ozone layer and I'll put a hole in your face. And if you cut down my rain forests, you'll live to regret it. *Am I making myself clear?*"

Years ago, my brothers and I were running and laughing in the woods when I tripped and fell over a log and landed in a pile of leaves. I stood up and felt something squirming in my shorts. I put my hand in my pocket and pulled out a frog. My brothers thought this was hilarious. What strikes me now is that I wasn't disgusted or frightened but I was amazed. It seemed like a prank by Ma Nature. Her version of slipping an ice cube down my back. And that's always been my relationship to Nature—a source of amused astonishment.

We arrive at the spot near the theater where the Painted Bunting was last seen. Opal points out several

large trees that we should search. It seems improbable that the bird is still here but migrating birds frequently stay in the same area for a few days while feeding and resting. There are several other birders also scanning the trees when our group arrives, and if the poor bird is sighted he'll be more scrutinized than a presidential candidate. We have several false alarms while we're looking.

THERE IT IS!

A reddish House Finch is momentarily mistaken for the Bunting by a birder who is not with our group. Martin says disgustedly, "I *knew* it was a House Finch."

We spend another half hour looking for the Bunting but without any success. Opal finally decides to move on. The disappointment in her voice makes it sound as if it's her fault that we haven't seen it.

"I'm *really* sorry. We can try to swing back later but I feel that we shouldn't spend any more time searching for this one bird."

The Painted Bunting customarily lives only in the South and Southwest. But it's possible during spring or fall migration for a few birds of any species (usually males) to turn up outside of their normal range. When one of these birds is sighted and reported this is what is called in the argot of the birder's world, a rare bird alert.

Most serious birders keep a "life list," a record of the different bird species seen in North America above the Mexican border. And each new species sighted by a birder is called a life-bird. The Painted Bunting would be a life-bird for me.

I hadn't heard about this sighting because I rarely call our birding hotline. Most regional bird organizations across the country have a local birding hotline that plays a recorded message of recent unusual bird sightings. During spring migration, the hotline tapes are updated almost daily, giving exact directions as to where hard-to-find or unusual birds were last seen. Birders always strive to give the most accurate directions because they want to make certain that you have enough information

to find the exact same bird. It's reassuring to have such specificity in an age of verbal imprecision. A birder won't say, "I saw this red bird in a tree at Central Park yesterday." He would say, "In Central Park on Monday, at approximately 3:17 P.M., I saw a Rose Breasted Grosbeak on the lower branch of the Swampy Pin Oak near Bow Bridge next to the small gazebo that was occupied by a heterosexual couple who were bickering over whether to visit his parents in Ohio this summer or try to get parts in the road company of *Grease*." If we held our politicians' promises to the same exacting standards of veracity as birders do for one another it would revolutionize our political system.

Our group moves toward the Castle, a large Victorian folly that is one of the park's landmarks. Opal stops for a moment and then asks the group, "Is that a Northern Parula?" During our birdwalks, Opal is often able to locate a bird by listening for its song. If she suddenly stands still and then after a moment says, "There's a Solitary Vireo. Let's try to find it," we are usually able to do so, making her seem like an ornithological medium.

There are several tapes and even CDs of bird songs available that theoretically enable anyone to master her ability. But I haven't attempted to do this yet as it seems too hard core. Only the most enthusiastic birders have all of a species' albums.

We find the Northern Parula, a beautiful blue-gray bird with a bright yellow throat and breast and a distinctive greenish patch in the middle of its back. We also spot a Palm Warbler, one of the earliest migrants through the park each year. The male Palm Warbler is a bright yellow with a rufous-colored cap, and it bobs its tail almost constantly. Two weeks before, Palm Warblers came through the park in a huge wave of migration. For a day or two, they seemed to be everywhere. We stood on the Castle, the highest point in the park, and as we watched warblers flying overhead, Opal looked in the

sky and shouted, "You can *actually* see migration today!" There were so many Palm Warblers in the park that they were hopping around on the ground like sparrows. It was astonishing, and it isn't easy to find a pleasant, inexpensive, and legal source of astonishment in the middle of Manhattan.

Opal spots another bird. "There's a Veery."

A Veery is a beautiful brown thrush. She then smiles and adds, "That's a *Veery* good bird for today."

Throughout the birdwalk, Opal makes bad puns. For instance, if we saw a *Least* Flycatcher she might say, "Well at *least* we saw it." When I hear her do this, I think she's mental.

I see something moving on the edge of a large maple tree and aim my binoculars toward the movement in the leaves. I spot a yellow-green bird with a black throat that's too large to be a warbler. I think I know its identity but I feel reluctant to announce it in case I'm wrong. If I'm correct this is a really good bird for Central Park. While keeping the bird in focus with my binoculars, I say tentatively, "I think there's a juvenile male Orchard Oriole in this maple tree."

The juvenile male Orchard Oriole looks like an entirely different species than the mature male, which has a black head and rust-colored body. Only a few species have this generational distinction that I have somehow remembered. Immediately, every other birder in our group aims his or her binoculars almost accusingly at the tree.

Rick gets the bird in focus and says, "Yep, that's a juvenile male Orchard Oriole."

The rest of the group gets the bird in focus while Opal asks with maternal concern, "Does everyone have this bird? Bob, thank you for sharing this."

At that moment, I feel such a sense of pride that I briefly consider putting this identification on my resume. I frequently try to improve my birding skills by looking through *The Birds of the Eastern United States* in an

attempt to learn the identifying characteristics of unfamiliar species. In birding, you never know when you're going to run into a Sprague's Pipit, and there is nothing more satisfying than being able to put a name to a face, especially if that face is on a Hepatic Tanager. One of the satisfactions of birding is that I never have to worry that a Xantus's murrelet will take umbrage if I mistake it for Kittlitz's murrelet. Even after all of my presearch, I find it difficult to remember the field marks that distinguish one confusing species from another. As I read, I tell myself: *Remember the Nashville warbler has a white eye ring, a gray head, and a yellow throat and breast contrasting with its olive green back while the Connecticut Warbler looks exactly the same except that it has a gray throat.*

Out in the field, I can never recall all of these details. Instead, I have to learn to really see each bird and then later compare my observations of its appearance and behavior with the field guide. This is the basic training of a good birder. Every birder must look at each bird as if trying to identify a feathered criminal and our testimony is crucial: *What color was its head, beak, feet, tail? Was it in a tree, a bush, or on the ground? In or near water? Did it have wingbars? An eye-ring? Did you notice any unusual behavior?* For example, the first time I saw a Winter Wren was at Muir Woods in California. It was running through the roots of a redwood tree, and its dark brown color and the way it scampered led me initially to believe it was a mouse which is exactly how the "mouse-like" Winter Wren is described by Mr. Peterson in his *Birds of the Western United States.*

My field guide shows that the female Painted Bunting is a solid green. For some Darwinian reason, the males of most bird species are often more brightly colored. There has been speculation that this helps attract the females because somehow garishness indicates good genetic potential. It's fortunate that humans don't mate on exactly the same system or else during the 1970s

thousands of children would have been fathered by the rock band Kiss.

I've sometimes heard fashion designers during interviews trot out this natural history fact as a justification for their own preposterous creations for men. It's as if they think of Mother Nature as some sort of Coco Chanel. Fashion designers don't seem to understand that a male Baltimore Oriole is bright orange and black with white wing bars after thousands of years of genetic consideration, while their whim of seeing a grown man wearing a blousy, band-collar paisley shirt open to his waist is a setback for evolution.

Opal leads us to another area of the park known as the Ramble. The Ramble is the best area of the park to bird because it is heavily wooded and has several ponds and a small stream. It also happens to be a notorious gay cruising spot that the very conservative *National Geographic* in an article on Central Park once euphemistically called a "historic gay meeting place," making some bushes and park benches sound like a Unitarian Church founded in 1753. Gay men and birds do like to congregate in many of the same areas. I first started birding in Provincetown, which is the best place to bird and boy watch on Cape Cod, and I've also birded in Key West, home to rare endemic species such as the Magnificent Frigatebird and the Brown Noddy, and the more common species of gay tourist, the Extremely Buff-breasted Blond, the Swan with an Ugly Attitude, the Lovebirds, and the Jaded Owl.

Bird watching and boy watching aren't always compatible activities, though. I once brought my binoculars to the beach in Provincetown and then realized that everyone would think that I was using them to stare at cute guys. But most gay men would at least understand that motive, whereas many of them would think that I was weird if I used my binoculars to look for the endangered Roseate Tern. It made me feel like an avian voyeur.

Suddenly Miss Shoup tries to get the attention of our group by stage-whispering, "Oh, here's a marvelous Scarlet Tanager!"

Jack bellows, "Miss Shoup has a Scarlet!"

Martin then exclaims, "Oh, that's one of my favorites!" Martin's enthusiasm for every species of bird is unconditional. After almost every bird we see, from Canada warblers to whippoorwills, he can be counted on to say, "Oh, that's one of my favorites!" He even has an aesthetic good word for starlings ("I love their iridescent color"), a species despised by American birders since 1888, when they were introduced here from England by a kook who wanted to establish in our country every species of bird mentioned in Shakespeare's plays. He inadvertently created an ecological disaster by releasing a cage of starlings in Central Park because the aggressive starling spread across the continent usurping the nesting holes of native species. Historians should note that this may be one of the earliest instances of an obsessed fan doing something really stupid after being influenced by popular culture.

Our group is entranced by Miss Shoup's Scarlet Tanager. Miss Shoup's only comment is, "Oh, splendid!" Looking at a Scarlet Tanager could yank the phrase "It's fabulous!" out of the farmer in Grant Wood's *American Gothic*. This fairly shy bird is perched on a branch surrounded by green leaves. The male's color is not just a bright red but actually scarlet, and it has such a vivacity with its contrasting black wings that it almost leaves an afterimage on your retinas.

Later, when Opal points out two distinctively plumaged male Rose Breasted Grosbeaks sitting on a branch together, Martin says with a leer, "Two males? Well, it is the Ramble after all...." Martin has said this lame joke on other occasions when two breeding males have been spotted together; when he does there's an uncomfortable silence that makes me inwardly wince and chuckle at the same time.

Every birder in Manhattan must be out in the park today. As we proceed, Opal cheerfully informs an awkward-looking teenager with binoculars about the location where we saw the Scarlet Tanager. He is wearing a pair of goggles that are held on by an elastic headband inscribed with the words, JR REC SPECS. The poor guy's a major dweeb. Martin looks him up and down and whispers, "When I first started bird-watching I thought that's how all bird-watchers looked. Well, some stereotypes are true." The kid could just as easily say the same thing about Martin. Martin eyes the other birders in the park as carefully as he does a Ruby Crowned Kinglet. His passing comments can sometimes be so catty that I'm surprised the birds don't avoid us completely. He savors each biting remark as if it's the most malicious thing that he's ever tasted. But Martin is more of a house cat than a saber-toothed tiger:

"Look at Jungle Jim in the safari jacket. He probably puts it on to watch the Discovery Channel."

"Let's go. If I hear about her trip to Alaska again, I'll *never* want to visit the state."

"You know how he's always got that camera with him? So you'd think that he's a wonderful nature photographer—I finally saw some of his photos. The bird could take a better picture of itself."

Our group is looking at a Wood Thrush scratching in some fallen leaves when a large Golden Retriever shoots up the path, scaring the bird into flight. Martin huffs, "I think it's *so* inconsiderate for people to let their dogs off the leash in the park. It's illegal. When I've seen the police giving them tickets for doing it—it's made me so happy that I actually went over to the policeman and said, 'Thank you.' Martin also hates to see birders stepping off the paths and trampling fragile vegetation in a quest to see an elusive bird. "The paths are there for a reason!" Martin is possessive of the park. He

reminds me of the neighborhood crank who chases children from playing on his front lawn. Someday I fear that he and Roger will become urban recluses living in a filthy apartment stacked with twenty years of *Audubon* magazines and forty pet peeves running wild.

"Look at that!"

Opal points to four birds flying in formation over our heads. We're slightly unsure of what we've seen because they're four large parrots. They flew by so quickly that I could only make out their green color and long tails. Opal says the scientific name of their genus and then apologizes for not being able to identify the species because she didn't get that good a look. She also adds that they normally live in Colombia and Venezuela. For a moment, I'm terrified that the greenhouse effect has accelerated climate change to the point where palm trees will soon start sprouting on Park Avenue, but then Opal mentions that exotic birds occasionally escape from shipments at Kennedy Airport.

One of our stops in the Ramble is called Azalea Pond, where a depressing bird-feeding station is located, which is frequented by a group of loitering pigeons and starlings. The bird feeders are a shabby assortment of homemade models fashioned out of old bleach bottles and other plastic containers. Several trees also have disgusting, oozing wads of pink suet wedged beneath small screens on their bark, making the trees appear to have hastily bandaged open wounds. The area has the grim atmosphere of a soup kitchen for birds. I almost expect the house sparrows to cough and hack while they eat.

Azalea Pond empties into the Dell, the only small stream in the park. This little waterway is one reason why Central Park is such a good spot to bird. It's one of the few places where migrating birds can find food, water, and shelter in New York City. The park is the only rest stop on this stretch of the Jersey Turnpike of migration—the birds seem to know that they don't have any other dining options.

We head down to the Point, an aptly named small peninsula on the park's largest lake. It's covered in a mixture of shrubs and trees, making it a very good bird habitat and—judging from the amount of used condoms on the ground—a popular trysting spot. This place must see a lot of action. The condoms littering the area have given the soil the impermeability of linoleum. I wonder when these trysts occur and if a passing birder has ever had the temerity to ask, "Excuse me, could you hold off humping for a minute? You're going to scare an Ovenbird."

We've covered the best areas of the Ramble and since it's almost ten-thirty, Opal informs us that she plans on ending our birdwalk by heading toward the east side of the park where we can witness one of the most exciting events of the park's natural history. Everyone in our group sits down on benches and watches through their binoculars a pair of red-tailed hawks that have built their nest on the window ledge of a building on Fifth Avenue. Someone mentions that the nest is supposedly right next to Woody Allen's apartment and that he became disturbed when he thought that strange people were staring at his apartment with binoculars. The hawks have nested on this ledge for three years, but this is the first year that any of their eggs have hatched.

Manhattan seems to be in the midst of ecological gentrification. Many animal species are returning to the old neighborhood or just moving in. Last year, a family of green herons successfully nested for the first time in the park's history, and recently *The New York Times* reported that a wandering male manatee, a native of Florida, was spotted swimming in the East River.

While watching the hawks feed their young, I tell Martin that my boyfriend, Tom, was recently riding his bicycle in the park when one of the hawks, carrying a struggling rat in its talons, flew right in front of him.

Tom, who doesn't share my interest in bird-watching, said that I would have loved it. Martin listens intently and then says, "Oh, that sounds wonderful. Now all we need is a bird of prey that feeds on roaches."

The birdwalk ends after everyone admires the hawks. People begin to disperse and I'm preparing to walk out of the park on the west side at the 72nd Street entrance when Martin suggests that we again try to find the Bunting. Rick and Jack are also going to head back that way and Martin and I quickly decide to join them.

We take a different route this time, stopping only for a Red-Eyed Vireo and Louisiana Water Thrush. As we walk past the Delacorte Theater, we see a group of about thirty birders standing with raised binoculars looking toward one tree located almost exactly near where we had looked this morning. Galvanized by the sight, we hurry over. A group of birders standing with raised binoculars is a universal symbol of a good bird.

When we reach the group, Martin is trying to contain his excitement as if it was a small overindulged, yapping dog. He says to no one in particular, "Do you have the Bunting?" Several birders confirm this while their binoculars remain locked on the bird. Jack soon says that he has it and then Rick does also. While I fruitlessly search the tree in the area that they seem to be looking, Martin says, "I've got it!" as if he has finally invented a really flattering lightbulb.

I still can't find it. I continue to scan the tree, looking for any small movement before raising my binoculars to focus. I'm afraid that the bird will fly off at any moment. In frustration, I whine, "I don't see it."

Martin tries to help me but his excitement makes his directions unusually vague, "Just *look* for the blaze of color!"

Rick puts down his binoculars, but before he can help me, Jack takes charge. He speaks to me, slowly and clearly, as if he's speaking to a telephone operator in Djakarta:

"Bob, do you see the larger of the trees, the one with the bare branch at the top?"

"Yes."

"Can you follow it up from the base and see where it branches off into a Y?"

"Okay."

"Follow the Y up and then see where it branches outward?"

"Yes."

I am forcing myself to follow his directions exactly. I feel like a cursor on a computer screen.

"It's near the front of that branch."

I see something move. I pick up my binoculars and focus on that area and there it is—a purple head, red breast, and green back—nibbling on a cluster of seeds. Its colors are more muted than in the guidebook, and when I comment on this someone says that it's probably a juvenile male without the full brilliance of the adult. Somehow I knew that someone would have an explanation. We stand there, thirty or so adults transfixed by a small bird while people walking by call out, "Hey, whadya lookin' at?" Behind us people are playing baseball and a rehearsal is being held in the theater. For a moment Central Park is one of the most remarkable places on the planet. The bird is still sitting there when we finally leave.

I've got my Painted Bunting, life-bird number 154.

Remembering the Alamo

OM'S PARENTS live in an adult retirement community, Rancho Verde, in the town of Cypress Creek, located forty-five miles north of Orlando. Every building in Rancho Verde is required to be built in a semblance of California Mission style. No expense has been spared to re-create the historic car washes and convenience stores of eighteenth-century Baja, and to my astonishment, I like it. I've reached the point between snotty youth and resigned old age when comfort and convenience are starting to affect my aesthetic values. Your tolerance for imperfection increases when the wrinkles on your shirt become less noticeable than the wrinkles on your face; it becomes increasingly difficult to muster outrage over the ugly facade of a building when the appearance of your ass is a daily affront.

My favorite building in Rancho Verde is the bowling alley, a replica of the Alamo in San Antonio. I'm disappointed that the architect couldn't convince the developer to call it the "Alley-mo." Persnickety architectural critics should be aware that it's not any more historically inappropriate or gauche to build adobe-style or New England–saltbox houses in Florida than it was for Thomas Jefferson to build a Palladian-style villa called Monticello in rural Virginia.

Tom's parents' two-bedroom "Sierra Hacienda" is built on a golf course, an architectural caprice that seems odd to nonduffers. (Aficionados of billiards don't clamor to live above pool halls.) Last year we stayed with Tom's parents for a week to attend the wedding of one of his nephews. Every afternoon, we tagged along with Tom's father as he drove his golf cart to pick up their mail. Golf carts are my favorite form of transportation. Only in America would someone build a vehicle for the sole purpose of making a form of exercise less taxing. I picture the inventor, the Henry Ford of sloth, tinkering in his garage as he built the first prototype; although I wonder how a man with such a propensity for indolence ever roused himself to start the project.

I believe that laziness has always been a major stimulus to inventiveness. Anthropologists have propagated a theory that over millions of years the size of our brains expanded as our ancestors began to use tools. Isn't it more probable that our mental capacity developed to avoid using tools? It takes much more ingenuity to get out of doing something than to do it. Call it the Tom Sawyer Theory of Evolution.

It's much easier to imagine that an important evolutionary leap—or more precisely, an evolutionary stroll—was made when a bored caveman, chipping away at his fourth arrowhead, thought, *I hate doing this. Hmmm...I wonder if I can get someone else to do it for me? If I became our tribe's spiritual leader, then I wouldn't*

*have to do any manual labor—of course I'd have to invent
some spiritual beliefs but that shouldn't be too hard....*

Our remote ancestors probably only evolved to stand
erect just to enjoy being able to sit down.

We were driving with Tom's parents in their Lincoln
Town Car. The name is apt, because the trunk is capa-
cious enough to contain a small village.

As we passed a new house being built, Tom's father
casually mentioned, "It gets so hot down here that the
construction workers take off their shirts by eight
o'clock." Tom and I avoided glancing at each other, as
we both had the same response: *Believe me. We've no-
ticed.* I've often thought that the signs posted on high-
ways, SLOW DOWN CONSTRUCTION WORKERS are not
only meant for their protection but to prompt my ap-
preciation.

I like visiting Tom's parents. Being an in-law is an
enviable social position; you're a family intimate, but
unless you're completely intolerable, the family treats
you with the same hospitality as they would a guest. It
makes me wish that I was related to my own family by
marriage.

I try to be on my best behavior in front of Tom's
parents, which means that I refrain from mocking and
swearing as I do when I visit my parents. Tom's rela-
tionship with his parents is much more formal than my
relationship is with mine. I've never heard Tom in a
conversation with his mother refer to someone as an
"asshole," a term that I somehow find frequent cause to
use when I'm speaking with my mother. My foul mouth
can't be blamed on my parents, though. My father
hardly ever swore and my mother might occasionally call
someone a bastard now and then, but they never cursed
with the boyish zeal that I do now. I became a feral
child *after* being raised by my parents.

Tom's parents are about ten years older than mine,
making Tom's father old enough to have served in the

Navy during World War II. One of Tom's most prized possessions is an oak-framed, over-sized sepia-tinted photograph of a Ships Dance with a big band held at the Hotel Pennsylvania in Manhattan on October 27, 1944. Tom's parents were on their first date and it always takes us a moment to find them standing in the middle of a hundred posed couples. It's an impossibly romantic photograph that we both find poignant, especially knowing that more than fifty years later their romance hasn't faded. Their devotion to each other is still apparent to the most casual observer. Somehow, having that history with another person is almost more of an accomplishment than winning that war.

When Tom's mother recalls the first year of her marriage, I listen intently. I especially enjoy her digressions, for she's a master of the tangential anecdote. "The first time I traveled to San Francisco during the war, by train, I was a nervous wreck because my mother warned me not to talk to any Chinamen because they take young girls and make them slaves. Back then people didn't know any better."

One of the reasons other people's parents are easier to enjoy is that you haven't heard all of their stories yet. I particularly enjoy when Tom's parents let slip a telling anecdote about Tom: "When Tom was four years old, we bought him a new pair of shoes and he started walking funny. So, we took Tom back to the shoestore and Mr. Noodleman checked his shoes and said that they were the right size. So then we took Tom to our regular doctor and he couldn't find anything wrong with Tom's feet and he sent us to a podiatrist and he couldn't figure it out. Well, it turns out that Tom was walking funny because he didn't want to crease his new shoes. Can you imagine? At four years old."

I didn't answer her but—*yes*—I could vividly imagine that. Tom has spent most of his life trying to balance his fussbudget. Right after our move to Los Angeles,

Tom did an insurance inventory of our apartment that will someday make as valuable a historical document as the *Domesday Book* of 1086 that listed for William the Conqueror all the properties of England's landowners. Tom had read somewhere that most people don't realize that if all of their possessions were stolen or destroyed, it would be incredibly expensive to replace, all at once, small items such as potato peelers, socks, plastic storage containers, paper clips, et cetera.

This cautionary tale is probably spread by insurance salesmen to encourage people to make sure that they have enough (or even too much) insurance to replace all of their property. I'm certain that they have actuarial tables that prove conclusively that most people would rather pay more money for unnecessary coverage than have to actually inventory all of their belongings.

Ha! Foolish insurance companies! They hadn't reckoned with the statistical anomaly of a meticulous man between jobs with way too much time on his hands.

A gauntlet had been thrown down and Tom picked it up because he hated the untidiness of the gesture. He knew that having as complete an insurance inventory as possible could save us some money on our premiums. Tom accepted this challenge to his thoroughness and decided to take a census of all of our possessions. He counted *everything*: forks, sponges, books—*by title and author*. When I questioned him about whether this level of comprehensiveness was necessary, he said, "I'm not going to get carried away. I'm only doing the hardcovers."

Once Tom started listing our worldly goods, he literally became a bean counter. His idea of taking a rough estimate of our possessions was not to tally all of the aspirins in the bottle. At one point, I stopped eating because I thought that he might have to re-inventory the contents of our refrigerator. His survey was exhaustive and exhausting, but it taught me an important lesson:

Completeness is an overrated virtue that most idiots are capable of achieving. Tom stopped only when I threatened to remove one boyfriend from the final inventory.

Tom's parents had several chores that they asked us, or more accurately, Tom, to do—including cleaning out the gutters of the house and painting the floor of the garage. For Tom's efforts we were both well rewarded with more than ample meals. In some ways visiting your parents as an adult is like going to a spa. Only at Tom's and my parents', the guests are required to overeat. I sometimes feel that our mothers are trying to entomb us in the pyramid of food groups. After serving us a delicious and copious dinner, Tom's mother would frequently make a request: "C'mon, guys, finish up that last piece of pie. I don't want to have to put it back in the refrigerator." She made the appeal almost as if the refrigerator was trying to cut down and she didn't want to tempt it.

Tom and I are heavily salted, honey-roasted health nuts. Most of the time we eat well, but there's enough snacking and periods of what-the-hell in our diets to make us persona non granola at health food stores. For the most part, though, we are trying to avoid the dietary path trod by our fathers, the one where all roads lead to a triple bypass. The men of our fathers' generation watch what they eat like they watch television. Most of the time they're not really paying attention, but there's always something special—a favorite concern or a cherished worry—that they watch like the Super Bowl. They'll keenly focus on this one specific part of their diet for a few hours every year—either their intake of cholesterol, sugar, or salt—and then the rest of the time they eat and drink whatever they want. One definition of adulthood is when you start to worry about what your parents eat. There are times when I've felt like saying, *"Mom and Dad, strawberry ice cream doesn't count as a serving of fruit."*

* * *

Oranges and guilt are the two products most fre-
quently sold along the roadside in Florida. As you drive,
you pass dozens of churches, each with signs out front
proclaiming a different version of the sentiment: Have
a Nice Judgment Day! There's even one produce stand
that sells citrus fruit and promotes Christian fundamen-
talist beliefs with huge admonitory hand-painted signs.
When you drive by fast enough, the numbered passages
of the New Testament blur with the price of tangelos.
It's a strange blend of marketing and witnessing that
could be neatly reduced to one slogan: Christ Has Risen
but Our Prices Haven't! Perhaps it's misguided to try to
sell the Lamb of God by the pound.

On this trip, every morning for breakfast we drank
a big glass of fresh-squeezed orange juice, as if we were
trying to wash away the dietary sins of the previous
night. Several times we went with Tom's parents to the
highway citrus stand where they liked to buy their juice.
While Tom's parents were making their purchases, I no-
ticed that the stand sold much more than just citrus fruit.
The aisles were filled with wares that used oranges in
imaginative ways; many of which should have remained
inconceivable.

In Florida, the orange has been squeezed for more
ideas than the Bible, and like most of the interpretations
of that book, the results are either ludicrous or tragic.
The fruit stand sold concoctions such as Orange Ice
Cream, Orange Blossom Honey, Orange Salt Water
Taffy, Orange Air Freshener, Orange Furniture Polish,
and even an Orange Pesticide.

During my travels, I've seen how the example of
George Washington Carver, the man who discovered
over a hundred different uses for the peanut, has now
been emulated with agricultural products from all over
the United States. Blueberries in Maine, maple syrup in
Vermont, cranberries in Massachusetts, peaches in Geor-
gia, blue corn and chilies in New Mexico, jojoba in Ar-

izona, avocados in California, and raspberries in Oregon—
all have been used to demonstrate that American inge-
nuity is capable of creating products that, even after fab-
rication, still seem unreal.

I made the mistake of testing the Orange Air Fresh-
ener. And like Adam after he picked the apple, I im-
mediately regretted giving in to the temptation. The
spray didn't deodorize a room—it flavored it with an
even more persistent smell. The atmosphere in the store
had changed as completely as if I had made a blundering
remark. One that I would have done anything to retract.
The aroma lingered like hard feelings.

The day before the wedding Tom painted the floor
of his parents' garage. Months before, Tom's father had
paid for the driveway to be professionally painted in a
complex pattern of different shades of green trimmed
with contrasting hues of white. Florida can claim drive-
way painting as its first indigenous art form. Most of the
driveways in Rancho Verde are painted with the same
elaborate care and preparation that the Renaissance ex-
pended on the ceilings of churches. Will the work of
these anonymous painters ever be recognized and val-
ued? Someday driveway painting may also be proudly
claimed as a great American folk art and blocks of pave-
ment will be displayed alongside old weathervanes and
Pennsylvania Dutch blanket chests.

Tom's father insisted that the paint wasn't merely
decorative but also acted as a sealant that protected the
driveway. This allowed him to preserve the masculine
ideal of not doing anything merely out of a spirit of
frivolity. It's a shame that men always need to find a
practical reason for beauty. As if the only reason to ad-
mire a pretty face is because over the course of a lifetime
it needs a lot less maintenance.

I've found that heterosexual men feel comfortable
expressing their aesthetic and creative natures only when
decorating the outdoors. Putting up the Christmas lights

or the placement of rose bushes is okay for real men to discuss, but once those roses are cut and brought indoors any discussion of their arrangement is acceptable only for women and queers. It's a ridiculous posture to assume. Landscape architects are just brawny decorators who enjoy fussily arranging a grove of trees on a hilltop as if they were a bunch of lilies in a vase. In fact, ornamental grasses are really just the throw pillows of landscape architecture.

While Tom was painting the floor of the garage, I felt so lazy that even sitting in the rocking chair seemed like too much work. So I spent the afternoon lying on the couch, reading Tom's father's extensive collection of *National Geographic* books. My mind is filled with arcane information from years of armchair traveling. I'm the type of person who knows that the Inca did not invent the wheel, which is why at an authentic Incan restaurant you'll never see a dessert cart. I didn't feel guilty about not helping Tom because he really didn't want my assistance. Is it unhealthy that I often feel most truly loved when my participation isn't required in our relationship?

At one point, when I called home to check the messages on our answering machine, I noticed that all the pens and notepads in Tom's parents' house were prescription-drug related. I was writing down names and telephone numbers on a notepad that was either taken from or given at a doctor's office. At the top of each page on one pad was an illustration of a gold heart-shaped pill locket on a chain and at the bottom of each page was printed: "Kindhearted One A Day Lozol® Indapamide 2.5 mg. *The diuretic that doesn't compromise cholesterol.*" It was as if as our parents got older, they wanted to be reminded of their mortality on their grocery list. The pen I used promoted: "Dual Action Lotrisone® Cream, USP brand of clotrimozole and betamethazone dipropionate." After writing down that our friends Glenn

and Larry had called, I also jotted down my last will and testament.

On the day of the wedding, Tom's mother woke us an hour earlier than usual to allow us extra time to get ready. Tom and I both wore blue blazers and chinos. Before we left, we had discussed what to wear, but we didn't bring our suits because they were too hot to wear and too formal. So instead, our only choice was to dress alike and become one of those nauseatingly cute, same-socks couples.

We left the house promptly at one o'clock in order to arrive at the church by two. Tom drove and I sat in the front seat while his parents sat in the back. Tom's brother had given him exact directions to the church, but like my parents, Tom's parents questioned his every driving decision. "Tom, please don't drive so close to the car in front of us," Tom's mother said. "It makes me nervous." Then, miles before we were even near the church: "Tom, you better start to pull over to the other lane. Is that the supermarket that we're supposed to look for?" It was a reflexive action that I found very moving, since I wasn't driving. It was another bittersweet milestone in our relationship with our parents. We had passed the point where we always followed their advice and now we were really claiming our adulthood—we weren't even following their directions.

We drove past several of the small towns that Tom and I have thoroughly explored during our past visits. Their downtowns are rundown and only a few merchants valiantly try to stem or at least slow down the onslaught of mega-malls and discount warehouses. I noticed that every town always has a tired-looking neighborhood gin-mill, usually called Eddie's, Mike's, or John's Bar and Grill, the last two words added to foster the illusion that people also go there for the food. The bar's neon sign always has an unhealthy ruddy look and

it twitches on and off as if it suffers from bad circulation. Of course, Eddie, Mike, and John are no longer the owners, as they were unable to qualify for a liver transplant. Posted in the front window of one of the bars was a hand-written sign that modestly boasted "The Biggest TV in Leesburg," which, judging from the vacant storefronts along Main Street, is a title that could be claimed by a nineteen-inch black-and-white.

In the town of Eustis, the Eustis Center for the Arts pathetically attempted to promote a local theater company with another hand-written sign that said, IT'S MORE FUN THAN BOWLING!—a claim that probably would have filled O'Neill with despair but amused Chekhov.

We arrived at the church on time, and most of the guests were standing out front, chatting in the bright sunshine before going inside. Tom's nephew Greg, the son of Tom's oldest brother Joe, was getting married. As we said hello to everyone, I was grateful that I was no longer known as just "Tom's friend."

Right after college Tom had told his parents that he was gay, but he never told his brothers, who are twelve and fifteen years older than he is. Tom's parents had handled his coming out with tremendous poise and understanding. Tom's mother said that they had suspected that he was gay for a while but that they hadn't said anything because, "What if we were wrong?" I pointed out to Tom how farcical that situation would have been. What if you really were an extremely shy heterosexual actor who just happened to like musicals and your parents questioned your sexuality? I think that no man, whether straight or gay, wants to have his sexuality mistaken by his parents.

After our second trip to Florida, I told Tom that he had to tell his brothers because I didn't think that anyone was buying the idea that two men in their thirties were just "roommates." It was obvious that we weren't

still in college. Even if we had been taking only one course every semester, we would have Ph.D.'s by now. So Tom wrote to his brothers. They took his announcement with the same degree of surprise as someone opening a poorly concealed gift-wrapped bicycle or tennis racket. We were both relieved after he told them. I had never realized before that the most difficult part of being in the closet wasn't pretending to be straight—it was pretending to be stupid.

The wedding was held in a church that was built during the 1970s, *not* one of the great periods in ecclesiastic architecture. It looked like the Ranch House of God. Instead of being built up, the building spread out horizontally and the octagonal roof was topped with such a short steeple that it made me wonder if the architect was agnostic. At the end of the twentieth century, the stunted steeple seemed to symbolize the lower expectations that Man and God now have for each other.

Inside the church over the alter was a bronze semiabstract crucifix on which Jesus seemed to die while modeling. Behind the altar was a large stained-glass picture window that portrayed a typical Holy Family of 2.2 parents and 1 child.

The ceremony was simple and beautiful. I'm in awe of anyone who gets married. Standing in front of your family and friends and vowing to love someone for a lifetime is a courageous act of daring in an age when most people are afraid to promise to pick up someone from the airport.

Our attendance at this wedding must have triggered some thoughts on matrimony in other members of Tom's family. The previous night while watching television, Tom's father startled us by asking, "Tom, did you and Bob get married?" We were both thunderstruck for a moment, and Tom said, "No! If we did you'd know about it." At the time, I assumed that Tom had put the emphasis on the "No" because of the unexpected

nature of the question, not because the thought was abhorrent to him. Tom's father then said apologetically, "I just wanted to know," and resumed reading his golf magazine.

Later that night, when his parents had gone to bed, Tom and I shared our disbelief that his father had asked that question. I suppose that it could've been that we both wear matching rings. Shortly before we moved, New York City passed a domestic partnership ordinance allowing gay, lesbian, and unmarried heterosexual couples to officially register their relationship at city hall. "Domestic partnership" sounds like a business arrangement where each couple writes up a contract stating who does what in the deal—sort of a prenuptial agreement for couples who can't, or won't, nuptial. *"Tom will empty the litter box because it's his cat. If he'll do most of the cooking, I'll do the dishes. I'll plan the vacations if he'll pack the suitcases."*

Somehow, waiting in line to have a bureaucrat stamp a form doesn't have the same emotional impact as having your friends and family witness your marriage. I'm probably just speaking for myself, since when I turned sixteen I wasn't that excited about getting my driver's license. They should probably also consider making a vision test mandatory when a couple applies for a marriage license. Only it wouldn't measure the clarity of your sight but the clarity of your imagination. You'd look through a viewfinder and be shown marital scenes of happiness, pain, strife, sickness, pettiness, boredom, affection, and joy and then afterward—if you still wanted it—they would give you the license.

I don't want to settle for domestic partnership, the wax facsimile of the right to marry. It looks almost like the real thing but even children know it's not. I hate when people try to pass off something second rate as if they're doing you a favor. For example, during our first visit to Orlando, Tom's parents took us to Disney World. The only part of the theme park that we didn't enjoy

was Disney World's Epcot Center World Showcase, which featured small-scale replicas of the Eiffel Tower, an Aztec Temple, and the campanile of St. Mark's in Venice. The concept's brilliant: It was designed to appeal to Americans who want to travel but don't like foreigners. Domestic partnership is the Epcot Center Civil Rights Showcase.

Here's how to ensure that gay marriage is legalized. I know that it's a stereotype, but there are a lot of gay men who work as waiters, caterers, florists, hairdressers, clothing designers, and priests. All we need to do to force straight people to legalize our weddings is to just stop helping them with theirs.

After the ceremony, we left the church and then headed to the reception at a nearby country club. I don't think I've ever really enjoyed myself at a wedding reception. It's a party where every detail has been thought out beforehand and the parties I've most enjoyed have always had a certain spontaneity. Too many traditions have accrued to wedding receptions and the obligatory fun always feels contrived. I almost expect the bride and groom to bang their spoons against their water glasses as a signal every time the guests are expected to enjoy themselves.

It's not that I felt unwelcome. Tom's family made that an impossibility by their genuine warmth. When we offered our congratulations to the bride and groom in the receiving line, they hugged us and we were told how much they really appreciated our coming "all the way from California."

But the real proof of our welcome was that we weren't seated at what I call the "Socially Handicapped Table," which is where the square-peg guests are seated. If the tables are numbered at the reception, this table should always be zero. This is the table filled with guests who fulfill social obligations. The couple who represent a different race than the majority of the guests. De-

pending upon your background, it's the African-American-Asian-Hispanic or Caucasian guy and his wife who you had to invite from work because his cubicle is next to yours. There's also the spinster or confirmed bachelor neighbor. The mentally retarded cousin. The loud couple who have stayed drunk since their own wedding six years ago. And, of course, the gay or lesbian couple. Tom and I have been unfortunate enough to sit at this table at other weddings. Conversation flows like seepage in a damp basement. It's difficult to make small talk when the only thing all of these guests share in common is the centerpiece.

Tom and I sat at his parents' table. The wedding cake was sitting on a small table near us. A cake with bride and groom figures on top is a tradition that should be carried on throughout the course of the marriage. Each year the anniversary cake's bride and groom figures would allow friends and family to know how the marriage was doing. According to the state of the marriage, the figures could be feeling ignored, drifting apart, staying together for the kids' sake, or even one of the figures could be scandalously seen on someone else's cake.

After we made a trip to the bar for two drinks, Tom's brother came over and said that they were going to take some family photos in the next room. I glanced quickly at Tom to see what I was supposed to do, but before Tom had a chance to react, his mother snatched our hesitation away by saying, "Come on, Bob. Come on, Tom." She possessed that maternal decisiveness that, depending on the situation, is either a source of misery or, in this case, comfort.

We walked into the next room where Tom's family was already being lined up by the photographer. As we hung back for a moment, Tom's mother turned to us and said, "C'mon," as if she was coaxing two little boys to try an unfamiliar vegetable. Tom's parents then moved into position, but as we were still unsure of ours, we waited. We didn't know whether to insert ourselves

or wait to be inserted. Tom's nephew then shouted, "Come on, Uncle Tom, come on, Bob, get in the picture." The photographer echoed him by shouting at us, "Come on, Uncle Tom, come on . . ." When he paused the groom laughingly said, "Come on, Uncle Bob."

Our hesitation stemmed from the fact that there are still social situations where it's impossible not to feel self-conscious about being a gay couple. But we were outgrowing our gay bashfulness and learning to enjoy feeling awkward because our lives, and not just our sex lives, were so different from our relatives.

We hurried over and as we were two of the tallest people in the shot, the photographer had us each stand at the end of the group. Later I made Tom laugh when I suggested that our lateral positions in the picture make it that much easier for us to be cut out of the photo.

After the photographs were taken, dinner was served, and then the disc jockey starting playing music. Soon, after the traditional first dances, a large group was dancing. Dancing at wedding receptions is still at this time unfairly restricted by social convention to heterosexual couples. It's not that I particularly want to dance with Tom at wedding receptions. I don't because I'm the exception to the common belief that most gay men dance well. Before I met Tom, when I went out to clubs, men offered to sleep with me just to get me off the dance floor.

After the cake was cut, one of the groom's friends had a seizure and collapsed while dancing the Macarena, a dance craze that has marked the 1990s as indelibly as the Charleston did the 1920s and the Twist did the 1960s. The reception came to a halt and paramedics were called. Later, we learned that the unfortunate young man had overdosed from taking a drug and not from hearing that song played for the umpteenth time that summer as I had suspected.

The reception never really resumed after that. It

didn't seem appropriate for the bride to be joyously throwing her bouquet when one of the guests was practically pushing up daisies. After the prostrate guest was taken away in an ambulance, the distraught bride told the DJ to pack up and go. For the next hour and a half, we waited to hear some news from the hospital. After we heard that he was going to be fine, everyone decided to leave. As we drove home, Tom's parents discussed what had happened. Tom's mother said, "I was once at another wedding when one of the guests had a fit."

Tom's father interrupted her. "He had a seizure, not a fit. A fit isn't the same as a seizure. All the kids in high school are doing this drug that causes them to have seizures. I think it's called 'Rugby,' or something."

Tom's mother now corrected him. "No, Hon. I think it's called 'Ecstasy.' "

His father was adamant. "*No*, it's not 'Ecstasy,' " he said. "It's the same stuff they give you in a hospital when you have an operation. Some of these kids in high school eat these mushrooms to get high and then they get sick."

No one said anything and so Tom turned on the radio, I think he was afraid that his parents might start arguing over the reported potency of Kona Gold versus Maui-Wowee.

The next day we went with Tom's parents to the local mall because they needed to buy a birthday gift for Tom's newest great-niece. Tom's mother suggested that we should go off by ourselves after Tom mentioned that we wanted to look at vacuum cleaners. In New York, we had never needed one because our apartment was small enough to clean with a Dustbuster. But we were thrilled to finally need an upright model for our much larger apartment in Los Angeles. We weren't going to buy the vacuum cleaner in Florida, but this was an opportunity to do some leisurely comparison shopping. I was happy that we were shopping for an appliance that was stored in a closet, because unlike buying a coffee maker, we

only had to consider how well it worked, not how well it looked.

Later, over lunch, Tom's mother announced that they would like to buy us the vacuum cleaner. "You really don't have to do that," Tom said.

"Listen, Tom, we've bought so many gifts for Joe and Rick and their families. There's no reason why we shouldn't buy you two something." Tom insisted again that it wasn't neccessary. But this time, Tom's father spoke up. "We know. But we want to do this."

Tom looked at me and I smiled, and then he said, "All right, we're not going to argue with you."

When we returned home, we bought a vacuum cleaner with the check that Tom's parents gave us. It's not the exact same as hearing our wedding march, but now the sound of a vacuum roaring is not only a symbol of our commitment to good housekeeping, but our commitment to each other, as well.

Pink Elephants

IN **INTERVIEWS**, Newt Gingrich has compared being gay to being alcoholic. Where did Mr. Gingrich develop this preposterous idea? He must be on a party circuit with extremely expansive standards of hospitality. I can't ever recall walking into a cocktail reception and hearing the host say, "Hi, Bob! Can I get you a man? Now I'm gonna get you the first one, but when you're ready for the second, just help yourself!"

Gay men and lesbians across America were dismayed to hear this comparison made by one of our nation's leaders because it only encourages denial in closeted gays. Now, if an inquiry is made on their sexual orientation, closeted gays will be able to waffle defensively and say, "*Me?* I'm not gay. I'm just a *social* homosexual. It's not like I have a problem being gay or anything. I

never touch a man until after work. Sure, I enjoy an occasional flirtation before dinner, but I never touch the hard stuff. And so what if I like a good stiff man every now and then?!"

Mr. Gingrich's claim is nothing more than the old discredited idea that homosexuality is an illness put in new clothes and sent teetering out on the stage of public opinion where it will stagger around and make a fool of itself before it crashes to the ground. If this is the most important "health problem" that he feels compelled to discuss in interviews, then he has a limited grasp of the real issues challenging our country. Let's make sure our tax dollars aren't wasted printing pamphlets that ask:

WHAT ARE THE WARNING SIGNS OF HOMOSEXUALITY?

Ask yourself the following questions:
Do you feel that you need to be gay in order to
 have a good time?
Have you ever been gay when you're alone?
Have you ever had times when you can't
 remember being gay the night before?

(Gay blackouts do happen. Many public figures spend their entire lives being gay and not remembering it.) One possible explanation for Mr. Gingrich's twisted view of homosexuality could be the very public announcement that his sister Candace is a lesbian. It sounds like he's yearning for the pre-Stonewall era when most gay men and lesbians were members of Homosexuals Anonymous. Next Mr. Gingrich will probably suggest that homosexuality is a condition that could be "cured" by a 12-step program. What would this "program" consist of? Meetings where gay men and lesbians would stand and tell their stories? This sounds exactly like what

already happens at gay bars—which means that the gay community must already be in "recovery"!

> Imagine the testimony at a meeting of Homosexuals Anonymous:
> "Hi, I'm Vince."
> Everyone: "Hi, Vince."
> "I'm gay. It got so bad for me that I would wake up and be gay first thing in the morning and then be gay all day long."

Mr. Gingrich's voting record and many statements about homosexuality make me suspect that he's under the influence of Homophobia. Maybe someone should point out to him that Homophobia and Alcoholism share many attributes: Homophobia is also a chronic condition. Its many sufferers are easy to spot in social gatherings where their heads shake *No* uncontrollably whenever homosexuality is even mentioned. They become all red in the face at the thought of gay parents, gays in the military, and gay marriages. Then chronic far-gone homophobes embarrassingly lose control and use words that slur.

The more one considers homophobes and alcoholics, the more they seem to have in common. They're both in denial because they don't think they have a problem. They never realize how stupid they look and sound. It seems to run in families. They both like parties—Republican and cocktail. And they both start seeing things that don't exist: Alcoholics see Pink Elephants everywhere while homophobes see Pink Triangles everywhere.

It's important to remember, though, that Homophobia is a disease, and we need to have compassion for the victims of this terrible affliction. From now on, when we hear a homophobic evangelist on television, we should nod our heads in sympathy and try to understand

2222

his hatred. *Oh, no. He's hitting the Bible again. It's such a shame. For most people it's not a problem. But he can't handle it.*

> NOTE: What's the definition of a gay Republican? A White Square wearing a Pink Triangle.

Hurricane Bob

WHEN THE owner of the newsstand started talking about the weather, it was a relief to learn that she didn't want to discuss the recent rain but had actual news of an impending natural disaster. Hurricane Bob was now headed toward Provincetown. It was due to hit at one o'clock that afternoon. She sounded strangely satisfied about the storm, as if she was pleased to offer gratis a little extra bad news to her steady customers. As I paid for my copy of *The New York Times*, which had a banner headline about a military coup in the Soviet Union, she mentioned that she had already been to the supermarket to stock up on candles, food, and water, and suggested that I do the same. Since I had never been in a hurricane, buying emergency supplies seemed like a sensible precaution. My previous experi-

ence of a natural disaster was being trapped in the house
with my family for three days during Buffalo's Blizzard
of '77. It pushed me beyond the limits of human en-
durance. By the end of the third day, I considered can-
nibalism—not out of hunger, but to ease the tension. As
I hurried home to tell Tom about the hurricane, I no-
ticed the owner of Cape Cards boarding up the windows
of his store. I then resolved not to take any steps to
protect the squalid house in which we were staying for
the summer—if the house was destroyed, it could only
improve our living situation. As I walked up Carver
Street, I ran into my friends Milt and Mark and we
stopped to talk about the hurricane. They had been to
the pharmacy again. Mark joked that he was going to
ask his doctor to have his name embossed on the pre-
scription pad. As we chatted, I realized why none of us
seemed overly concerned about the hurricane. It was a
relief to be the bearer of impersonal bad news, a calam-
ity without a last name attached to it.

The most prominent landmark in Provincetown is a
towering Renaissance-style monument commemorating
the first landing of the Pilgrims in the New World. It
was built in the early part of the twentieth century
shortly before Provincetown began its own renaissance
as an artists' colony. "Artists' colony" conjures up an im-
age of pilgrims of a different sort, also dressed in black
(but this time because it's cool), leaving their hometowns
in search of freedom of self-expression, the right to wor-
ship the sun, and to escape persecution from bewildered
parents. In America, the definition of an artists' colony
seems to be any small town with more than five happy
gay inhabitants and a store that sells *The New York
Times*. Provincetown fulfills both of those qualifications.
It has a year-round permanent population of three thou-
sand, which during the summer increases to more than
thirty thousand, and most of the influx is due to vaca-

tioning gay men and lesbians. For one or two weeks each year, Provincetown is a "Yoo-hoo!"-topia for gay tourists. What makes Provincetown unique among gay resorts is that it also features many forms of live entertainment. It's the Catskills of queer vaudeville—the Bisque Belt for stand-up comics, drag queens, singers, one-man shows, one-woman shows, and one man/woman shows of indeterminate gender and talents. Provincetown is where audiences learn that just because you're born gay, it doesn't necessarily follow that you're born *talented*. Tom, our cat Grady, and I were spending the summer in Provincetown while I performed stand-up comedy in a show called *Funny Gay Males* at the Firehouse Cabaret.

In June, when we had first arrived from New York, we had learned that only performers are capable of leaving Manhattan and finding even smaller and dirtier places to live. We shared a place with all the other performers at the club. The large gray Cape Cod–style shingled house on Bradford Street was built during the 1920s. At one time I imagine it had been lovely, with its fieldstone fireplace and oak floors. But Lois Monkarsh, the owner of the Firehouse Cabaret, had bought the house as an investment and was determined to spend as little as possible on its upkeep. The weathered "For Sale" sign on the weedy front lawn indicated that it had obviously been on the market for years. The overgrown backyard was returning to forest and the only evidence that a garden had once existed was a faded rose bush capable of producing only one bloom at a time. The single yellow flower was offered wearily, almost as if the bush was tired from standing in the garden all year.

The inside of the house was even more dilapidated. Every time someone took a shower in the upstairs bathroom, a cascade poured through the ceiling light fixture in the downstairs kitchen. The dancing waters finally

ended when one of our housemates, Hoss Burdock, repaired the problem, revealing to our astonishment that before he started doing drag he had been a plumber.

The furniture in the house had the same relation to real furnishings that drag queens have to real women. Everything was a parody, done either with affection or cruelty. Cobwebs draped each room like torn stockings hung to dry. All the wobbly tables in the house were temperamental divas capable of throwing dishes to the floor if taken for granted. No matter how much each table was propped up, we were always unsure of its stability. The couch had let itself go and its cushions sprawled in an unseemly manner. Its blue-flowered fabric incorporated enough dirt to grow real hydrangea.

We were living in a shelter for battered furniture. All the lightshades in the house were scorched and the crooked floor lamps flinched as if in fear of another blow. Each broken chair seemed to be struggling to get back on its feet, and in most rooms bare lightbulbs burned with resentment.

Henry James said that the two most beautiful words in the English language are "summer afternoon." After Provincetown, my vote for the two most appalling words would be "stained mattress." In every room, a filthy double-sized mattress and box spring appeared to have passed out on the floor. Our mattress looked as if someone had used it as a coffee filter. We were horrified. My one feeble note of encouragement to Tom was that at least it didn't smell. After some consideration, Tom finally double-sheeted the mattress in a prophylactic attempt at propriety. Our initial revulsion faded once the cobwebs were cleared away because that summer, although our living standards had fallen, we fell in love with Provincetown.

I could hear the telephone ringing as I approached the house. No one answered it because we always screened our calls in an effort to avoid talking to Lois.

There was only one telephone in the entire house that thirty feet of extension cord allowed to be technically called portable. As soon as the telephone was installed and the answering machine set up, we started receiving daily messages from Lois. In January, Lois, who during the off-season lived in New York with her girlfriend, Barb, had asked us to perform at her cabaret in Provincetown. The deal she offered was 80 percent of the door and a place to live for the summer. She made it very clear that there was no guarantee that we would make any money. Our income would depend entirely on how many seats we filled and Lois explained that our success would depend on "fliering." Lois fervently believed in fliering. She repeatedly said to us, before and after we arrived, "You've gotta flier!" Fliering entailed handing out small leaflets advertising our show. Lois informed us that the times and places to flier were one o'clock at Herring Cove Beach and immediately after tea dance at a bar called the Boatslip. Every week new tourists arrived in town and the fliers, although annoying to hand out and receive, grabbed their attention. When after our first week performing we received a thick envelope of cash, the embarrassment of hawking ourselves gave way to our greed. We fliered.

Lois was a plump woman in her mid-fifties who wore expensive designer clothes and favored heavy jewelry of mounted gold coins, which was befitting, since to Lois money was the most beautiful thing in the world. She divided all of show business in two simple categories: You're either a "Moneymaker" or "You Suck." Lois, although not a performer, was a moneymaker. She was a lesbian Midas—everything she fingered turned to gold. A former real estate agent, Lois had parlayed a small shop, P-Town T-Shirts, into several different businesses worth millions.

After getting to know Lois, we assumed that she had been initially attracted to Provincetown because, like her favorite drink, margaritas, it was also encircled by salt.

Lois was a happy lush who looked at the world through rosé-colored glasses. Although she frequently complained that compared to the gay men in her audiences, "the dykes don't drink," Lois disproved that statement nightly. During the day, she was an extremely capable businesswoman, but when the sun set, she sipped into something more comfortable. Playing back her latest message on our answering machine became a daily ritual at the house. It was like listening to a garrulous and usually libelous motivational tape:

"Hi, guys. It's Lois. This hurricane's . . . oh, can you believe it? I don't know. At least you don't have to flier. . . . Shut the windows in the house and let's not cancel the shows tonight. We don't want to lose the money. But then if no one comes, I have to pay the staff. . . . You think about it. Now Maxine said that someone had asked about hooking up the washer and dryer at the house. I told you: I DON'T WANT YOU USING THAT WASHER AND DRYER! It costs me money for the septic system to be emptied and I won't stand for it! I'm serious. Oh, and by the way, have you guys heard of an all-women band called, ¡Lesbomba!? They want to try to do a midnight show. I don't know . . . I might let them do it, out of the goodness of my heart. I won't make any money but—Oh, and you're not going to believe this! Marie Blue announced from the stage at the start of her show that she doesn't want her audiences to feel that they have to *drink*! When Maxine told me—Who does she think she is? I only gave her the six o'clock spot out of the goodness of my heart. Maybe you can do some jokes about her in your act. I called her manager and told him that she's very unprofessional. She's a mess. She's not even a moneymaker. She's not selling out. Barb and I saw her show—she's not that good—she's from Quebec—I know they drink

up there—what's her problem? All right, I'll talk to you later."

Tom took the news about Hurricane Bob and the coup in the Soviet Union with a serenity that was disconcerting. I hate pressing his panic button only to rediscover that it's controlled by a rheostat. However, one possible reason for the success of our relationship is that we complement each other's irrational behavior. I panic about things that Tom handles with complacency and vice versa. Tom agreed to accompany me to the A&P to take advantage of a rare opportunity: a looming disaster being one of the few times when impulse buying has a rational justification. Before leaving, Tom wanted to shower but I had made up my mind that we had to go *now*. I was persistent. My sense of urgency, once activated, is as annoying as a car alarm that needs to be shut off. I told Tom that good grooming wasn't necessary before a hurricane. Why wash your hair in anticipation of one-hundred-mile-per-hour winds? Tom reluctantly agreed to shower later, but he insisted on making a list of what we needed to buy before departing. List making is something Tom does compulsively. His lists can be divided into three categories: Things To Buy, Things To Do, and Things To Change. As a psychological profile, they're more revealing than a Rorschach test. Unfortunately, Tom sets himself up for unnecessary disappointment by regarding each item listed not as a task but as a resolution. His self-esteem takes forgetting to buy a can of cleanser equally as hard as not being able to quit smoking.

While Tom and I were talking, Kenny Jerome, a towel piled around his wet hair, came out of his room. "What's going on?" he asked. Kenny's panting voice always sounded as if he was trying to catch his breath and was afraid that he was going to drop it. He was always the last person in the house to wake up. Emerging

from his room wearing a thick, red, terry cloth robe, Kenny would remain so attired for the rest of the day, giving the impression of being a movie star waiting in her trailer between takes. His breathy voice was an asset, though, because Kenny's specialty was impersonating Marilyn Monroe. He also impersonated Judy Garland, Patsy Cline, Peggy Lee, and Eartha Kitt, and apparently he was eating for all of them. Kenny could no longer create the illusion that he was svelte because he had svelled. At a little over five feet tall, with a pudgy baby face and platinum brunette hair, Kenny fluctuated between zaftig and zeppelin. The extra poundage was becoming a problem professionally—now during his show when he did Peggy Lee singing "Hey, Big Spender," the audience's first thought was that he was referring to the last person who took him out to dinner.

I patiently tried to tell Kenny what I knew about the hurricane. I didn't bother to tell him about the Gorbachev coup because Kenny's knowledge of current events, like Marilyn's, ended during the Kennedy administration. It soon became apparent that when Kenny imagined an "act of God" he pictured a Las Vegas–style revue.

"I thought hurricanes only hit Florida."

"No, they can move up the coast and then move inland."

"Are we in any danger?"

I explained to Kenny that the storm would pass near us but that we wouldn't be directly in its path.

"Will I have to cancel my show?"

"Girrrl, you better get dressed and get your ass to the A & P." The unmistakable deep gravely voice coming from the bathroom was Hoss's. Hoss was a big, burly, and extremely loud drag queen, and years of drink, drag, and cigarettes had transformed his vocal cords into barbed wire. An unabashed redneck, Hoss also preferred

that color when he did his nails. Almost every sentence he spoke started with "Girrrl," a term that he considered to be the omnisexual pronoun the English language had always lacked. Hoss and Kenny had known each other since high school in their hometown of Lubbock, Texas. When Kenny started performing, Hoss quit working as a plumber and became Kenny's opening act, assistant, dresser, and sidekick. He was a one-man entourage if you included his drag alter egos.

Kenny asked, "Hoss, can't you just pick up a few things for me?"

"No. I can not."

"Why?"

"Because you'll just blame me for not buying something that you needed—that I should've known—that I didn't know—because you didn't know it yourself—all because you wouldn't climb down from your pumps and do your own goddamn shopping."

Kenny was self-absorbed to a degree known only to death row prisoners and drag queens. His impression of helplessness was similar to his impression of Eartha Kitt—impossible to believe—but the execution was always impeccable. Whenever he needed even the smallest favor, Kenny always gave a demand performance. First, he would make an expiration point by letting out a pensive sigh. Having gained your attention, he would make the preliminary inquiry, "Did I hear you say that you're going to have some wine?" He would ask this in a tone of disbelief as if you were flying to Bordeaux to stomp the grapes yourself. Then he would let slip, "I don't suppose..." He'd pause as if the thought was a sliver that had to be painstakingly removed from his brain. Finally, in a voice filled with trepidation he would ask, "Would you mind getting me a glass?" When you agreed, as his lips became a halo around his radiant smile, he'd add, "Oh, would you?! Thank you, darling. Thank you so much. You are *so* sweet."

To Hoss's surprise, Kenny agreed to go to the A&P without any further argument, saying, "Let me fix my face. I'll be just a minute."

Fixing his face was the only manual labor that Kenny ever performed. Being extremely vain, and having done drag for years, his idea of being out of costume was wearing *less* makeup and no wig.

While we waited, the doorbell rang. It was a delivery man from Federal Express. I yelled upstairs, "Danny! It's your FedEx!"

Danny McWilliams is a stand-up comic and one of my partners in *Funny Gay Males*. Every two weeks, since the beginning of the summer, he had received a shipment of pot from his dealer in New York. He had tried the local dope, but like a New Yorker who's convinced that it's impossible to get a really good corned beef sandwich west of the Hudson, Danny was convinced that New York marijuana was superior. Danny was a pot-smoking show queen, a combination of interests that suggests a black-light poster for *Gypsy*. It was easy to imagine Danny as a teenager, sitting in his bedroom in Ozone Park, Queens, getting high while listening to *Annie Get Your Gun* and raving, "Oh, wow. Ethel is *soooo* fucking amazing."

Danny was a post-Stonewall show queen who had been influenced by the values of rock and roll, unlike previous generations of gay men who had admired stars like Billie Holiday and Judy Garland and thought, Isn't it awful that they suffer from those terrible addictions? Rock music let all Americans realize for the first time, Why is it that only the stars get to be fucked up? I can have a drug problem too! After the delivery man left, I told Danny about the hurricane and suggested that he come with us to the store. His reaction was to confess, with evident embarrassment, that he loved stormy weather as if he were divulging an unsavory meteorological fetish.

I agreed to drive since Jaffe, the third member of

our comedy trio, had generously given me a set of keys for his car—a 1971 Buick Skylark that had originally been painted gold but dirt and rust had reduced the finish to the glimmer of unrefined ore. I loved that car because it was so New York: tough, ugly, and dependable. It was a wreck and yet we had used it to drive to gigs from Maine to Virginia. Tom and I sat in the front, and Kenny, Danny, and Hoss squeezed into the back. As we were pulling out of the driveway, Jaffe rode up on his bicycle and Hoss rolled down his window and shouted, "Girrrl, a hurricane's coming! We've got to get ready!" Jaffe left his bicycle sitting unlocked on the front lawn—it was possible to do that in Provincetown—and climbed into the car. Peering calmly through his wire-rimmed glasses, Jaffe announced, "I'm not surprised about the hurricane. Mercury's going retrograde."

"Oh, Jaffe . . ."

"Bob, of course, you don't believe in astrology. You're a Capricorn. Stubborn like a goat."

I laughed at Jaffe's astrological reading. Jaffe blended his New Age beliefs seamlessly into his Jewish heritage, a spiritual amalgam whose central tenet is feeling guilty from previous lives and that could be symbolized by a yarmulke in the shape of a geodesic dome. I gathered from Jaffe that Mercury going retrograde was to the adherents of astrology what original sin is for Roman Catholics, a convenient starting point for most of life's troubles. Although, in some ways, astrology is an improvement on Judeo-Christian causality, since Mercury only goes retrograde three times a year, making the bad times seasonal instead of perennial.

Jaffe asked me, "Did you tell Kenny and Hoss about Lee?"

I hadn't. Yesterday, Danny, Jaffe, and I were having a cup of coffee on the front steps of our house when a young man named Lee who had recognized us from our posters introduced himself. The dawn is as fatal for drag queens as it is for vampires. In the first rays of the sun,

BOB SMITH

drag queens no longer inspire awe but instantly crumble into a pile of face powder. Lee's age could have been anywhere from twenty-three to forty-three, and whatever age he was—he looked bad for it. His wispy blond hair had receded, as if resigned to the fact that most nights it was redundant. His skin was raw from the nightly removal of more makeup than most women wear in a lifetime. Even Lee's posture and body language were odd—he moved as if he had trouble walking *out* of heels.

Lee wanted some advice from fellow performers.

"I only do Carol Channing. Do you think it will limit my career?"

There was a pause as we considered his question. She was a performer that no rational person would consider in the top echelon of entertainers.

Jaffe finally responded, "No. *She* only does Carol Channing and it hasn't hurt her career."

"Think of yourself as a specialist," I added.

"Well, I'm not like some drag performers who do Carol. I never use bad language on stage because she wouldn't. I respect the integrity of the character."

"Have you ever met her?" Danny asked.

"Oh, yes. Several times. I've seen her do *Hello, Dolly!* in at least ten different cities."

I asked, "Is she nice?"

"She's mar-vel-ous." Lee ecstatically enunciated every syllable.

"The first time, I flew to Toronto—to give her a sweater I had knitted—she arranged for me to get house seats, fifth-row-center, and afterward I was invited backstage."

This was when I questioned his sanity. "You *knit* her a sweater?"

"Yes, it had a map of North America appliquéd on the front with rhinestone stars of all the cities she's played in."

There was a pause in the conversation as we tried

to envision this garment. Lee ended our conversation by informing us that he was on his way to the printer to pick up the fliers and posters for his show. He was performing for three weeks and graciously invited us to come as his guests on any night. We thanked him and promised that we would. As soon as Lee was out of hearing range, we began to talk about him.

I asked, "Is he mental or what?"

Danny said, "I can't wait to see his show. I love really bad drag queens."

Jaffe began to mimic him, " 'I only do Carol Channing. Do you think it will limit my career?' Oh, no. Devoting your life to a B-level celebrity. That's a sensible career choice."

Danny, Jaffe, and I had worked together every week for four years and one of the bonds of our friendship was that whenever one of us started a comic premise, the other two were able to effortlessly embellish it. We were on a roll.

"That's probably the same question he asked his high school guidance counselor."

"Yeah, and he probably advised him to do Tallulah Bankhead just to have something practical to fall back on."

"And knitting a sweater for Carol Channing. . . . How big a queen is that?"

"That's probably how he came out to his parents. 'Hi, son. What are you doing?' 'Oh, I'm just knitting a sweater for Carol Channing.' Then his mother burst into tears."

"You know as soon as he was out of her dressing room, she was telling her assistant, 'Put it with the rest of the drag queen gifts.' "

"Now even *I* almost want to see him perform." Danny and Jaffe were surprised to hear me say this, since they knew my aversion to bad drag. I believe that moving your lips to a tape isn't a talent. It's a learning disability.

"He has an eleven o'clock show. We can make that."

We agreed to see his show, *Hello, Carol!*

Kenny had listened to Jaffe without saying a word and his only reaction was to raise an eyebrow and then throw it over his shoulder with disdain.

Hoss dismissed him with the comment, "I'd like to meet a gay man who can't do Carol Channing."

The only supermarket for thirty miles on the Outer Cape is the A&P on Shankpainter Road in Provincetown, and as we approached it we saw that almost every parking space in the lot was filled with vehicles of other panicky shoppers. After parking, to my relief, everyone split up once we were in the store. Grocery shopping is like marriage—when two people walk down that aisle together, it's a big commitment. Sharing a shopping cart with someone shouldn't be taken lightly. There's nothing more intimate than having her L'eggs nestled next to his lunch meat.

Supermarkets are on the cutting edge of social change. Anyone can buy family-size packages, whether your family is nuclear, dysfunctional, or chosen. At the cash register, all relationships are treated with the same respect. Your right to purchase a family valu-pack of paper towels is never disputed—your family is always valid even if your coupons aren't.

Supermarkets are also one of the few places in America where we're encouraged to make a public display of our private desires. If you have a yen for pig's feet, it's considered unusual but not perverted, and although your desire may not be universally shared, no one will quarrel with your right to enjoy it. Vegetarians might argue that eating pig's feet isn't exactly consensual dining, but most Americans believe that you have the right to eat what you want in the privacy of your own kitchen.

With our nation's increasing emphasis on fat-free and healthy foods, I worry that eating heartily may someday become a disreputable activity. Supermarkets

will have to offer dimly lit aisles, toward the back of the store, where furtive shoppers can grab butter and pork wrapped in plain white paper before shamefacedly paying for them and hurrying out of the store.

The first item on Tom's list was bottled water. When we reached the beverage aisle, Evian and Perrier were the only two brands left. As we chose four bottles of Evian, I imagined our humiliation as we were shown being rescued on the national news, clutching bottles of trendy H$_2$Eau. The next items on his list were a flashlight and candles. The flashlights were long gone and the candle selection was rapidly burning itself out. There were several vacillating customers standing in the aisle trying to make a selection from the meager and unappealing remains: citronella, scented, and some unsold Christmas candles that a swift-thinking manager had decided to unload. The scented candles were down to bayberry, pine, cranberry, and other Cape Coddish scents. I said to Tom, "Why hasn't a paraffin entrepreneur come out with a line of scented candles called, 'Natural Disasters'? The smell of 'Fear,' the air of 'Panic,' a whiff of 'Death'?" Tom listened and then said "No" in the brusque tone of finality he used only to indicate that an idea or joke of mine was not funny and never would be.

Tom grabbed one of the last packages of tall tapers in peach—a color that I knew he would choose only under a life-threatening situation. He would relish burning them if only to get them out of his sight. Since the Christmas candles were the largest and cheapest, we also grabbed three waxen Santa heads and three snow-covered cottages. As Christmas is frequently a disastrous holiday, the selection seemed satisfyingly appropriate for the occasion.

Tom had already figured out some possible menus for last-minute last meals. He thought it was likely that the power might go out and suggested only buying food not requiring refrigeration. I hadn't considered this a potential problem because the ancient refrigerator in our

house didn't really preserve food—it merely delayed its spoilage. The small freezer compartment was useless; the door had fallen off in a previous Ice Cube Age, and a thick, permanent layer of frost buildup made calving a glacier necessary to remove a Frozfruit. Tom stocked up on bananas, apples, and oranges, but healthy foods aren't comfort foods—in menacing situations, people instinctively crave sugar and fat. It doesn't matter whether the peril is imminent extinction or another Saturday night without a date. I tossed a bag of chocolate chip cookies into our cart.

The mood in the store was almost merry. People weren't complaining about the long lines and everyone was talking to strangers. I had even observed a lesbian couple offering to share their package of four batteries with a gay man. The prospect of a disaster was bringing out the altruistic qualities of gay people. Will Judgment Day do the same for right-wing Christian fundamentalists? If it falls on a Monday, will they at least try to enjoy the holiday weekend? Perhaps gay Americans have seen enough disaster movies to realize that the heroic lead survives while the hysterical, selfish character who needs to be slapped always gets eaten by the shark or buried in lava.

We waited thirty minutes in the checkout line. Kenny bought nothing but soda, potato chips, tortilla chips, salsa, and other snack foods. Apparently he was preparing to entertain the National Guard before being rescued. Most important, he bought three cans of hair spray. When I pointed out to Jaffe that Kenny had bought hair spray, we launched into an impromptu fantasy about drag queen panic buying—fighting in the aisles over the last tube of mascara.

Hoss said to Kenny, "Girrrl, what the hell are you buying all that crap for?" Kenny had opened a package of cookies and was demurely plowing through a row while we waited. Kenny said, "I don't want to buy much food. I think it would be better not to be able to eat for

a few days." I understood why Kenny didn't like to go grocery shopping. For him, the act of purchasing any food was an admission of failure.

Meanwhile, Danny was slowly pushing his cart down the aisles like an elderly and indecisive woman doing her marketing. He had a small package of frozen carrots, a quart of half-and-half, coffee, and two cans of split pea soup. Jaffe, who never cooked, bought water, cheese, and crackers, and in case of a total breakdown in his social order, a can of ravioli. Before we left, Hoss ran next door to the liquor store to pick up his "disaster relief"—a half gallon of vodka.

Our room was the best one in the house. It was at the back and had probably been the den or study. The walls were paneled with knotty pine and there was a large picture window that, if the garden was cut back, offered a view of the ocean. Yet our room's most desirable feature was that it had its own bathroom—an important consideration in a house inhabited by nine people. On rainy days, we could shut the door and almost feel like we were living in a log cabin. Although with the hurricane approaching, the large window now looked extremely vulnerable. Tom had bought a roll of duct tape and began to apply a large X across the window. We were going to sit out the hurricane in the living room, located in the center of the house, as it was the safest and least exposed room.

As we were moving our TV, VCR, and my computer and printer into the protection of our closet, Rachel Bergman and Amy Musso knocked on the door of our room. Rachel and Amy were our other housemates. They had just returned from the wharf and reported that waves were already coming over the breakwater in the harbor. We talked briefly about the hurricane and the situation in the Soviet Union. Since my nine-day trip to the Soviet Union in 1987 during perestroika I considered myself somewhat of an expert on the subject. I had left

Moscow convinced that no one still believed in communism and that the system would someday collapse. I based my expertise solely upon my conversations with our tour guide, a bartender, and the two guys who I met in the lobby of the Bolshoi Ballet who introduced themselves by asking, "Do you like the gay boys?"

At the start of the summer, Rachel and Amy had arrived in their minivan from their hometown of Northampton, Massachusetts. Rachel and Amy were in their late thirties and into the natural look: Rachel wore absolutely no makeup and Amy wore even less. Rachel was slim with lovely green eyes and light brown hair that she wore in a ponytail. I came to think of her as Sappho, the long-lost lesbian sister of the Marx Brothers, although her mustache was much lighter than Groucho's. Amy wore her long, salt-and-pepper-colored hair in two braided pigtails and whenever she spoke her dark brown eyes winked in a nervous tic that emphasized her flirtation with reality. Rachel and Amy were of the school of fashion that favors comfortable shoes and uncomfortable earrings. Their earrings were their only concession to adornment, one that cleverly allowed them to express their femininity in the butchest possible manner. Hanging from their ears were semiprecious stones of such tremendous mass that if they turned their heads too quickly they risked either a concussion or demolishing a nearby building. I liked Rachel and Amy because they were extremely well educated, prided themselves on being political, and were able to converse about anything, from the novels of Willa Cather to the best pancakes in town.

Rachel's full-time job was working as an administrator in the Internal Revenue Service, and Amy taught creative writing at a community college to support her addiction to writing unwatchable plays. Rachel had the rest of her life and career completely planned. She would work for nine more years in order to collect her govern-

ment pension, then she would become a full-time performer at women's music festivals and gay prides from coast to coast. Rachel billed herself as "America's Number One Openly Lesbian Ventriloquist." A title that went undisputed as she was, in fact, America's *only* openly lesbian ventriloquist. Offstage, Rachel favored blue jeans, work boots, and embroidered blouses, but on stage she performed dressed in complete S&M regalia: a black leather motorcycle cap, a studded harness, and leather chaps. While I respected Rachel's right to proclaim her allegiance to S&M, I had doubts as to whether it should be the basis of an entertainer's identity. If the audience found it painful to sit through your performance, did that mean you were successful? Rachel believed that her act had crossover potential, and after seeing it I hoped that she meant from bad to entertaining. She performed with Butch, a dummy with extremely short hair, dressed in tiny work boots, blue jeans, and a T-shirt that said I'M A DYKE! Rachel's opening line was, "Hi, my name's Rachel Bergman and I'm an openly lesbian ventriloquist."

Butch then "said" accusingly, "You're moving your lips!"

Rachel replied, "No, I'm not!"

"I wasn't talking about those lips."

The jokes in Rachel's act were like the traditional accessories worn by a bride at her wedding to ensure good luck: Something old, something new, something borrowed, and something blue. Her act consisted of Butch making incredibly filthy and relentless pussy jokes. For example, Butch claimed, "I'm the only piece of wood that eats beavers." For variety, Butch also picked on different members of the almost entirely lesbian audience, "Hey, you. Yeah, you in the Birkenstocks. Boy, what a lesbian trendsetter. How about after the show you and I. . . . I make a great dildo. And don't worry, if I give you a splinter. I'll go back in and get it."

* * *

As the hurricane approached, even the rain seemed to be hurrying for shelter. Tom locked Grady in her carrier as a precaution, concerned that during the storm she might be able to escape. He was guiltily solicitous about her safety because Tom had, to his regret, agreed to a veterinarian's recommendation and had her front paws declawed when she was still a kitten. I wasn't as troubled by her supposed vulnerability because Grady had matured into a talon-tempered cat who hissed with astonishing hatred at anyone who attempted to pet her. Her formidable personality was an effective defense against any form of predation imaginable. After Grady's howling imprisonment was completed we received a telephone call from Milt asking if he and Mark could sit out the storm with us. They lived in a house on the bay and the Coast Guard had suggested that they evacuate. I invited them to stay with us during the storm and then asked if there was anything that we could do. "No, I'm putting myself in the hands of God and Valium." Milt said this without a trace of levity, which indicated to me that he was really worried.

Milt Tatelman was in his early fifties; he had a dark, bushy mustache and a toupee as blatantly artificial as leopard-skin wall-to-wall carpeting. Milt joked about his toupee before you had a chance to pity him, which eliminated our having to pretend that we hadn't noticed that he was wearing one. Toupees are a poor bargain—they conceal your baldness while revealing that you're an idiot. When men start losing their hair they should pay for a personal trainer, not a hairpiece. One of the great unacknowledged recent contributions to masculine self-worth has been by balding men who instead of thinking that their hair loss is a liability have instead decided to make it an asset. They work out religiously and often even accentuate their loss by wearing their remaining hair closely cropped or even completely shaved. Thus they become Anti-Samsons, who demonstrate that the

more hair they lose, the hotter, and stronger, they become.

We first met Milt in New York when, after seeing one of our performances, he invited us to his annual Academy Award party. At the party, prominently displayed on the buffet table, were five giant custom-made hero sandwiches spelling out the word "OSCAR." Using hero sandwiches in a tribute to show business was a perfect example of Milt's style: Regular Gay. He couldn't resist taking something ordinary and giving it a campy twist. When Milt discovered that we were going to be spending the summer in Provincetown, he said that he had a house there and invited us to his annual Fourth of July Party. Provincetown's Fourth of July celebration is a Norman Rockwell illustration as drawn by Tom of Finland. The annual parade down Commercial Street has the traditional procession of fire trucks, local politicians riding in convertibles, and troops of boy and girl scouts, but it also includes drag queens, dykes on bikes, and floats from all the local gay bars. The parade is, like Provincetown itself, a sweet and savory blend of Americana and Queericana.

Our friendship with Milt flourished because he loved to throw parties almost as much as we loved to be guests. Milt came from a very wealthy family, which allowed him to entertain more lavishly than the income from his part-time career as a film and theater critic would normally have allowed. Over the front door of Milt's house hung a sign, WELCOME TO CAMP TATELMAN, and he meant camp in both senses of the word. Each wall in the house was covered with framed movie posters whose titles referred to beaches or the sea, including everything from *Muscle Beach Party* to the 1950s post–nuclear holocaust melodrama *On the Beach.*

Milt's enthusiasm and knowledge of show business was encyclopedic. He also seemed to possess an anecdote about meeting every star of the stage and screen from the last half of the twentieth century. While listening

to a song on Milt's CD player, Tom once asked, "Milt, what show is that song from?" Milt paused, and then in his mellifluous voice said, "That's from the musical *Chicago*. It was sung by Mary McCarty. You know, I'll never forget, I saw *Chicago* on opening night. The word of mouth was that the show was in trouble—but Bob Fosse must have done wonders at the last minute—but of course, Bob Fosse was *wonderful*—and you had the sense, in the middle of the first act, that everyone suddenly knew that they were seeing a smash hit musical, which of course it was."

I have absolutely no interest in musical theater—in fact, I hate musicals—whenever Tom's talked me into seeing one, I always hope that the show-stopping number will actually do what it promises. The sight of people breaking into song always makes me think that they're suffering from gay Tourette's syndrome, yet when Milt talked about musicals even I was enthralled. He had a deep, engaging voice and included enough detail, dramatic pauses, and mimicry to make every anecdote, however ludicrous, spellbinding.

The hurricane struck Provincetown almost exactly at one o'clock. The house seemed to be shivering as the rain and wind made every window rattle. After Milt and Mark arrived, everyone huddled in the living room, with the exception of Rachel and Amy who remained upstairs in their bedroom. We tried to reassure Milt that his house would be all right, but our confidence was as doubtful as our hope that Mark would also be all right. Mark calmly reminded Milt that his house, unlike most others in town, had metal storm shutters covering every window. Milt had brought his portable CD player and several discs of original cast albums, and after he settled into the red vinyl easy chair he put on his headphones, shut his eyes, and tried to listen to *Stormy Weather* instead of thinking about it.

Tom had made a pan of brownies. When they were

almost done, Kenny entered the kitchen. When food was being prepared, Kenny became as friendly as a cat hearing a can of tuna being opened. Kenny never cooked and usually depended upon the calories of strangers. He was always hungry, and if anyone was cooking something, he would glide into the kitchen, like a sofa on casters, and purr, "Oooooh, that smells soooo good." You had to be careful though, because if Kenny initiated an interest in eating, then it was permissible to offer him something to eat; but if the offer was unsolicited, he took it as an aspersion on his weight.

"Kenny, would you like a bagel?"

"No, Bob! What are you trying to do? A bagel has 438 calories!" Kenny knew the amount of calories in everything, from an apple to zabaglione. When food was placed in front of him, he always reacted with the same level of all-this-just-for-me incredulity, no matter what he was being served. The size of the portion was irrelevant. It could be a cracker or an entire leg of lamb. Kenny would make a perfunctory protest, "Oh, please. That's too much." His demurral would usually provoke Hoss into shouting, "Fill her plate! She'll eat the whole damn thing!" Hoss and Kenny's relationship was peculiar, even in a town that celebrates unorthodox relationships. Hoss constantly talked about Kenny behind his back, a maneuver that required some agility as his physique became increasingly prominent. He would tell us over coffee, "She has to go on a diet! Last night I got bloody fingers tryin' to zip her in that dress!" On other occasions, however, I overheard Hoss reassuring Kenny, "Girrrl, you're not fat! You're soft and voluptuous."

While we devoured the brownies, Hoss told us about what he and Kenny did the previous night. They were infamous for their licentious evenings out on the town. The night would commence after their show, when Hoss would announce, "Girrrl, we're going out to find us some straight husbands!" Before venturing forth, they would drink several vodkas while changing into their drag out-

fits. Hoss and Kenny had reached the point of jadedness where dressing up in women's clothes was the same as a fast-food employee putting on his uniform. They would transform themselves into their bad-girl alter egos, "Connie" and "Tina." Hoss and Kenny worked diligently on their look—the desired result being to have the slutty appearance of a whore while maintaining the sexually aggressive personality of a john. "Connie" was Kenny in a huge, long blond wig, and "Tina" was Hoss in a long auburn-colored wig. The next day they would recount in pornographic detail their adventures at the "Dick Dock," the nickname of a notorious pier that was Provincetown's late-night cruising area.

"Kenny and I met these two hot-hot guys. Girrrl, they had muscles out to here and I said to this hunky blond, 'Honey, show us your cock.' Well, he whipped out this big thick thing that was harder than a calculus test. Damn, if I didn't give him a handjob that's better than you can do yourself."

None of us was prepared to argue his assertion.

"Hoss, have you talked to Jerry this morning?" Kenny asked.

"No darlin', I haven't." He added waspishly, "You'd think he would've called *you* before a hurricane."

Kenny's manager was Dr. Jerry Bissell, a dentist from Baltimore who in addition to managing Kenny also wanted to be a cabaret singer. The previous week he had taken Danny, Jaffe, and me out to dinner because he also wanted to manage our careers. It's an unfortunate fact of show business that the people who proclaim the loudest that they can help your career usually need the most help themselves. Jerry didn't grasp that it's not reassuring for a performer to have a manager who has two other careers to fall back on. Since our dinner he had been pressing us to sign a contract with him. We considered his offer in our customary manner:

Jaffe said, "Imagine if you were one of his acts. He's drilling your teeth while talking on the phone trying to

sell you to a club owner: 'These guys are hilarious. You should book them immediately. Spit, please. *Oh, not you.* Um . . . it's an old show business expression . . . ' "

"Our headshots would be X-rays," I added.

Danny said, "Hey, but think of the benefits—not only would he manage our careers, but we'd probably get a deal on getting our teeth capped."

"Yeah, and we'd probably get a lot of work because every six months he'd send out notices reminding the club owners that it was time to book us again."

"And what about him singing cabaret?" Jaffe asked. He proceeded to mimic Jerry talking on the phone again: " 'Well if you don't want comedians or a drag queen, then how about booking me? I can sing. . . . ' "

Danny said, "He probably has a one-man show, 'The Singing Dentist.' "

I added, "Yeah, but his one-man show refers to the size of his audience."

Kenny had signed with Jerry because Kenny's dream was to appear in Las Vegas in his own show, *Me, Myself, and Eyeliner.* ("Isn't that title clever?" he would ask.) Jerry assured Kenny that he had a lot of contacts in Vegas but before he could do anything for him he needed Kenny to sign a three-year contract. I suspected that Jerry's contacts were probably fellow members of the American Dental Association.

A beeper went off. Mark needed to take his AIDS medication. He tried to pass over the moment by nonchalantly saying, "Time for my pills."

Hoss said, "Girrrl, do you need some water?"

While Mark swallowed his pills, Jaffe said, "My friend Peter's medication costs two thousand dollars a month."

Danny burst out with, "Two thousand dollars? How can anyone afford that?"

Mark said, "You know what pisses me off. Reagan and Bush and the entire Congress have government health insurance but they hypocritically claim that

they're opposed to everyone else having the same thing. If they're so against it, they should give up their own coverage."

Danny, who only read newspapers for show business gossip, nevertheless had strong feelings about this issue. He had watched his best friend, Michael, die without health insurance in one of New York's more gruesome public hospitals and the experience had infuriated him. When one of Danny's friends or family is wronged, his easygoing disposition disappears and he has a vindictiveness equal to another son of Ozone Park, John Gotti, head of the Gambino family. But Danny never becomes physically violent; he settles the score with cursing. Describing Danny as foul-mouthed doesn't do him justice. His vocabulary, like a rank, ripe Roquefort, was initially unappealing yet I had learned to savor it. His curses were spontaneous vivid tirades that combined elements of hilarity and horror.

"Reagan, that dried-up old fuck! I bet he cums in powder. He should get ball cancer!"

"Oh, Danny . . . stop!" Jaffe said. We couldn't stop ourselves from laughing.

It was impossible not to laugh at Danny's shocking outbursts, because his maledictions were delivered with such gusto. Most people cuss with one or two words, but Danny could spit out an entire paragraph. Danny's anger was like fireworks—the explosion was a show of force that was more entertaining than threatening.

Danny continued. "No. I want to see him end up in diapers in a hospital and I hope he smells so bad that no one wants to visit him."

"*Danny!* Stop."

While we laughed, Kenny excused himself to call his manager and grab a couple more brownies in the kitchen. "Kenny has quite an appetite," Mark said.

"Girrrl, are you kidding?" Hoss said. "When he visits friends in the hospital, he finishes their IV bags."

Mark laughed. "Kenny told me that he's going to start jogging."

"I can see Kenny jogging," Tom said, standing up to mimic Kenny jogging as Marilyn. Tom clutched his shoulders, one arm crossing the other, then he swung each shoulder in and out rapidly as if Marilyn's bosom was heaving as Kenny ran. Everyone exploded with laughter.

Hoss was about to resume his tale of last night's exploits when we heard Amy shouting from upstairs, "Rachel, why don't you respect my work? You moved the books on my shelf! That's where I keep my plays!"

"Now, Amy. I didn't deliberately move your books."

We rolled our eyes, acknowledging the familiar sounds of Rachel and Amy's bickering. It was quite an accomplishment to have your argument drown out a raging hurricane. Rachel and Amy never had petty quarrels. Everything was argued with a vehemence normally reserved for a lawyer's closing statements to a jury. And yet, their relationship had the true stability of two people who find contention to be a source of contentment. Rachel and Amy's dispute soon subsided.

The rain-streaked windows made the world look immersed. Every few minutes, Milt would remove his headphones and listen to the storm with a look of resignation on his face. Meanwhile, Danny had set up his TV and VCR in the living room because at the last minute he'd rented *The Poseidon Adventure*. Just as we settled in to watch the movie, there was a huge crack of thunder and the power went out. Milt deadpanned, "Even God can't bear to see that movie again."

A police car with the siren wailing pulled up near our house. When we looked outside, we saw that a large tree had fallen next door, taking down some power lines. The color drained from Milt's face, and toupee, when he saw the damage.

To distract Milt, Mark suggested that he tell every-

one about the time Lucille Ball had appeared on *The Tonight Show*. Danny and Jaffe seconded Mark's encouragement because they had both recently read her biography. All summer, as each of them worked their way through the book, they had discussed the juiciest stories with a thoroughness that made it unnecessary for me to read it. Milt, with the calm assurance of a storyteller confident of his talent, waited for everyone's attention, then he began. "Lucille Ball, years after her retirement, appeared on *The Tonight Show* with Johnny Carson during the mid-eighties."

Milt delivered his opening line the way a mother would say, "Once upon a time . . ."

"Lucy was wearing a long-sleeved emerald green pantsuit—to set off her hair color—and the large tinted eyeglasses she wore in her later years. She had already done her spot and had moved to the couch to make room for the next guest—the actress Michele Lee. Michele was eager to tell Johnny about her recent visit to the White House, where she was a guest of the Reagans. She went on and on about the pomp and the glamour. The evening had been incredible and the menu was the best part. Now Lucy had been listening with growing impatience, and she could be seen tugging at the sleeves of her pantsuit as if to distract herself from the long-winded story. When Michele started to reach into her handbag for the menu, apparently Lucy had heard enough. She asked Michele in astonishment, 'You're *not* going to read them the menu, are you?!' Lucy gestured with her arm toward the audience as if enlisting their support. Michele stammered, 'Uh, yes. I was. I think people are interested—' Lucy barked, 'You're *losin'* 'em! You're *losin'* 'em!' At that point, Johnny diplomatically cut to a commercial." It didn't occur to me until much later why we found this story so appealing. Lucy's single-minded determination to hold on to the audience perfectly exemplified our outlook.

Then I urged Milt to tell everyone about the time

he met Bette Davis: He had recently told Tom and me, and it was classic Milt. He hesitated until everyone gave him further encouragement.

"I went to see David Rabe's play *Streamers* and after I was seated I heard a very distinctive voice coming from the woman sitting in front of me. It couldn't be. I heard her speak again. It *had* to be her. I leaned forward to get a better look, and to my delight, *she* was sitting directly in front of me—Bette Davis. She still looked wonderful—this was before the stroke. She was wearing a beautiful dark blue wool dress and she was sitting with a black couple—as it turned out their son was in the play and she'd agreed to see him perform. Of course, I couldn't concentrate on the play—it was good but not great—because I couldn't wait until the intermission.

"I *knew* she would have to go out for a cigarette. Sure enough, at the end of the first act, she was up and out before the rest of the crowd. I wanted to speak to her but I didn't want to bother her—people can be so rude—but I knew this might be my only chance. I had thought carefully about what I wanted to say. I didn't want to be just another gushing fan. A small group of people had gathered around her in the front of the theater. When I saw my opportunity, I went up to her and I said, 'Miss Davis, we have something in common.' She gave me a quizzical look that was polite but not friendly. I said, 'We're both graduates of Newton North.' You see, we had both attended the same high school, a fact, that of course, I knew. Well, that was all I needed to say. She smiled and said, 'Aaaah, dear old Newwwton North.' " Milt had easily broken into a startling impression of Bette Davis's voice.

Milt continued: "She instantly became charming and we started a conversation. She didn't care for the play—the foul language. But the actor's parents were old friends. As we talked, they rang the bell to indicate that the second act was about to start, but Bette paid it no attention. They rang the bell a second and then a final

time, but when she pulled out another cigarette, *I knew* I was in for a treat.... After I lit her cigarette—I don't smoke but I always carry a lighter just for those occasions."

I was unsure if Milt meant the occasion of a woman needing a light for her cigarette or keeping a Hollywood film legend engaged in conversation.

"Well, we talked until the lobby was completely empty. Then she stubbed out her cigarette and said grimly, 'Weeell, we'd better go in.' She held out her arm and I took it. I escorted her into the theater and when we entered, the entire audience stood and gave her a rousing standing ovation as we proceeded down the aisle—and this was a New York audience, they were used to seeing celebrities. It was magical. They had held the curtain, as I'm sure she knew they would. When we arrived at our seats, she turned and smiled and said, in that voice, 'Milt, thaaank you so much. It was a pleasure to meet you.'"

Milt stopped speaking and basked in the glory of the moment. Although I'd heard the story before, Milt had told it just as well the second time. He gave the line, "*I knew* I was in for a treat" exactly the same preposterous and yet affecting emphasis. The hurricane still was raging but we were momentarily oblivious to it. It was storytime for boys who found tales of treasured moments more riveting than tales of pirates' gold.

By 3:30, the wind abated and the storm seemed to be passing. The rain was falling softly now, and Tom and I opened the door to check on our room. The picture window was intact but completely covered with a thick paste of shredded leaves that caused the room to be filled with a murky greenish light. When Grady was freed from her carrier, she didn't hesitate to release her pent-up feline contempt. Milt and Mark were anxious to check on their house and they asked if Tom and I would go with them. When we stepped outside, we saw the

front lawn littered with shingles blown from our roof and the streets strewn with leaves and branches. An emergency crew was already chainsawing and removing the fallen tree. Milt asked Tom to drive, and at first it didn't seem as if the storm had done all that much damage, but as we drove down Bradford Street, we saw several large elms that had been toppled across from the Town Hall.

Soon we saw more evidence of the storm's force. The roof of the Wayfarer Motel had been blown off and landed in the motel's pool. It looked as if the roof was trying to relax after all the commotion. Milt let out a strained "Oh, my" as we slowly drove through the crowd that had gathered to see the damage. I felt uneasy as Tom parked the car.

Milt's house wasn't visible from the street, and after parking the car we had to walk past several homes to reach it on the beach. Milt and Mark walked slowly, and Milt seemed resigned to whatever had happened. As we turned the corner and saw the undamaged house, Milt let out a giant sigh of relief. "Oh, thank God," he groaned. Camp Tatelman had come through the storm unscathed. Milt's instinctive hospitality returned and he asked if we wanted to stay for dinner. We declined because I had the show to do.

We headed back to our house. Commercial Street was crowded as everyone in town was gawking at the damaged buildings and uprooted trees. The hurricane had been over for only thirty minutes when we saw Kirk, an acquaintance of ours, dressed as Dorothy from *The Wizard of Oz*, carrying a small basket in which a stuffed dog played the part of Toto. To the amusement of passersby, he was walking down the street stopping occasionally to reenact a scene from the movie. Two guys holding hands had written in bold letters on their rain ponchos, I GOT BLOWN BY BOB! and a lesbian couple passed us who had made their own storm souvenir T-shirts, HER-ICANES ARE MORE FUN! One guesthouse

played over and over a tape of "Raindrops Keep Falling on My Head" while a block away another one blared the old disco song "It's Raining Men." It seemed as if the entire gay and lesbian population of Provincetown had spent the duration of the storm planning their triumphs over adversity.

When we returned to the house, we found another message on the answering machine from Lois. "Hi, guys. It's Lois. Oh, I'm glad the phones didn't go out. That would've been a real disaster. Thank goodness, the restaurant's okay. I'm having them stay open tonight. They can't serve any hot food, but out of the goodness of my heart, I thought they could sell cold sandwiches and potato chips. I mean the meat's just gonna spoil.... Oh, and they can't use the blenders..."

The mention of the "blenders" made me laugh as I pictured a panicked Lois attempting to hang solar panels in order to whip up a batch of frozen margaritas.

"Oh. It's a mess. Anyway, I think we should do the shows tonight. I mean we shouldn't lose the money. People will want something to do. We can still sell drinks. I'm getting bottled mixers. And for now, I'm charging fifty cents for water. Those paper cups cost me money. Not every restaurant in town can close. You know the visitors have to eat . . . and drink. Now I'm getting a portable generator—you wouldn't believe what it's costing— and I'll try to have the power back on soon but if it doesn't happen, we can put candles on the stage and light you with a flashlight. Make it part of the act. All right, call me."

The Firehouse Café and Cabaret was located on Commercial Street, in a former firehouse that Lois had converted into a restaurant serving breakfast, lunch, and dinner downstairs and a cabaret upstairs. The cabaret was an hourglass-shaped room filled with a haphazard collection of chairs, stools, and benches, and the cheap

tinselly Mylar curtain on the stage gave the place just the right touch of crass. As Lois said, "It's not fancy but it works for comedy." The showtimes were Kenny at 7 o'clock. *Funny Gay Males* at 8:30. Rachel at 10.

Tom worked as waiter in the restaurant after Lois had generously offered him a job. She had immediately taken a liking to Tom and told me repeatedly throughout the summer, "Tom's a class act." The manager of the restaurant and cabaret was a man known as Maxine. I never learned his real name because he was always called Maxine by everyone in town. The name had lost whatever campiness it had once held and was now used matter-of-factly, as if it were Joe or Bill. Maxine was slightly buck-toothed, had red hair and a red beard, wore pinkish oversized eyeglasses, and was renowned as one of the rudest people in P-town. Maxine also spoke with a striking lisp. His pronunciation of the word "sister" could blow out candles on a birthday cake. The normal sound of Maxine's voice was a tone of exasperation. He was like a simmering teakettle always on the verge of having a hissy fit. Whenever one of us would walk into the cabaret, before we had a chance to speak, he would ask, "*Now* what do you want?"

Maxine was the biggest queen in town—in a town where that title would be contested. He is the only gay man that I've ever met who actually was limp-wristed. He walked with his elbows touching his hips, his arms holding his boneless hands as if they were two icky starfish. I didn't think of Maxine as being stereotypical, he was archetypal. He's the standard by which I measure and compare anyone referred to as a "big queen." In appearance, Maxine was a man who had gotten in touch with his feminine side and asked to borrow some clothes. He wore silver bangle bracelets on both arms and his eyeglasses hung around his neck on a strand of glass beads. He looked like a drag queen who had started getting dressed for a show and had been interrupted before he could finish.

The waiters of the cabaret—Andy, John, and Trudy—loved thinking up new ways to aggravate Maxine. All summer, they sang a parody about him: "Poof, the Magic Drag Queen, lived by the sea..." The staff was entertaining enough to do their own show for Lois. Andy was a cheerful, muscular blond who had recently won the Best Pecs contest at the Vault, Provincetown's leather bar—you could ride a donkey down his cleavage. Not only was Andy good-looking, he had just graduated near the top of his class from Harvard Business School and was starting a high-paying job in New York in the fall. Everyone had the same reaction after meeting Andy: He was too good to be true and too bad he wasn't single.

John was a country-western singer from Oklahoma who was dark haired and slightly less muscular than Andy. He was a tough guy who also occasionally enjoyed acting very silly. John was a shit-kicker who could also jeté. All summer he had wanted someone to heckle us just to give him the opportunity to give them the heave-ho. But to his disappointment, John learned that gay audiences heckle the performers *after* the show.

Trudy was a tall, stunningly beautiful, auburn-haired Australian woman who during the winter lived in Palm Springs, where she made her living scuba diving to retrieve balls from the water hazards of golf courses. Trudy had recently become girlfriends with Mary, who ran the cabaret's lights and sound. Mary was barely over five feet tall and had long, unkempt brown hair and horrifyingly stained teeth. They looked as if you could drop one of her bicuspids in a cup of hot water and brew tea. Mary introduced each act from her soundbooth, but at the first opportunity, she would go to the back stairs of the club to smoke the remains of a joint and make out with Trudy. Trudy and Mary kissing was an exhilarating and romantic image: Beauty and the Beast, but much hotter than anything by Disney.

Harry was an elderly black man who ran the door at the club. A former college librarian, he was dapper in

a town where having a crisp tan line was much more important than the crease in your pants. Harry always wore a jacket and an ascot, which to his delight prompted numerous compliments. Before opening the door to the club, Harry would order from Maxine the first of the several rye and gingers that he would drink during the shows. Harry spoke so slowly that I was unsure if he was drunk all the time or if it was just his habitual manner of speech. He always greeted every performer and when I would ask him how he was doing, I never received a perfunctory response. His cryptic replies ranged from "Poorly" to the mysterious "The dykes are driving me crazy."

After the hurricane, I arrived at the show forty-five minutes early because I was apprehensive about whether we could do the show without a microphone or lights. I went up on stage to try out a few of my jokes and discovered that to be heard in the back of the club, I literally had to shout. Lois had some workmen installing a portable generator, but according to Maxine it wouldn't be hooked up by the time our show started.

After my sound test, I sat at the bar and listened to Maxine and John discussing body piercing. John was considered an expert on the subject because his optional bodily orifices now outnumbered the set he had been born with. John had six earrings, a stud through his nose, his nipples were pierced with small bolts, and, according to Maxine, "His dick has its own door knocker." Trudy casually interrupted. "John, be a sweetie and show Bob yer cock."

John smiled and said, "Bob doesn't want to see my cock."

Trudy said, "Yes, he does. Ev'ryone likes to see a nice cock."

Maxine leered, "Bob, you have to give him some encouragement."

At that moment, I thought, *What would Hoss do in my situation?* "Girrrl. Whip it out."

John's smile grew as he started to undo the buttons on the fly of his cutoffs. He quickly yanked down his white underwear, proudly displaying his cock as if he was a little boy and he had just caught a frog. Hanging through the end of it was a large silver hoop. John had mounted the family jewels in an engagement ring. We frankly stared in astonishment—not so much at what we were seeing, as the fact that he was showing it with such poise. Having someone display their genitalia for public admiration is usually a cause for alarm.

"See, Bob. It's lovely," Trudy said.

I wouldn't have used those exact words to describe it. When asked to admire penis mutilation, do you admire the look, the ability to endure the process, or the sheer insanity of it?

I asked the obvious question: "How much did it hurt?"

"It was worse then even I imagined." John's intonation left me uncertain whether that was a good thing or a bad thing.

Trudy asked, "What about when you pee?"

"Oh, it sprays all over the place. I have to sit down."

Our respect drooped. Somehow after that admission, John wasn't Lord of the Rings anymore, but just another Frodo wannabe. Maxine stopped our discussion. "Okay, John. Put your dick away. Lois and Barb just pulled up."

Just as John finished packing his piece, Lois and Barb walked in the backdoor. They attended the shows only a few times each summer, and when Lois arrived the staff stopped goofing off and tried to look busy. It was folklore among the staff that no matter how much Lois drank, she remembered everything. Somehow her black outs were never accompanied by a loss of power.

Barb was in her mid-thirties and looked like one of the tough greaser girls in high school who had finally grown up and washed her hair. She was a brooding extrovert. Barb loved to dwell on her own problems by sharing them with other people. Whenever she showed

up at the cabaret, I made every effort to avoid conversing with her. We went over and said hello and Lois immediately embarked on one of her monologues. In person, as on the telephone, Lois sounded as if she was thinking aloud.

"Hi, guys. There's already a line out front. Oh, it looks like it's gonna be a good house. Maxine, I'll have a margarita, darlin'. Just a little one. The candles look good on the stage...."

There were two tables of burning candles on the stage, giving it the appearance of an altar. Harry had opened the front door of the cabaret and the audience started to enter.

"I hope they don't violate the fire laws.... Oh, it's just for one night. You've already got thirty reservations for tomorrow. You draw in the men. And the women too. But the dykes don't drink. I don't get it. Trudy, don't just stand there. Go push a round of drinks. She's beautiful but... can you believe her and Mary? I don't get it. Oh, it's a goof. So you met Ted at the Hook and Sinker? Oh, I know. I drink. But only at night. He's a mess. I don't know how he runs that club. Now Danny, don't go on too long tonight."

Lois came to the club infrequently but she kept track of how the shows were doing by calling Maxine at the bar and having him hold the telephone receiver aloft to allow her to listen to the audience's response. Whenever Lois came to our show, I felt like the boss was looking over my shoulder as I worked.

Danny did an impression of her that was uncannily accurate. Our nightly ritual, as we stood next to Mary's sound booth waiting to be announced, was for Danny to whisper as Lois, "OK, guys. Have a great show. Remember: In comedy, silence equals death and one last thing, *I don't want you using that washer and dryer!*"

Our show consisted of Danny, Jaffe, and me coming out and doing a bantering opening together and then each of us doing a twenty-minute set of stand-up. The

show was completely sold out. When we came on stage, we were nervous but we knew the show would go well when Danny commented on all the candles and then I made a lame joke that our next performance was going to be at St. Patrick's Cathedral. This received a huge, undeserved laugh. Our audience had clearly decided that The Show Must Go On, and they weren't going to let our acts be a hindrance. They had survived a hurricane and in the candlelight all of our jokes looked golden.

The biggest difficulty with doing the show was overcoming the distraction of Lois's conversations. During every performer's set, Lois talked until her voice became too loud and then with a shock of realization that someone was making too much noise, she would put her index finger up to her mouth and gesture for *quiet* while shushing everyone but herself. It was the liquor talking in a monologue that had started twenty years ago. The three of us shared a fantasy that someday Lois would do her own one-woman show. The posters would read: SECOND SMASHED YEAR! HUNGOVER TWO MORE WEEKS! LAST CALL FOR TICKETS!

After each of our sets, Lois would invariably call us over and say either "You're my favorite" or "Oh, you're the best." When two of us were together, she might combine the two phrases by saying, "Danny, you're my favorite, but Jaffe, you're the best." It's a measure of the performer's need for praise that on some level we thought her compliments were sincere.

After our show, Lois and Barb insisted that we stay for a drink, so we sat through the opening of Rachel's show. That night Rachel's audience was rather unresponsive and Lois attempted to assist her by spurring their laughter. On slow nights, Lois worked harder in the audience than the performers did on stage. If the audience was dead, Lois would take a word from the set-up of the joke and say it aloud as if it were the funniest thing that she had ever heard. When Rachel started a joke with "My brother-in-law Warren is so...," Lois

would loudly say, before the audience had a chance to laugh, "Oh, *Warren*..." She would then laugh uproariously as if she had never heard the word before. If the audience didn't join in, she would abruptly stop laughing and then try again during another joke. We admired Lois's perseverance—she worked it.

Rachel said, "Have you ever been to the deli and noticed..."

"Oh, the *deli*..."

Lois's boozy laugh started and stopped like someone rattling ice cubes in a glass. After three attempts to perk up the crowd, Lois turned to us and said, "Rachel's a very sweet girl but...she sucks. Oh, she sucks!" Lois finished her thought with a dismissive shrug. After an interval that was long enough to be sociable but short enough not to be unbearable, we told Lois that we were going to leave. We didn't want to stay until Lois became completely blotto and started singing songs that only she knew the lyrics to—Lois said to Maxine as we headed towards the door, "Lemme have another one, darlin'. Just a little one. Are you guys going? Okay. Thank you. You guys are the best."

The electricity was still out, and as we made our way down the dark street the flashlight beams of passing pedestrians made it look as if a few lighthouses with a wandering eye had decided to take a stroll. The sky had cleared and the stars reminded me of the night of shooting-star gazing at Herring Cove Beach, which I had organized a few weeks before after I read that the annual Perseid Meteor showers were anticipated to be the most spectacular in forty years.

What prompted me to do this is that I feel that anything that truly interests me can, under the right circumstances, be interesting to other people. An absurd belief that has comforted notable bores throughout history. I share my enthusiasms with an eagerness that makes missionaries uncomfortable.

On an impulse, I had decided to ask people who had never demonstrated any interest in natural history to share one of my passions. When I suggested my plan to Kenny and Hoss, they were intrigued by the idea but couldn't commit to it. It didn't occur to me that drag queens are resistant to the appeal of natural phenomena. They find watching the movie *Niagara* more memorable than seeing the Falls itself. If I was prudent I might have given the idea more consideration before inviting people who consider a man in a black dress and pearls to be the epitome of subtlety and whose standards of dazzlement are more attuned to watching a career plummet. Hoss warned me, "Girrrl, it will be freezing on that beach at night."

I said, "Not if you wear men's clothes."

Kenny concurred with Hoss, whining, "I hate the cold. Can't we just watch from our front steps?"

I explained that it would be easier to see shooting stars the farther away we were from the lights of town.

Hoss said, "Darlin', why don't you just come with us to the Dick Dock? I'll show you some shootin' stars."

Convincing Rachel and Amy to join us wasn't too difficult. Amy earnestly inquired, "Now, Bob. Why do these meteors appear at the same time every year?"

"I think our planet passes through the same group of asteroids in its orbit around the sun." I wasn't sure if that was the correct reason but it sounded fairly plausible.

Rachel backed me up: "I read that also. In the 'Science' section of the *Times*."

Amy said with a smile, "You know, I read that the Earth could be struck by a major asteroid at any time. But it wouldn't destroy all the life on the planet. Just mankind."

Rachel said, "Really? That's interesting. I should try to get a book about meteors."

By now I understood that the love between Rachel and Amy was bibliophilic as well as Sapphic. They

needed to read about a subject in order to be able to enjoy it. Whether it was orgasms or the afterlife, they spent more time reading about the experience than they would ever spend undergoing it.

Everyone agreed to come when Danny offered to bring several joints.

The night of August 12, the peak night of the meteor shower, was perfect for stargazing. It was cloudless and there was no moon. We drove out to the beach in Rachel and Amy's minivan and during the ride smoked one of Danny's joints. In addition to everyone in our house, I had also included Milt and Mark. After we had arrived, we chose to sit on the closest dune near the parking lot. I had brought several blankets because I knew that this group would complain about having to lie on the cold sand. After we sat down, Danny had trouble lighting the second joint. The match kept blowing out. After several unsuccessful attempts, he became frustrated and yelled, "Fucking lick my taint!" The first time I had heard Danny use this expression I had asked him what a "taint" is. As he explained, "Taint the balls or the asshole—it's the part in between." Hoss impatiently said to Danny, "Give it to me." He took the joint and lit it on his first try. I was impressed. Hoss was like a delinquent Eagle Scout who could start a fire in the wilderness if it was necessary for the survival of a good time. As we passed around the potent joint, I said, "Jaffe, what's Lois's sign?"

He replied, "Are you kidding? She is the Big Dipper."

Danny said in Lois's voice, " 'I don't want the Big Dipper, darlin'. Just a little one.' "

Kenny asked, "Where is the Big Dipper?"

"There it is." I pointed.

"Now I see it," Kenny said, adding reverently, "The sky's beautiful. It looks like sequins."

I mentioned that if you follow the two stars at the

end of the bowl of the dipper they point to the North
Star, Polaris.

"Girrrl, how do you know this shit?"

Amy said, "Bob, has anyone ever told you that you'd
make a good forest ranger?"

"Yes."

Tom squeezed my hand. "Oh, he'd love that."

"Some of those park rangers in those uniforms are
hot. Honey," Hoss said, "they can put out my fire any-
time."

The pot must have affected my judgment because I
continued, "And if you look closely, the middle star in
the handle of the Big Dipper is actually a double star."

Danny had completely assumed Lois's identity and
said, " 'I'll have a double, darlin'.' "

After we finished the joint, everyone lay back on the
blankets. The first meteor appeared shortly thereafter,
followed by others in a steady and wondrous succession.
I was relieved that the night wasn't a dud. After a few
minutes of awed appreciation, Danny-Lois started re-
sponding to the shooting stars, " 'Oh, that one was the
best. . . . Oh, that one's my favorite. No, *you're* the best.
Oh, but *you're* my favorite.' " When there was a mo-
mentary lull while we waited for the next meteor to
streak across the sky, Danny-Lois would say, " 'Darlin',
lemme have another one. Just a little one.' " Then after
one would flash, Danny would add, in the same tone
Lois would use with a bartender who had just set down
a drink, " 'Thank you, darlin'.' "

After an hour everyone started to feel cold from sit-
ting in the wind blowing off the ocean and we decided
to leave. As we walked back to the parking lot, Hoss
summed up the evening when he said, "Girrrl, that was
a good show." I knew he was talking about the meteors,
but I said, "I know. Danny was hilarious."

The next morning the power was restored in Prov-
incetown at about the same time power was being re-

stored to Mikhail Gorbachev in the Soviet Union. Within a few days after the hurricane, I noticed that the leaves on all the trees and bushes in town started to wither. Soon the entire Cape looked blighted. The local newspaper reported that this was due to the amount of saltwater that had been blown ashore by the storm. Green dimmed to brown as if someone had turned off the power on the summer itself. Autumn had slipped and fallen on Provincetown.

Before leaving Provincetown, we went to see Lee's show, *Hello, Carol!* He performed in the back dining room of the Jib, a restaurant whose walls were decorated with lobster pots and fish nets, pertinent symbols for a tourist trap that lured in customers with "Complete Lobster Dinners for ONLY $12.95." The Jib claimed to offer "fine dining," but it was a pretentious coffee shop—a greasy demitasse spoon. Judging from the Jib's unappetizing appearance, I could tell that the boiled lobsters were the only thing in the joint that had ever been touched by hot water. It was an "authentic Cape Cod" restaurant that could be found anywhere, only the seafood restaurants in Kansas served fresher lobsters.

In the large back dining room, a small black box stood in a corner. It was the stage, but it looked as if it was intended as a place of punishment for bad performers. A black cloth had been hastily and clumsily hung as a backdrop, giving it the grim air of a scaffold. The tables in the restaurant were spread out adequately for dining, but they were too far apart to create the cohesion necessary for an audience. Each table was an island, and unfortunately for Lee most of them were deserted. After the glum waitress took our drink orders, Milt said with concern, "This doesn't look good."

Milt knew Lee, which wasn't surprising since Milt managed to meet all the local performers. Lee had also recently asked him for advice about his career. Milt said that he tried to be supportive, but before he could elab-

orate on that ambiguous statement the show started. The emcee was a perky blond man in his late thirties with a boyish quality more chorus than Huckleberry Finn. He was wearing a tuxedo with an iridescent-spangled bow tie and cummerbund that instead of making his outfit look festive just reiterated that he was gay. He seemed to be trying to warm up the audience with friction as his singing caused everyone to fidget in their seats. After he finished, Lee was introduced with Brag Queen bravado as "The foremost Carol Channing illusionist ever to appear in Provincetown."

Lee started the show by walking through the audience, moving rapidly, as a follow spot tried to keep pace with him. He beckoned the light, in a charade of an impersonation of Carol's voice, with the comment, "I'm over here." Then he would move to a new position and say, "No. I'm over here." Lee did this repeatedly until he reached the stage. The audience didn't react. We understood what he was doing but were mystified as to its purpose. Jaffe leaned forward in his seat and said à la Lucy, "He's losin' em! He's losin' em!" I started to snicker but Milt gave us a look of disapproval that would have hushed a stadium. Once Lee reached the stage, "Carol" greeted the audience with a short, chatty monologue that elicited a few chuckles and then he segued into singing "Diamonds Are a Girl's Best Friend."

After Lee finished "Diamonds," he went behind a screen for a costume change. While changing, Lee continued to talk to the audience in an attempt to keep the audience's interest. Before each of Lee's reappearances, the audible click of someone pressing a button on a tape player could be heard followed by the sizzle and crackle of his music starting. Throughout his performance, the sound system heckled Lee with feedback. Twice the tape became stuck in the player, causing the show to be interrupted, each time giving false hope to the audience. The second time it occurred, the look of panic on Lee's

face was painful to observe, but he earned the biggest laugh of the night by saying, in character, "Carol's becoming angry."

Lee's show was such a disaster that his drag name should be "Miss Fortune." After his third song, Lee's makeup started to run for the exit. The most disturbing moment of the evening was when the owner of the Jib started a loud conversation in the back of the room. Judging from his slurred speech, I thought a more apt nautical name for the restaurant would have been "Three Sheets to the Wind." Milt silenced him when he said in a commanding voice, "Would you please be quiet?"

We applauded enthusiastically when the show was over *because* it was finished. We paid the check, and Milt said, "I don't think we should wait for Lee. He might not be up to it. Why don't I thank Lee for everyone while you walk down to Spiritus? I'll meet you there for an ice cream." Milt usually insisted on waiting afterward to congratulate a performer, especially if the performer had invited you and knew that you were in the audience. We agreed to Milt's plan with relief, but as we were departing Lee came out front looking for us. He appeared more like a bedraggled queen than ever. But to our astonishment, he smiled and said, "Thank you all for coming. There are still a few rough spots to work out but the show keeps improving." This put everyone on the spot; now we *had* to talk about the show. I never worry about what to say to an untalented performer. I always lie. I try to remember that even if I give a bad performance, it's still probably better than the one I just saw.

We paid our compliments with counterfeit currency. I said, "Lee that was . . . unforgettable."

Lee said, "Thank you. It went well but that room was hard to work in."

I thought, *No. That room was hard to sit in.*

Everyone struggled with their pseudo-kudos. Tom said, "You did a great job considering . . ."

I wanted to finish his sentence with... *that you have no talent.*

Hoss gushed, "Girrrl, your Carol makes me want to quit doing drag!" The unspoken reason for Hoss's wanting to retire had to be repudiation, not admiration.

Kenny impersonating sincerity said simply, "Darling, thank you."

Lee's and Kenny's acts were the worst fashion choice a drag queen could make—they were old hat. Instead of imitating celebrities, modern drag queens want to be celebrities. During the summer, we had a few friends in their early twenties staying with us, and one of them had mortified Kenny by asking, "Who's Peggy Lee?" Is anyone really still interested in Judy, Bette, Marilyn, or most doubtfully, Carol? Soon their legends will seem as distant as Jenny Lind's or Sarah Bernhardt's.

A recent obituary in *The New York Times* was headlined, RED THUNDER CLOUD, 76, DIES, AND THE CATAWBA TONGUE WITH HIM. It reported:

Red Thunder Cloud, a member of the Catawba Nation who was steeped in the history of American Indians, died Monday in Worcester, Mass., apparently taking to the grave the last human link to the ancient language of his people.

It made me wonder if in the year 2036, Kenny Jerome's obituary will read: "Kenny Jerome, 76, Dies, And Marilyn Impersonation With Him."

The day after Labor Day, Provincetown becomes a tranquil small town again. We stayed one more week because there were still enough tourists to make doing the show worthwhile. But now there was no pressure from Lois for us to fill the house. During our last week, Tom and I attempted to do all the things that we hadn't done during the previous nine weeks. We rode our bicycles over the few remaining trails that we hadn't trav-

eled and we finally rented a boat and spent a leisurely
day on a deserted beach. One night we even made a fire
in the fireplace since there were piles of freshly cut wood
neatly stacked all over the Cape now—a practical use
for all of the trees downed by Bob. Everyone came the
night of our last show: Milt, Mark, Rachel, Amy, Kenny,
Hoss, Lois, and Barb. During my set, I realized that I
could pick out each of their laughs from among the
crowd. It must have been a good show because Lois
didn't try to prompt our audience.

The day before we returned to New York, Tom
drove me to the town of Orleans to pick up our rental
truck. Hoss had been packing all morning. He was
having Kenny's costumes and wigs shipped to Las Vegas.
Jerry had actually found a booking for Kenny. It was in
a show of female impersonation with a doppelgänger of
drag queens called "Ladies Are Gentlemen!" The show's
tacky slogan was "They're Men by Day but Ladies of
the Night!" Kenny was very excited. "It's in a gay bar.
But it's nice. They do brunch on Sundays and put potted
palm trees on the pool table."

Hoss was already trying to talk Kenny out of buying
new costumes. "Girrrl, your life savings are going to be
in wigs." After half an hour of desultory packing, Kenny
said, "I wish I was a stand-up comic. You can wear what-
ever you want." Hoss said to him, "Darlin', if you were
a stand-up comic, you'd probably have more props than
any drag queen." I suggested to Kenny that he consider
becoming America's first drag ventriloquist—"He
Throws His Voice Like a Girl." Hoss said, "Oh, no. Then
he'd have to buy clothes for the dummy. He'd lose
money on the act."

Saying good-bye to Hoss and Kenny was like saying
good-bye to two elderly aunts. They warned us to drive
safely. They insisted we stay in touch. And we had to
kiss them each on the cheek before they departed to the
airport.

Rachel and Amy had left very early that morning.

We had stayed up late talking and had already said our good-byes. But when they left shortly after dawn, I awoke with a bang on the stairs and then heard Amy snap, "Rachel, please be careful of my computer!"

Lois had called earlier and left one last surprisingly brief message on our answering machine: "Hi, guys, it's Lois. I know I'm going to see you later but before you go, would you please put out the garbage? Thanks, guys." I considered bagging the entire house and leaving it by the curb, but they recycle in Provincetown and there wasn't enough time to separate the house from my memories.

We stopped by Lois's house to pick up our last envelope of cash. After we knocked on the door, she came out in a housecoat. Lois didn't appear to be used to seeing people in the morning. She had attempted to pull herself together but a few parts were still missing. She said, "Oh, I can't believe the summer's over—just keep the keys to the house—you'll be back next year—I'll talk to you over the winter—I mean, we live in New York—we'll have you over during the holidays—if I can get our new apartment ready—oh, the contractor's doing a good job but he's taking forever—I shouldn't complain because I got a great deal—are you sure that you don't want to stay another week? How about coming back Columbus Day weekend? I mean—c'mon—oh, the money!" As she said this, Lois shook the envelope of cash like a happy baby with a rattle.

"Guys," she said, as she turned to go back into the house, "this was your year!"

The Dark Side
of the Honeymoon

I T IS a truth that should be universally acknowledged that all couples will someday need counseling. To state this fact of modern life is not to prepare oneself for failure; it is an admission that should be accepted with the same equanimity as the knowledge that everyone will someday need the services of a dentist. My feelings about dentistry and therapy are comparable. Before the first visit, I'm certain that the doctor is going to find something horrible that can only be corrected by numerous excruciating and expensive sessions in the chair. Usually, my fears are unfounded and the initial examination is not painful, it's only uncomfortable. Although, at some point during the visit, both dentists and therapists have to prompt their patients to spit it out. Examining your own behavior is as difficult as exam-

ining your own mouth—it's impossible to adequately view in its entirety and you will surely overlook something. But I always leave both offices resolving to do better in the future. (I *will* floss and express affection regularly.)

Some people may be asking: Didn't the human race flourish for eons without couples counseling? Surely there must be couples who have gone through a long-term relationship without conflict? The inevitability of problems in a relationship can be proved by the syllogism:

1. All couples quarrel.

2. I'm not trying to start an argument.

3. *Would you just let me finish?!*

It is true that the human race flourished for thousands of years without couples counseling as it also flourished without sun screens, anesthetics, and effective birth control. But only a few reactionary crackpots are unwilling to concede that these aren't necessities of modern life. How did humanity seemingly thrive for generations without couples counseling? It's important to remember that our ancestors had one major advantage over modern man: Their life expectancy was forty years or less, which ensured that bad relationships were at least of limited duration. It's quite possible that an early checkout time may have been preferred by people stuck in miserable relationships without the tools or knowledge to improve them. The phrase "till death do us part" held out hope to couples when often the only legal, moral, and economic way out of a bad relationship was to expire.

It's not surprising that an increase in life expectancy and the development of therapy occurred simultaneously. There was no incentive to improve life expectancies if it only meant being neurotic or living with a neurotic longer. As life spans slowly increased in Europe

and America, the development of psychotherapy became inevitable. We now have over twice the time of previous generations to make ourselves and others miserable.

I say this as a veteran of couples counseling. Tom and I have gone through two different bouts of couples counseling with two different therapists. After seeing our first therapist, we thought that we had solved all of our problems. The second therapist stopped us from ever thinking that again. Tom and I during our eight years together have had "our ups and downs": a euphemistic phrase that gives only the most superficial sense of the range of motion possible in a relationship. The turbulence and G-forces of a relationship are comparable to the sudden decompression of a passenger jet at thirty-five thousand feet.

How did Tom and I come to realize that we needed couples counseling? There were several warning signs: Our pet names for each other became rabid. We started taking separate vacations while sitting in the same room. We had sex less frequently. Then we had sex less frequently than people in full-body casts. We stopped having sex. Finally, our relationship stopped other people, gay or straight, from wanting to have sex. Eventually, the chill in our relationship liquefied nitrogen. We became superconducting—the colder we were, the easier it became for negative energy to flow.

After months of misery, one day Tom sadly announced that if things didn't change he wanted to break up. I became angry. I wanted to be the one to threaten to break up. Of course, I only wanted to threaten this, I didn't want to do it. Tom suggested that we try couples counseling. After some hesitation, I agreed. My intentions weren't the best because I assumed that the therapist and I would be the couple who would counsel the obviously fucked-up Tom.

After deciding to seek counseling, we had to choose a therapist. A process that in itself can cause a relationship to deteriorate. In retrospect, I would advise: Don't

spend less time picking a therapist than you would choosing a movie. Instead of researching the subject, we decided to just ask our friends who were already in couples counseling for the name of their therapist. Before doing this though, we made the mistake of trying to assess the quality of our friends' relationships (which is especially difficult to ascertain when you're unsure of the quality of your own). How do you gauge happiness? A physician can measure your heart rate, but we lack an electrocardiogram for what makes it pound. Observing our friends we tried to determine: Is their relationship stable or ossified? Satisfied or complacent? Permanent or chronic? Close or oppressive? Deep or abysmal? Over dinner with our two closest friends, Sharon and Patty, I mentioned, "We're thinking of doing couples counseling. . . ."

Patty interrupted and said, "Bob, you'd better do it or Tom's going to break up with you."

I became defensive. "I will."

"Well, you have no time for anyone else and you're obsessed with your career. Don't give me that look. I know because I'm the exact same way and you just have to get over it."

Patty is also a stand-up comic and the only woman in New York brassier than her is the Statue of Liberty. Patty's personality sets off metal detectors.

Tom said, "We're looking for a therapist. How did you find yours?"

Patty said, "I love our therapist. She always agrees with me that Sharon's wrong."

Sharon didn't appreciate Patty's referral. "Patty! You asshole! Don't say that!"

"Sharon, I'm kidding. You can't take a joke."

"No, Patty. That wasn't a joke."

Tom said, "Do you want me to give your therapist a call? Maybe she can see you two tonight?" It wasn't awkward or embarrassing anymore when Sharon and

Patty argued in front of us. We were as accustomed to their disagreements as if they were our own.

"Sharon, I'm sorry," Patty said without sincerity. She gave her apologies as if they were tax-deductible charitable donations. Patty thought of herself as being generous for doing something that usually benefited her more than the recipient.

Patty said, "Okay. You guys can't break up because we hate most of our other friends. And Bob, you have to start doing more work around the house. You're so fucking lazy. When he stayed with me in L.A., he didn't clean up a goddamn thing."

Tom had also complained that I didn't contribute enough to the housework. He had some justification. My idea of cleaning up was erasing the messages on our answering machine.

After a very brief moment of deliberation, we decided not to ask Sharon and Patty for the name of their therapist. If Patty and I shared a therapist, at some point the temptation for us to mock him or her would be irresistible. We would notice a mannerism and turn it into a running joke. It would be handing Tom and Sharon the reason to break up with us.

Instead, we asked our friends Bill and Michelle for the name of their therapist. They seemed to have a good relationship—basing our assumption upon their ability to go out for dinner and a movie without brawling in public. (An erroneous belief, because subsequently Bill and Michelle have broken up while Sharon and Patty are still together.) Unfortunately, we didn't ask what type of therapy Bill and Michelle's therapist favored. If we had inquired it might have saved us a considerable amount of time and money. Going into therapy without knowing the therapist's approach is hazardous. (I once had a therapist who took such delight in hearing about my problems that I concluded he was Schadenfreudian.) It's like seeking treatment for a medical problem and

not knowing the physician's specialty. Dr. Schweitzer's treatment for a headache would differ drastically from Dr. Frankenstein's.

Choosing a therapist is like choosing a religion. There are many differing doctrines but most forms of therapy expect you to participate once a week, "donate" money, and believe in salvation. And converts to therapy, like all true believers, have a boring tendency to talk too much about their newfound faith.

On Bill and Michelle's recommendation, Tom made an appointment with Sheila Carmody, a clinical social worker. It's important for captious couples to remember that whoever makes the first appointment can feel superior for taking the initiative. We were to see Sheila on Tuesday, 10 A.M., at her office on West 74th Street. Around 9:15 on the morning of our first appointment was when I decided to discuss whether we could afford spending eighty-five dollars a week on therapy. It's important to find out what the therapy is going to cost because if you're already having money problems this can be one issue you can fight about in therapy *and* have the added satisfaction of complaining to one of the sources of the trouble. Tom became furious that I had waited until the last minute to discuss this. For some inexplicable reason, Tom looks with disdain upon "waiting until the last minute." He feels that I do this deliberately to torment him. Tom doesn't seem to understand that premeditation in a relationship isn't necessarily a sign that things are going well. Our trip on the subway only created more hostility. I had to give Tom a token or we would've missed the train. When I handed it to him I added, "Well, obviously I don't wait until the last minute to buy my tokens." Considering that both of us have absolutely no interest in competitive sports, we're adept at keeping score.

We arrived at Sheila's office, and after announcing ourselves on the intercom we were buzzed in. The sign

on the door said: THE SHORT-TERM THERAPY CENTER. I said to Tom, "They should call it 'The Short-Term Therapy Center for People with Long-Term Problems.'" He didn't even smile.

When I feel nervous, I try to obey E. M. Forster's plea to "Only Connect." But I only connect odd thoughts because establishing a relationship between two disparate ideas is much easier than connecting with another person. Sometimes I entertain my thoughts as if they're a restive audience and I'm afraid that at any moment they could turn on me.

The waiting room had a small brown leather couch and a couple of chrome-and-leather chairs. There must be a Therapist Waiting Room Furniture Store where the choices are limited to three styles: Scandinavian, Shaker, and Modern. Which is apropos since they could also be considered the three most popular styles of guilt and anxiety. On a small table was an ample selection of magazines, the titles of which hinted at the problems of the waiting couples: *Time*, *Us*, *Harper's*. (The perfect magazine for a couples counseling waiting room would be: *MAD*.) I picked up a copy of *Time*. I find it soothing to read about unsolvable world problems before attempting to deal with the unsolvable problems of my own world.

The magazines in a therapist's waiting room allow couples who are already having trouble communicating to avoid further conversation. Who knows? If there were no magazines, Tom and I might have talked more and finished therapy months sooner. It was ironic that our therapist's waiting room was filled with reading material because Tom had accused me of always having my head in a book or magazine and not giving him the attention he deserved. I didn't feel that it was fair that he should be strongly reminded of this moments before we attempted to resolve the problem. If our childish behavior was any indication of most couples starting therapy, then our reading material should have been limited to coloring books.

After ten minutes, the door to Sheila's office opened and another couple walked out. It was two men who were approximately the same age as Tom and me. There is an unspoken therapy-waiting-room etiquette where you try to avoid making eye contact and ignore the other patients. I can't decide if it's out of respect for another person's privacy or because you're afraid to see the unflattering reflection of your own problems.

After the two men departed, Sheila opened the door and welcomed us. Sheila was in her early forties. She had long graying blond hair and was wearing a black designer skirt and jacket with a Navaho squash blossom necklace and Hopi silver earrings. She looked like a Native inhabitant of the Upper Southwestside of New York. Sheila's office was empty except for three Barcelona chairs and a small table with a telephone. Don't worry about having an initial revulsion to your therapist's office. It could be that your reaction is just a reflection of an office that you disliked in your childhood. Your feelings will change. During therapy, it's common for even the most fastidious patients to undergo an aesthetic transference and fall in love with the ugly possessions of their therapist.

Sheila had a serene demeanor. She spoke in a well-modulated voice that expressed concern and authority yet kept her distance. It's a timbre most often used most by deities, therapists, and the operators of directory assistance. Before making our appointment, Tom had asked Sheila if she had experience in counseling gay couples. She replied that she did and that the problems most couples develop are similar. Perhaps the strategy for gay civil rights is misguided. Instead of seeking the recognition of our love, maybe it would be easier to first bond with straight couples over our mutual grievances. We may not do the same things in bed but we all hate being the one who always has to make it.

The first session of couples counseling is a getting-to-know-your-problems get-together. A couple who have

been diligently practicing their quarrels for years are allowed to give a recital of their most rehearsed and polished duets. The temptation is for each of you to use this opportunity to display your grievances in such an impressive manner that by the end of the session the therapist will insist that your partner do a solo in individual therapy. But a good therapist is a conductor who reminds both of you that you need to work on your technique.

Sheila based her treatment for couples upon *Imago Relationship Therapy*, which was developed by Harville Hendrix. According to Hendrix, everyone has an "Imago," a composite inner picture of the people who most influenced us at an early age. He believes that each of us is compulsively searching for a mate who has the predominant character traits of the people who raised us, and we enter relationships seeking to restore the feelings of wholeness that we experienced in the womb. So that's it. We've tripped over our own umbilical cord. We suffer from wombsickness. *Mom, remember when it was just me and uterus?*

Or as Hendrix puts it in his book *Getting the Love You Want*, "You fell in love because you had your partner confused with your parents." An idea that should bolster everyone's self-esteem. Instead of wondering why someone broke up with you, always assume that, like your parents, he felt that you could do much better. Hendrix claims that "we are trapped in an infantile perspective although we are now adults capable of keeping ourselves fed and warm and dry, a hidden part of us expects the outside world to take care of us. When our partners are hostile or merely unhelpful, a silent alarm is triggered deep in our brains that fills us with the fear of death. This automatic alarm system plays a key role in marriage." (What is a "silent alarm"? A mental pager giving off bad vibes?)

If someone being "merely unhelpful" filled people with a fear of death, then the entire population of New

York City would live in a constant state of suicidal depression from encounters with snooty salesclerks or brusque waiters. Equating death with unhelpfulness is quite a burden of guilt for Tom to assume whenever he's unable to bring me back a newspaper or pick up my dry cleaning. I have my doubts about some of Hendrix's theories. Most of my friends have been dealing with their mortality on a conscious level since their early twenties. It wasn't our fear of death that was being triggered, it was our fear of life stuck in an unhappy relationship.

For the first few weeks of our therapy, Sheila had us discuss another aspect of Hendrix's theory, our "childhood wounds." This didn't mean a remembrance of scraped knees and skinned elbows; she meant the cutting comments, blistering remarks, sore feelings, broken promises, bruised egos, strained relationships, painful memories, and heartaches that are an inevitable part of growing up.

Tom and I weren't novices to therapy. We had already done individual therapy in which we learned that the couple we should probably be in counseling with was our parents. Reviewing the worst moments of your childhood in therapy is like looking at a family photo album where all the pictures are negatives. It's excruciating nostalgia: It's *neuralgia*. It's being sentimental with the emphasis on mental. (Excuse me. I need to get all the plays on the word "nostalgia" out of my system: *Noshtalgia*—remembering favorite foods or meals. *Notstalgia*—remembering someone or something that you never want to see or do again. *Nosetalgia*—remembering your face before cosmetic surgery. Thanks—I feel much better.)

Individual therapy helps you write your autobiography. But remember, even though it's *your* favorite story, don't ever delude yourself that it holds the same appeal for other people. After individual therapy, Tom and I had made peace with ourselves. Now if we could

only make our well-adjusted personalities bearable to each other.

For the first month with Sheila, Tom and I discussed our lives and families, and while very little of what we said to each other was new, it was said with a clarity that eighty-five dollars an hour makes unforgettable. To put our childhoods in a nuts-shell: When I was a kid, my mother had a nervous breakdown and her problems loomed so large that it made it difficult for me to ask for any of my needs to be met. Guilting the lily, as a child, I was told by several unthinking idiots that I was directly responsible for her breakdown: "Raising four kids is enough to put anyone in a mental hospital." I withdrew into reading—ignoring my feelings—and like my brothers and my sister, distracted myself with work and other interests, which unfortunately is what I still tend to do. No wonder I liked the character of Mr. Spock on the television show *Star Trek* when I was growing up—he was an alien from another planet where the inhabitants didn't believe in expressing their emotions— he's the hero of the repressed.

Tom's upbringing was much different from mine. Tom's parents are like him: They have no major addictions and they're loving and thoughtful. (Since gay marriages are still illegal, should I call Tom's parents my out-laws?) His childhood wasn't unsettled, although his parents were, like all parents, capable of unsettling remarks. Tom never doubted his parents' love but he was sometimes encouraged to doubt himself. It doesn't take a Gregor Mendel to figure out that in addition to inheriting eye color from our parents, we usually inherit their vision of the world. Tom has a habit of excessive worrying that is uncannily like his mother's habit of expressing her anxieties through horrific family anecdotes. *"Tom, please be careful when you're cutting the lawn. You know cousin Eleanor was cutting the lawn when she had her accident. They almost had to take off her foot."*

For some reason, all of her cautionary tales end with the loss of a limb.

During our weeks of therapy with Sheila, Tom and I became more familiar with each other's upbringings, and since my childhood was more melo-traumatic than Tom's, I later tried to use it to my advantage. "Tom, I know it's my turn to do the laundry but it's hard . . . the suds bring back too many memories of my father's drinking and the spin cycle reminds me of my mother's breakdown." Tom never fell for it.

I have a problem with Hendrix when he describes all children as victims of their parents. Certainly, as a comedian, I've sometimes been the beneficiary of my parents' "wounds." In some ways, I was at cross-purposes with a form of therapy that purported to heal childhood wounds because I needed to hold on to mine—they made such good material. When I finally came out to my mother during a visit home at Christmas, four months after I had moved to New York, she said in complete seriousness, "You're gay . . . well, it could be worse. Look at the Gardiners across the street with those retarded grandchildren." Causing me to laugh and say, "Thanks, Mom. I love that comparison." Then two weeks later, after I had returned to New York, she wrote me a long sweet thoughtful letter of acceptance that she ended with:

> Our family's gone through so much. My breakdown, Dad's heart attacks, Carol's divorce, and now this.
> Love, Mom
> P.S. Keep up the good work with the comedy.

Tom and I both knew and, more important, felt that our parents did the best they could. Our parents didn't fail us. There are no perfect parents. Even Jesus had a distant father and a domineering mother. (I would have trust issues if my father allowed me to be crucified.)

Concurrent with rehashing our childhoods, Sheila had us practice "Intentional Dialogue," an exercise of Hendrix's designed to restore trust. It involved three steps: Mirroring, Validation, and Empathy. I wish therapists suffered from an inhibition in creating jargon. The new terminology sounds Freudulent. Speech Therapy should be available not just for the manner of speaking but for the content. To my ear, the use of the term "closure" in everyday conversation is much more of a speech impediment than a lateral lisp. And "inner child" should refer only to gestation. We can blame the overuse of jargon on the Fathers of Psychotherapy, Freud and Jung. They were the Shakespeares of Psychobabble, who originated the id, anima, and the Oedipus Complex. Freud was the Moses of the Subconscious who discovered a new set of Commandments: Thou shall not kill thy father and covet thy mother. Thou shall not covet thy neighbor's penis. It took a man with a poet's mind to create the term "Penis Envy." Not that Freud's ideas aren't debatable. My theory is that women don't suffer from penis envy. Every man just thinks his penis is enviable. Maybe Freud suffered from Penis Doubt?

Sheila kept the psychobabble to a minimum and after an initial introduction to the idea just referred to Hendrix's technique as the Dialogue. We did his exercises in our sessions each week and Sheila also asked us to do them as homework. For example, Tom and I took turns saying a simple statement that the other had to paraphrase and repeat back. No interpretation or emotional reaction was allowed. In relationships, hostility without adrenaline is whining, but the formulaic nature of the exercise made the whining acceptable because we took turns. It went something like this:

TOM: When you read the newspaper while I talk to you it makes me feel hurt and unwanted.

BOB: When I read the paper while you're talking

it makes you feel hurt and unwanted. I can understand that must make you feel frustrated, rejected, and angry. Did I understand what you said and felt?

TOM: Yes.

It was like an argument between two bureaucrats. Perhaps every couple should be forced to write out all of their arguments. Reading ours only makes me see how trivial they were. Then it was my turn.

BOB: When you don't take me seriously about spending too much money it makes me feel that we'll never get ahead.

Then Tom would paraphrase what I said.

We suffered from a lack of communication, a phrase that in itself is an example of the phenomenon it describes. Like many couples we seemed to have developed a pattern of *in*communication that we practiced in all areas of our life. Whenever Tom tried to get in touch with my feelings, I'd let my emotional answering machine pick up while I screened his calls. Later, I might decide to respond long after Tom had given up on my ever returning his message. But most of the time I'd just feel guilty about not calling back or, even worse, become angry and accuse him of harassment. Finally, out of frustration, Tom stopped trying.

Getting in touch with someone's feelings is often like necking. As you fumble and grope to undo buttons, instead you press them and receive a slap in the face.

The Dialogue was helpful because it didn't restore intimacy. The stilted dialogue restored distance, which is what we needed. It's always easier to be polite and considerate to a stranger than a lover. We slowly learned more about each other and began to base our behavior on that knowledge. We began to communicate by find-

ing a common language, *Desperanto*—the universal language of neediness.

The most difficult part of couples counseling was discussing sex. Talking about sex was for us just like having sex. It had been a while since the last time. We were never in the mood. We both resented having to initiate it. The only difference was that having sex by yourself is socially acceptable, but talking about sex by yourself is not. And oddly enough, in a committed relationship, paying for sex with a stranger is never acceptable, but paying to talk about sex with a therapist is.

Tom and I needed to perk up our sex life. Our same-sex relationship had become a same-old-sex relationship. It was starting to feel like a 9"-to-5" job. We were ho-hum-sexuals. We knew of couples who had sex outside their relationship. But we never considered it. How awful would that be? You'd be in an unsatisfactory relationship, plus have the added miseries of dating. Sheila asked if we still found each other attractive and we both answered yes. But there was so much hostility between us that not having sex was just another way of not communicating.

As we made progress in therapy, we kept Sharon and Patty up to date on how we were doing. Patty, who was competitive in every aspect of her life, asked us every few months, "When was the last time you guys had sex?" Sharon had stopped trying to keep Patty from discussing their sex life and was satisfied that she limited her discussions to ours. After we answered Patty's question, she said, "Sharon, I can't believe that Bob and Tom finally had sex last weekend."

Sharon congratulated us as if we had just had a baby (and it had been almost nine months). Then she said, "It's been so long since Patty and I have had sex."

Patty blurted out, "Sharon, we just had sex last month!"

We all laughed at that declaration.

"Patty, we had better have sex this weekend." Sharon and Patty were going to spend the weekend at their house in Provincetown. I have a theory that many couples buy a second house just to give their sex lives a second chance.

After six months, we progressively reduced our therapy from once a week to once every two weeks to once a month. Then finally, Tom and I thought about quitting. How do you know if it's time to quit therapy? I quit individual therapy when my therapist started suggesting joke ideas for my act. With couples counseling, if both of you start thinking that the money spent each week on therapy might be better spent on a going out to dinner then it might be time to quit. We told Sheila that we wanted to stop our sessions. She thought it was time but suggested that as "closure" we attend a gay and lesbian couples weekend workshop. Tom was much more enthusiastic about the weekend workshop than I. He was an avid reader of self-help books and attending a weekend workshop to work on his "problems" was like sending his inner child on a trip to Disney World.

Sheila gave us a phone number to call for information about the weekend. The price was two hundred fifty dollars apiece. We were sent a brochure and cover letter in the mail. The cover letter welcoming us was written in the mandatory stilted language used by people who refer to themselves as members of the "helping professions." The letter started:

There are two things you can consider that will enhance your weekend. First, think of sitting long hours on a hotel chair. Think how your body might feel.

I thought, *Oh, great. That sounds like my worst nightmare.*

Now think about what you could bring with you to sit on that would help you to be comfortable and relaxed—a back support—a beach chair—a bean bag—quilts—pillows—whatever you think of, be sure to bring it with you. You will be glad you did!

The letter was as strenuously cheerful as Christmas decorations in a funeral home. Reading their suggestions, I thought that anyone in a relationship with the non-ironic owner of a bean bag chair should break up. I would have responded better to a more adult appeal: "Bring something comfortable to sit on because the last thing you two need is for one of you to be pissing and moaning all weekend."

Mentioned in detail were all the snacks and meal breaks planned for the weekend.

Each morning we will break for fresh fruit and a nut mixture for a high-energy snack.

The obsessiveness about food seemed reasonable because when your relationship is in trouble and your sex life kaput *Getting the Lunch You Want* may be the only satisfaction you receive.

If you have special food needs, please come prepared to take care of those needs. You may always have a cooler with you with the foods you need.

Oh, God. It sounded like the weekend was going to be devoted to helping the lactose-intolerant resolve their childhood wound of being breast-fed.

Tom called and signed us up to attend. (I know, there's a pattern there.) The workshop was not only going to cost five hundred dollars, but since it was to be held in New Jersey, we would also need to pay for our transportation, a hotel, and our meals. It felt like we were deliberately planning a bad vacation. Our schedule

was going to be from six until nine on Friday; from eight to eight on Saturday; and from eight to seven on Sunday. Conjugal visits at penitentiaries are less supervised.

We arrived at the hotel around five and checked into our room, then at a quarter to six we went downstairs. There was a sign:

⟵ Ballroom One: The Lieberman Wedding
Ballroom Two: Couples Workshop ⟶

I silently wished the Liebermans good luck. I hoped that their relationship was going better than mine. At least if they started having problems during the reception, they'd know where to turn for help. We walked in the meeting room and sat down. Promptly at 6:00, our "facilitators," Raymond Bergman and Arthur Craig, introduced themselves. Raymond was a psychotherapist in his late forties. He was dressed like a man who wants to appear youthful but remains unsure of what decade to recapture. He had a teenage pair of running shoes, blue jeans from his twenties, a black turtleneck from his thirties, and the blue blazer he had bought three years ago. Arthur, Raymond's "life partner," was in his late thirties and the holder of an unspecified B.A. who had been "clinically trained by Dr. Hendrix and facilitated couples workshops nationwide."

Arthur wore his long blond hair pulled back in a ponytail and was handsome, although he had obviously once had a very bad complexion. Raymond announced that as a couple of twelve years they had been through Imago Therapy together and that it had greatly enhanced their relationship. Arthur then added fervently, "We know what each of you is dealing with and applaud and support your doing this workshop."

A few latecomers straggled in and Raymond said to the assembled group, "Everyone take three deep breaths. Let's release our anger for the people who are late."

After that comment, I suspected that Raymond's and

Arthur's auras were on but nobody was home. They were New Age airheads who enjoyed the cranial breeze that tinkled their inner wind chimes. Arthur then asked everyone to join hands. Joining hands in public is a gesture appropriate only for environmentalists protecting redwood trees or the cast of a play at a curtain call. I didn't think establishing superficial intimacy was a promising beginning for a workshop to help couples deepen their relationship.

After welcoming us Raymond said, "This weekend may be intense for some of you. At any time, please feel free to use the stuffed animals around the room."

I whispered to Tom, "*Use* the stuffed animals? For *what?*" Tom's face flashed a warning like a traffic signal.

My animosity that night wasn't unexpected. Whenever I travel, I always carry a universal adaptor for my hostility. I'm never unable to find an outlet. If I discover that my two-pronged relationship isn't working, I'm quickly able to convert my frustration into a three-pronged anger directed toward other people.

Each couple had to stand and introduce themselves and explain why they had decided to attend the workshop. There were twenty-eight couples and as they proceeded to go around the room, I secretly hoped that one couple would start arguing bitterly about why they were there. Two men stood and introduced themselves and one of them said, "Well, before I met Ted, I wanted to do couples counseling but I was never in a relationship." I wanted to ask him: If you were yearning to do couples counseling while still single, then what was your idea of a desirable man? "He's perfect for me. As soon as we met, I wanted to break up!"

Next, two women stood up and introduced themselves as Joanne and Robin. Joanne said, "Well, Robin and I have been going out together for a week, and I was really glad when she agreed to attend the workshop." *They've only been together for a week! How did Joanne bring up the subject?* "*Next weekend, for our sec-*

ond date, what sounds more appealing? Dinner and a movie or intensive therapy?"

Two women named Linda and Diane stood up next and Diane announced, "We decided to attend the workshop because for the past year we've been trying unsuccessfully to have a baby and its been creating conflicts."

I whispered to Tom, "Well, you're both women. Have you tried sperm?"

"Shut up," Tom mouthed.

When it was our turn, we each said our names and then Tom said, "We've been in therapy for several months and we thought this would be a good way to consolidate our work."

Arthur handed out to every participant a three-ring notebook filled with an entire course of Imago Therapy. That first night, we reviewed the basic principles. The first principle we discussed was what Hendrix called "The No-Exit Decision." We had to resolve to close our "Catastrophic" and "Terminal" exits in order to help our relationships. Examples of Catastrophic Exits were affairs, addictions, and insanity. Examples of Terminal Exits were suicide, divorce, murder. We were asked to fill out a work page, "Closing the Exits." Sample resolutions were provided:

"I agree to keep you safe—No murder."
"I agree to stay in the relationship—No divorce."
"I agree to limit my TV viewing and spend an
 hour with you each evening."

What's sad is that for many couples the last resolution is probably the hardest one to keep, and for the deeply troubled losing the distraction of watching murders and divorces probably increases the chances of their commiting those actions.

On Saturday morning, the first thing we were asked to do, in an attempt to heal our "childhood wounds," was to lie on our backs and using "guided imagery"

imagine ourselves "journeying back in time" to our childhoods. I wish I had been warned beforehand. I hate time travel. You always have to wait three hundred years for your luggage. Arthur put on a CD of New Age music to help us get "in the mood." It put me in a bad one. The music was insistently soothing without being enjoyable. It was like a ice-cold whirlpool bath.

For the rest of the morning and afternoon we did therapeutic exercises. We made a space on the floor of the meeting room and each of us started filling in our Imago Exercise sheets with a number 2 pencil. Much of what we did that weekend we had already done with Sheila. One new exercise was called the Parent/Child Dialogue. It involved role playing where we each had to pretend to be the other's parents. The work sheet offered sample lines of dialogue such as:

"I am your mother. What is it like living with me?"
"What is your deepest hurt and frustration with me?"
"As your mother what do you need from me?"
"Now, as your partner, what can I do to begin to
 heal all that?"
"I want you to have all that."

After that last statement there was a note in parentheses that said: "Remember you don't have to give it, you just have to want your partner to have it." A philosophy of giving that I wanted Tom to remember on his birthday and Christmas. Tom didn't appreciate the first question I asked while pretending to be his mother: "Why don't you have any girlfriends?" (If I worked out my glutes as much as I work out my smartass, I'd have the best butt in the world.)

The workshop was obsessed with taking care of our childhood wounds. I hated that my childhood was getting more attention than me. It was like having a sibling rivalry with myself. What we needed to deal with was why Tom and I fight about who does the laundry. Ar-

thur and Raymond were trying to make everything better with our childhoods—after the damage had already been done—in the shortest amount of time possible. Isn't that exactly what our parents would try to do?

After lunch on Saturday I started a fight with Tom because I suddenly wanted to go home. It was one of those moments of irrational behavior that in retrospect looks even more intemperate. I was completely in touch with my feelings and they were all excessive. Tom was alarmed, sympathetic, and angry. Without warning, I had selfishly decided to stop dealing with us in order to deal with me. I was furious because I felt that too much of this weekend was wasting my time. We could have done all the Imago exercises in one day if Arthur and Raymond had skipped the New Age mumbo-jumbo. Maybe an old childhood wound was resurfacing. When I was younger I also hated being bored.

Boredom is when Father Time becomes an abusive parent. As I get older, I realize that while I don't support any of their political goals, I'm a Temporal Republican. I'm a selfish big spender of my own time but I deeply resent someone else spending it for me. My suddenly demanding to leave was proof of my belief that in every couple, there is one person who is relatively easygoing and pleasant and there is one person who is a pill. My behavior on that day confirmed what I had always suspected. I'm the pill. A big Pill.

Mea Culpa.

I have more unfinished business than an accountant who drops dead on April 13.

Difficult? I'm Me $= mc^2$.

Impatient? I'm next.

Bitter? I'm an unripe grudge.

Vacillating? I'm not sure.

Sensitive? I can feel the word "pea" under twenty mattresses.

Phony? I'm Trojan horseshit.

Childish? I want YOUR Mommy too!

Know it all? Wrong!

Smug? Thank you.

Selfish? I?

Tom asked me to stay and I did. Only later did I realize that by my sitting through something I detested I was demonstrating to Tom my commitment to him and to our relationship. Although I refuse to equate love with suffering—it's *too* Catholic—sometimes true love is the ability to be bored for someone else.

I've often found that the anticipation of boredom is sometimes more dreadful than the actual experience. My desire to escape from the workshop was intensified because I knew that the next day would also be excruciating.

On Sunday, instead of examining our childhood wounds, we spent the morning making lists of how we could help heal our partners. By lunchtime, I had done more healing than Saint Jude. After completing our healing, we were asked to write a list of what Hendrix called "Re-Romanticising: Caring Behaviors and High- and Low-Energy Fun Activities."

I have to admit that writing down what Tom and I like to do did teach me something that I didn't realize about our relationship. Our low-energy activities were going to the movies or theater, reading, travel, and flea marketing, and our high-energy activities were biking, dancing, and going to the gym. (I've since been told that the way I dance counts as a low-energy activity.)

Realistically, though, Tom and I went dancing only a few times a year, we rode our bicycles only when we lived in Provincetown for three summers, and with our schedules we usually went to the gym at different times. What Tom and I discovered was that our relationship was based upon a mutual appreciation of laziness. On our separate lists of caring behaviors, under the category

"I feel cared about/loved when you...," I put down "Make dinner for me," and Tom put down "Bring me coffee in the morning." Is being inactive a solid foundation to build a relationship upon? I think so. (Most likely, however, someone else is doing the actual construction.) Inactivity is an interest that can be pursued at any age. It's inexpensive, unless you order room service, and if you ever feel that your relationship is stuck in a rut, for a change of pace all you need to do is stand up.

We also had to make lists of our good and bad qualities. While I wrote my list of Tom's qualities, I kept trying to make suggestions for Tom's list of my qualities. "Hey, you forgot to put down that I'm bossy." Tom's good qualities have always been readily apparent. He's thoughtful, affectionate, generous, smart, funny, and handsome. Tom's one bad quality though was that he was uncertain about what he wanted to do with his life. He had a B.F.A. in Acting from S.U.N.Y. at Purchase, but he had stopped auditioning when I met him and he was unsure of what to do next. I've known since high school that I wanted to write and perform comedy, and after a few years I found his indecisiveness frustrating. He would start a new job and then after a few months quit with a plausible list of reasons why it wasn't exactly right for him. But after this happened several times, I found it increasingly harder to muster any enthusiasm when Tom proposed embarking on yet another career. Tom would then accuse me of not taking an interest in him. He was the boy who cried "Work."

Our final task of the weekend was filling out a Conscious Marriage/Relationship Worksheet. At the top of our list, I wanted to suggest that we write, "We never do another weekend workshop." Our list started with noble aspirations:

We are healthy.

We communicate our feelings openly.

We support each other's goals.

We have many rewarding friendships.

We're close to our families.

We have a satisfying sex life.

As we proceeded, though, our list started to sound as if we were writing a letter to Santa Claus:

We want to own our own home.

We want a dog.

We want to travel more frequently.

What was encouraging was that Tom and I do share our lives. Our goals, interests, likes, dislikes, and even our differences are compatible. For example, even though Tom has no interest in bird-watching, he always has been supportive *and* sardonic about my hobby. One of the things I love about Tom is that he knows that the two feelings often can and should go together.

Finally, seven o'clock neared and the weekend was almost finished. Raymond and Arthur passed around a sheet of paper and a pencil, giving us the option of having our names and phone numbers placed on a group list. Tom and I both immediately agreed that we didn't want to be included. I realized that this was another trait we shared: We both try to avoid loser friends. We were making a Conscious Relationship Decision to avoid people who need to talk about their Conscious Relationships. We were "closing the exit" on a "catastrophic" weekend.

Before we departed, Raymond and Arthur handed everyone candles, which were lit as a symbol of "keeping the light alive within us and our relationships." Unfortunately, this ceremony only rekindled my resentment

of the whole weekend. I couldn't wait to get back to
New York where people light candles in order to curse
the darkness better.

As we headed into the city, I apologized to Tom for
freaking out and he admitted that the weekend probably
wasn't worth it. I was touched when he said this. Then
we started discussing our impressions of which other cou-
ple had the most frightening relationship. And somehow
our being nasty together filled me with renewed hope
and love.

After the Lost Weekend Workshop, we saw Sheila
one last time. In the year that followed, our relationship
seemed fine, but then some of our problems reappeared.
Unfortunately, it didn't matter that Tom knew why I
was being selfish or that I knew why he was indecisive.
I still felt like a passenger in a plummeting airplane who
doesn't find it helpful or comforting that he's been told
by the pilot that the cause of the problem is engine
failure.

Tom had started group therapy to work on his ina-
bility to decide upon a career. So when we decided to
try couples counseling again, instead of returning to
Sheila we made an appointment with Tom's new ther-
apist, Brian, who practiced cognitive therapy. Cognitive
therapists direct a patient's attention to "automatic
thoughts," the things that people say to themselves that
result in unpleasant feelings. Cognitive therapy is based
upon the Cartesian Theory of Neurosis: I think,
therefore I feel bad. It's like the classic joke: A man
walks into a doctor's office and says, "Doctor, doctor, my
arm hurts when I go like this." The doctor says, "Don't
do that." We were going into Brian's office in emotional
pain and saying "Doctor, doctor, it hurts when I think
like this." Brian said, "Don't think like that." And it
worked.

Brian was a gay man in his forties who always sat

curled up in his armchair, looking like a very wise, comfortable cat. When Tom and I started talking about our problems, Brian made it very clear that we were basing our feelings on assumptions that we couldn't possibly know the truth of. If I said, "When Tom says that I'm not supportive, I feel he's blaming me for his not being able to decide on a career," or if Tom said, "I feel that when Bob reads while I'm talking, he's rejecting me," Brian told us, "You're both saying that based upon what you think the other one's thinking. We can never know what another person is thinking. Therefore, your assumptions are based upon a false idea. If you stop doing that, you might really communicate and start to hear each other. There is evidence in your relationship that both of you care for each other. You wouldn't be here if you didn't. But that doesn't excuse hurtful behavior. Bob, it's not right for you to ignore Tom when he's talking. And Tom, Bob has nothing to do with your choice of a career. It's your decision."

This was an important breakthrough in our relationship. (I know what you're thinking: *What is this, a testimonial for cognitive therapy?* Except according to Brian, I can never know what you're thinking. He'd say that I'm just telling myself that because I'm feeling insecure.)

We also weren't allowed to make what Brian called all-or-nothing statements. For example, if I said, "Tom is always complaining about the papers on my desk," Brian would say, "*Always?* So that's all he does twenty-four hours a day?" He earned my respect when he started mocking my assumptions, because in his place I would've done the exact same thing.

It's been over a year since we stopped seeing Brian, and one indication of how much our relationship has improved is that during that time, we moved from New York to Los Angeles without killing each other. What has thousands of dollars worth of couples counseling

taught us? We've learned that nothing in life is beyond dispute. The key to all relationships is: Know Thy Self-ishness. I think I know mine. All I want is Tom's undivided attention for the next forty years and then I'm all his.

Untitled

JONATHAN **SWIFT** in his story *The Tale of a Tub* wrote that books are "the children of the brain." His writer's fancy became real for me when I had to choose a title for my literary offspring. The naming of a book and the naming of a child often reveal more about the creator than the creation. Each is a repository for the grandiose hopes and dreams of their authors. In fact, if children and books truly expressed the unspoken desires of their creators, they'd all be named "Great Expectations."

The naming of a book should differ from the naming of a child. A good title should either entice, reveal, or sum up the book. Whereas a name for a child should never attempt to do any of those things. Novelty has become an overrated virtue in picking names or titles.

If the name of your child is unique, it may only ensure that his or her mental problems will also be unprecedented.

From my experience, the worst thing that a writer can do when choosing a title is ask the opinion of his friends. I made that error without considering that my friends can never agree on a restaurant, let alone agree on *Dinner at the Homesick Restaurant* as a title. It quickly became obvious that when offered a list of possible titles that the Sallys of my acquaintance wanted something more striking while the Gwendolyns preferred something simpler.

An author and a parent live with the same hope. Ideally, a person and a book should be treated with the same consideration. Don't judge a book by its cover. Give it a trial and render your verdict after sentencing it.

In our era of full disclosure, I've decided to reveal some of the titles, that, for one reason or another, weren't chosen. (NOTE: *One Reason or Another* sounds like a possible title.)

My Favorites:

These are the titles of books that I know I would have to pick up if I saw them in a bookstore. I have been persuaded, though, that I would probably find many of these titles in the $3.99 bin. I've included my working title for the book that no one liked but me. (NOTE: *No One Liked but Me.*)

Mental Notes [My working title]

Snap Judgment Day

Cyclops Winked

...And Now This

Just Because You're Coming Home for Your Father's Funeral Doesn't Mean That We Can't Have Fun

*A Full Life** *(*The Contents Are Measured by Weight, Not Volume, and Some Settling May Have Occurred Through Handling)*

How I Beat Low Self-Esteem and Other Essays

Trying Too Hard to Be Funny

Since I was writing a book of comic essays, there is a danger in picking a title that tries too hard to be funny. Of course, a funny title lets the reader know immediately that the book is supposed to be comic, but striking the right balance between the clever and a title that rudely grabs your attention is easier said than done. (NOTE: *Easier Said Than Done.*)

Is Being Starved for Affection an Eating Disorder?

Do Porno Writers Ever Get Writer's Block?

Can a Vegetarian Eat Carnivorous Plants?

Never Accept Candy from a Stranger, or Candy As Your Name

I'll Cross That Umbrage When I Get to It

Get Rid of That Tub of Laundry on Your Washboard Abs!

Gay

Since the book is written from the point of view of a gay man, it seemed sensible to allude to that in the title. Although I quickly realized that the words "Out," "Gay," "Queer" were all played out. (NOTE: *Played Out.*)

Status Queer

Loud and Queer

His and His

More Than Just Friends

Out Smart

Outbursts

Out of Sorts

Out Wit

The Man in the Cucumber Masque

It's a Multiple Choice

Blame My Parents

It Takes Balls to Be Gay (Even If You're a Lesbian)

The Only Balls I Ever Caught Are My Own

The Manly Art of Homosexuality

The Way to a Man's Heart Is Through His Penis

I Wish Someone Would Open a Not-Good-at-Sports Bar

It's My Parents' Fault That I'm Funny

A Domineering Mother and Distant Father Caused Me to Be Sarcastic!

A Drag Queen Once Kicked Sequins in My Face

Stonewall Is My Favorite Color

Dirty

I've always admired the titles of Joe Orton such as *Up Against It* and *Prick Up Your Ears*. So I tried my hand at something with more oomph. (NOTE: *More Oomph.*)

Blown Away

Square Peg at the Circle Jerk

Below the Belt

My Dick Joke's Bigger Than Yours

Blow Your Own Horn

Come Off It

Easy Come, Easy Go

Come Full Circle

Parting Shots

Rubbed the Wrong Way

Sit Tight

Two Heads Are Better Than One

You Said a Mouthful

Lip Service

Swallow Your Pride

Trying Too Hard to Be Gay

The "F" Word Is Fabulous!

Hissy Fitness

It's a Wonderful Lifestyle

A Pec on the Cheek

Loose Lisps

Silence = Death (in Comedy)

Do I Have to Spell It OUT for You?

Swished at Birth

People, Places, and Miss Things

Proud Mary

Meaner Than an Antique Shop Cockapoo

I Don't Care Anymore

Finally, I became desperate. Every title I thought of seemed terrible. I was ready to quit and throw in the towel. (NOTE: *Throw In the Towel.*)

My Hometown Is Sodom

If I Was in the Three Stooges, I'd Be a Big Moe

No More Mr. Nice Gay

Sometimes Being Gay Is a Pain in the Ass

I'm Gay but My Book Isn't

Real Men Suck Cock

Anyway, It's Too Late Now, The Die Is Cast, The Fat Is in the Fire, I Made My Decision, and Now I Have to Live with It. (NOTE: *All of the Above.*)

The Skull of
Georgia O'Keeffe

Canyon Road

THE **MOUNTAINS** surrounding Santa Fe are called the Sangre de Cristos, which in Spanish means "Blood of Christ." I've always thought that the mentality of Coronado and the other conquistadores who first arrived in New Mexico during the 1540s is summed up by that name. If the first image that comes to mind after seeing those beautiful green mountains in the red glow of a sunset is the blood of Christ, I would guess that you possess the unbearable self-righteousness and lack of humor that has always been the hallmark of conquerors.

The conquistadores were looking for seven mythical cities of gold. They were the first in a procession of kooks

who have been drawn to Santa Fe in search of something fantastic. Soon after Tom and I arrived for a weeklong visit to see my friend Michael, he introduced us to one such kook: a gray-haired woman who worked at the environmental store that he managed. She called herself Sunshine. Now I'm aware that anyone named Sunshine has been an easy target since the late 1960s and that I'm not the first person to find odd chosen names amusing. Although, here's a good tip. Never rename yourself after a type of weather. Trust me, Rain, Wind, Hail, Sleet, and Snow are not better names than your given one.

What I found truly fascinating about Sunshine was that when she applied for the job, I was told that she used her real name, not her *nom de climat*. It was only after she had been hired that she went around to her fellow employees and said, "Oh, by the way, my name is actually... *Sunshine*." She *knew* that her name was preposterous and took pains to hide it. I found this to be disgraceful. Now even people without common sense are shrewd at business. At least the conquistadores were up-front about their delusions. They told the Native Americans that they were there to claim their lands for themselves, and then proceeded to do so.

We were staying with Michael and his boyfriend, Richard, for a week. This was Tom's first visit to Santa Fe and I wanted him to love the city as I do. I'm still completely enthusiastic about Santa Fe, even though by now the look of "Santa Fe style" is usually without either quality.

In a recently published book called *The Myth of Santa Fe*, the author, Chris Wilson, explains that early in this century the regional style of adobe architecture was intentionally fostered and encouraged by a small group of artists in an attempt to create a distinct identity for the city. Most of the authentic, ornate nineteenth-century buildings on the "historic" plaza have been altered, and even older buildings like the Palace of the

Governors were "restored" to a style that is based entirely upon conjecture. Santa Fe can proudly claim to be the first city in America that learned how to impersonate its own history.

Santa Fe takes pride in its heritage of being a meeting place for three distinct cultures: Native American, Hispanic, and Anglo-American. I won't describe the area as a melting pot because Santa Fe already has too much earthenware for sale. During our first day, Tom and I dutifully visited the shops and galleries along Canyon Road. Shopping in Santa Fe allows Anglo consumers to demonstrate their broad-mindedness. It's a way for white people who have never had a Native American or Hispanic guest in their homes at least to offer their hospitality to things manufactured by those two cultures.

Throughout the West, white people have to decide whether to dress up as cowboys or Native Americans, and the choice of fashions is psychologically revealing. For most of the people who wear cowboy hats, the Code of the West is driving a Bronco, smoking Marlboros, and ordering a salad with ranch dressing. Whereas the white people who dress like Native Americans usually appear to be trying to make amends—almost as if, in compensation for taking their lands, the whites want to give them a good laugh. In Santa Fe, though, a cowboy dressed in black is probably less a sign of villainy than a sign of another artist who wants his work to be taken seriously.

After visiting our third art gallery, I came to the disturbing realization that for some people, the ultimate acquisition would be owning the skull of Georgia O'Keeffe. Her presence seems only to have increased since her death. A new museum has been built to display her work, and her house has become a shrine to Our Lady of Abiquiu.

Georgia O'Keeffe is so revered in Santa Fe that it's the only city in the world where fashion models can find

work past the age of eighty-five. In Santa Fe, every Caucasian woman over forty with sun-damaged skin seems to believe she can emulate O'Keeffe's style by wearing long flowing dresses and buying so much turquoise and silver jewelry that her buried remains could be mined.

When I travel, my favorite souvenir to bring back is a new deposit of cholesterol on my arteries. In an attempt to add to my past acquisitions, Tom and I stopped for lunch at a place recommended by Michael that served delicious New Mexican–style food. In a mockery of history, the conquistadores are remembered now less for their carnage than for *carne*—bringing tortillas, chiles, and cheese to New Mexico. As someone who loves to eat and thinks that the permanent members of the Security Council of the United Nations should be the five culinary superpowers—the United States, France, Italy, China, and Mexico—I've always thought that one reason the Germans lost World War II was that no one wanted to be ruled by their cuisine. A nation's food has always been a more effective tool of conquest than an ideology anyway, since most people would rather read a menu than a manifesto. In our country, I've never understood why anyone would ever consider joining groups like the Aryan Nation or Ku Klux Klan; their xenophobic hostility must extend to non-Aryan foods, and how can any American live without bagels, pizza, burritos, and spring rolls?

After lunch, we stopped in and visited Michael, who was managing his friend Leo's environmental store, "of the earth." I wondered if the name of the store was lowercased as a measure to conserve ink. Michael introduced us to Leo, who was in his early forties and had a neatly trimmed beard and wore a pair of silver wire-rimmed eyeglasses, blue jeans, work boots, and a plaid flannel shirt that barely contained his pumped-up physique. It's embarrassing for a gay man who considers himself to be an environmentalist to admit it, but I think Paul Bunyan is sexier than Johnny Appleseed. Why are

do-gooders so rarely sexy? Nice guys always finish last in the looks department. Scrawny Jesus usually appears so gaunt in paintings that he doesn't look like he has the strength to wear a cross around his neck, let alone carry one across his shoulders. Buddha was probably always telling his disciples that this was definitely going to be *his* last supper—*"starting tomorrow, I'm going on a diet."* Albert Schweitzer, Mahatma Gandhi, Eleanor Roosevelt—the list of homely paragons goes on. Samson was probably an exception to the rule, but he also got killed because he was a nice guy. And I'll bet that Michelangelo's statue of the ultimate good guy, David, is more an indication of Michelangelo's fantasies about Goliath than an accurate portrayal of David's face and physique.

Leo definitely wanted his customers to feel that they were paragons of consumption. The interior of the store looked like a log cabin owned by an extremely fussy lumberjack. Attached to the plain pine shelves were neatly handwritten labels that gave a short sermon on every product and why you should buy it. On the front of the shelf that held the store's house brand of shampoo, a label said:

> Every hour an acre of rain forest is being destroyed, but our Gaia shampoo is made from all-natural ingredients that are harvested in a sustainable manner from the Amazon. Gaia shampoo not only helps keep the rain forests intact but keeps your hair soft and manageable.

The store was unsure about what it wanted to do. Did it want to alarm its customers about the earth's environmental crisis or soothe them into making a purchase? When I finished reading about the shampoo, I felt equally confused and concerned about the environment and my hair.

Environmental stores are misleading. The environ-

ment isn't going to be saved by shopping, because shopping is what fucked up the environment in the first place. If you want to help the environment, don't buy something; return something that you already bought but don't really need. When Americans try to be environmental it only gives us an excuse to make more products. Let's make regular plastic garbage bags *and* blue plastic recycling garbage bags.

While I was talking to Leo, Tom excused himself and headed toward the store's section of greeting cards. Tom is a greeting-card squirrel who believes in keeping an ample supply of carefully chosen blank greeting cards on hand at all times. He once explained to me that, since you have to send a certain number of cards throughout the year, instead of running out to try to find the right card for each person it's much easier to find the right person for the perfect card. I suspect that Tom has actually struck up friendships just to be able to use the Diane Arbus photograph *A Woman with Her Baby Monkey, New Jersey, 1971* as a birthday card. I'm not complaining, because I've dipped into Tom's greeting card stockpile on the many occasions when I've forgotten about Mother's Day or a birthday. While Tom looked, a passing thought whispered: *You're in love with someone who actually has a lifetime strategy for purchasing greeting cards.*

Leo sold a line of overly virtuous greeting cards in which the seeds from various species of trees were embedded. The recipient of the card was then encouraged to plant a blue spruce seed, growing a tree that could eventually be turned into more greeting cards. Receiving one of those cards would almost be worse than receiving a chain letter. I was surprised that the cards didn't also threaten you with seven years' bad luck if you didn't plant the seed. And why does the recipient of the card have to do all the work? The sender should assume the responsibility for growing the tree, since he's the one who sent the card in the first place.

The idea was lovely, but in practical terms it was an imposition. If the store was going to make growing your own products part of its corporate philosophy, then I felt that it was inconsistent not to attempt to do this with everything it sold. None of the wallets for sale came with a vial of bovine semen and a pamphlet suggesting how to raise your own leather.

Every product in the store was like medicine. It was good for you and the environment, but it was hard to swallow. As Tom and I looked at soaps that cleaned your conscience and undyed, unbleached cotton towels that were extra-absorbent of guilt, we came across a product that caused me to become discouraged that we'll ever be able to save the environment. It was a set of place mats made from the leaves of rain forest trees by an Amazonian tribe.

It's sad that it's not enough of a reason to save the rain forests just because they're millions of years old and contain most of the biological diversity of our planet; no, the rain forests have to prove their value for frequent entertaining. How smug the customers must feel after buying these place mats: *"I've been doing my part to save the rain forest. Every night this week I've had dinner guests. It takes a lot out of me but I feel it's important."*

I was reminded of the night that I'd been passing hors d'oeuvres at a party on Park Avenue, when the hostess pointed to a bench in her living room that was made from the legs of a real zebra and said to one of her guests, "I felt guilty when I bought it, but Donald and I visited Africa and there are still thousands of zebras—they're not endangered." My reaction was "Hey, there are thousands of assholes on Park Avenue, they're not endangered, but I wouldn't use them to furnish my apartment." She probably thinks that the only reason Noah saved two of every animal was for end tables.

Tsankawi

Michael almost stepped on the two-foot-long snake that was lying along the ledge of the mesa that we were hiking. It was a creamy yellow with dark brown blotches, and it tried to avoid being noticed by remaining motionless. But as soon as Richard pointed out that it was a nonvenomous gopher snake, Michael and I quickly moved in to get a better look. Tom held back at a safe distance, his curiosity about the snake having already been satisfied by its frequent appearance in his worst imaginings. With all four of us staring intently, the gopher snake then tried to scare us by imitating a rattlesnake. It hissed and wiggled just the last inch of its ringed tail. Most impersonations don't fool anyone. Nonetheless we were impressed by the snake's performance. From our vantage point, its tail did appear to rattle. To their credit, unlike human impersonators, gopher snakes don't want to draw attention to themselves; they just want to be left alone. Gopher snakes are delighted when their audiences walk out during their performances.

It's incredible that evolution has led one species to impersonate another, a process that makes the survival of the fittest into the survival of the most talented. Over the course of millennia, the gopher snakes that did the best imitation diamondback had the best chance of surviving to pass along their thespian genes. Nature has discriminating taste, though, and untalented gopher snakes were devoured by predators, a system of criticism that should be considered for our performing arts.

Before we continued along the path, a family approached from the other direction; when they were about to pass us, Richard shared our discovery with them. A little blond-haired boy was shown the snake and his awestruck face perfectly expressed what my own reaction would have been at his age. He asked, "Is it a rattlesnake?"

Richard said, "No. It's a gopher snake."

The boy's father then said, "That's not a gopher snake. That's a king snake."

The boy's grandfather backed up the father with "Yeah, that looks like a king snake."

Like the gopher snake, they were bluffing, and their display of knowledge didn't deceive us. Only a few months before, Richard and Michael had seen another gopher snake, and we knew that Richard, who has spent hours looking in field guides to find the exact name of a lizard or a tree, wasn't likely to be mistaken.

In the midst of the ruins of an Anasazi settlement, our prehistoric natures were revealed. It almost seemed as if these strange men felt threatened that their spouses would leave them for men who knew reptiles better than they did. But Richard didn't try to argue with them. For one thing, we definitely weren't challenging them for their mates, and we had met too many know-it-alls over the years to feel anything but annoyance. Someday when I meet Jane Goodall, I must ask her if after years of studying chimpanzee behavior, it has ever occurred to her that male primates may back down not out of fear or intimidation but out of sheer exasperation.

It was appropriate that this timeless confrontation would occur as we were hiking at Tsankawi, unexcavated Indian ruins that are a unit of Bandelier National Monument. Michael had suggested going to Tsankawi instead of some of the other, more spectacular ruins in the Santa Fe area because it was visited by fewer people.

I've known Michael for fifteen years; our friendship was formed when we both moved to New York from Buffalo in our early twenties, and it grew while we both tried to figure out what we wanted to do with our lives. We've remained friends even though Michael's been in Santa Fe for eight years while I was in New York, Provincetown, and now Los Angeles.

In some ways, your relationships with your friends are easier than your relationships with your spouse or

your family. One of the things that I like about my friends is that we have a satisfying relationship with a strong emotional connection, but we never have to have sex or live together. With your friends, it's as if you're always dating, with the added bonus that you never worry that you'll have nothing to talk about or you'll feel awkward when you say good night at the end of the evening.

There are times when we get on each other's nerves, but I can't ever imagine needing to do couples counseling with my friends. It's worth noting that I've never even heard of a form of therapy for troubled friendships, and I'm certain that if there was even the slightest market for friendship therapy some psychologist would be offering it. Friendships have remained out of the sway of therapy because your closest friends often act as de facto therapists.

The view from the top of the mesa of Tsankawi was a Georgia O'Keeffe landscape. We could see the red rock cliffs of the surrounding mesas, while below us was a piñon-juniper forest that spread out for miles. In one of the arroyos on our ascent, we passed a beautiful, massive, old ponderosa pine with a trunk shaped like a tuning fork. Michael mentioned that if you sniff the crevices of a ponderosa pine's thick orange bark, it smells like vanilla. My curiosity aroused, I immediately poked my nose into the underarm of a tree branch and detected a sweet tangy scent that did remind me of vanilla. I urged Tom to try it. He looked around to make sure no one was watching before he reluctantly took a hesitant whiff. He acted as if sniffing the private parts of a tree was committing an illegal act of botany. When it was Michael and Richard's turn to savor the tree's scent, Tom turned the other way, almost as if he wanted to give them some privacy.

Sniffing trees and walking in the footsteps of prehistoric Indians were not dreams of Tom's. The night before, I had read aloud to him a line from a travel

guide that said, "Visit Tsankawi for a day . . . and re-
member it for a lifetime!" His response to that bit of
hyperbole was to say, "Is that a promise or a threat?"
Due to our enthusiasm, Tom had agreed to come today,
but he reserved the inalienable right of the reluctant to
be sarcastic.

As we hiked, Tom reminded me to put on some more
sunblock. To protect myself, I wore a baseball cap and
the strongest sunblock sold. When I put it on, clouds
would form. I had to wear sunblock because a few years
before I had had a precancerous growth removed from
my left shoulder. It was a freckle that smoked three
packs a day. After completing the procedure, the der-
matologist tried to reassure me by saying, "Bob, there's
absolutely nothing to worry about. Just try to avoid the
sun." His medical advice was as practical as telling some-
one who's overweight just to avoid gravity. He made it
sound like our planet's circuit around the sun was social,
and evading the pervasive source of life on Earth was as
easy as dodging a dull guest at a party. I do feel resentful
about all the years I spent getting a suntan. Maybe Cop-
pertone should come up with a new ad campaign to
promote its products. It could feature an adorable little
dog pulling the bandages off a tumor.

As I applied some lotion to my face, Richard found
a shard of Native American pottery. On one side, it was
a dark gray that matched the color of the soil, but on
the other side, it was a dark red with black zigzag lines.
Richard was the only one of us to have grown up out
West; he had spent every summer as a child at his fam-
ily's cabin in the Sierras, where he and his brothers
frequently spent hours searching for and finding Indian
arrowheads. Since moving to Santa Fe a year before to
live with Michael, he had already found three exqui-
sitely carved arrowheads while hiking. One was made
out of translucent smoky quartz, another was obsidian,
and the third resembled one of the more primitive Fol-
som points named after the town in New Mexico where

they were first discovered, embedded in the bones of mammoths. Finding an arrowhead in the late twentieth century is fabulous—a word that is too often used to describe merely the expensive, and a word that I believe should never be used more than seven times in every person's life.

We all started scanning the ground. On the mesa, there were no obvious ruins. There were trails, but most of the mesa was covered with clumps of grass and piñon and juniper trees. Under one grassy mound we discovered the remains of the foundation of a pueblo. I bent down and picked up what looked like a piece of rock or wood, but to my amazement it turned out to be a fragment from the lip of a pot. It was cream-colored and the brush strokes of the decoration were striking. Now I was really faced with a dilemma. I really wanted to keep my pottery shard, but it's illegal to remove anything from a national park and I knew I would feel guilty about it. But I assumed that Richard had found his arrowheads while hiking in a park, and I had already decided that if I found an arrowhead, I was going to keep it.

I used to collect rocks and fossils when I was a boy— a hobby that is so boring that rockhounds are picked on by coin and stamp collectors—and sitting on my desk is a fossil brachiopod, an impression of a prehistoric clam, that I found in Allegany State Park and swiped because I didn't know any better. But it's probably my favorite possession, and the only way it's going back to the park is if I leave instructions to have it returned in my will. After I found a handful of pottery shards, I slipped one piece in my pocket but put the rest back.

At the entrance to the park, I had purchased a Tsankawi brochure for fifty cents. It offered a self-guided tour that explained various numbered points along the trail. I was intrigued by the information offered for Number 8 and read it aloud: "In the valley to the northeast are the remains of a home and school built by Madame Vera

Von Blumenthal and her friend Rose Dugan in 1918. They wanted to revive and improve the quality of pottery at nearby Indian pueblos, an effort shared by a number of individuals and institutions during the first half of this century. The project resulted in improved native ceramic art and also enabled craftspeople to get better prices for their wares." When I read this, my gaydar rattled like the gopher snake's tail. Two women sharing a home could be construed as having a lesbian relationship, and while it's not always advisable to assume a relationship because of its appearance, it's equally ridiculous to discount it. I found the story of Vera and Rose intriguing and I wanted to be able to reconstruct their lives from this one shard of information.

A half hour after reading about Vera and Rose, we met two women in their late fifties who could have been them in the flesh. After we'd eaten lunch on the mesa, Michael had taken us off the marked path and was leading us down on a steep unmarked trail. As much as I like to think of myself as being adventurous, I have to admit that my spirit of derring-do is usually limited to impulsively ordering dessert. I tried not to look down because we seemed to be unscaling a cliff. Just as I was about to complain to Michael and Tom, I saw that our Vera and Rose were also following our pathway and I was heartened by their example. I honestly don't mind if other men, gay or straight, think of me as being a wimp, but I do want to keep the respect of lesbians.

That same day, we ran into a group of six men and one woman hiking. I didn't have to guess if they were gay. One guy was wearing a T-shirt that parodied a box of Cheer laundry detergent with ALL-TEMPERATURE QUEER, while another guy was wearing a T-shirt that was emblazoned with the Gay Rainbow Flag. (If that wasn't enough information, beneath the flag was the word QUEER.) Maybe I'm just cranky, but I feel that clothing that tells people that you're gay should stay in

the closet. Whatever happened to the good old-fashioned way of letting people know that you're gay through your behavior?

Any romanticism I had about the idyllic life of cliff dwellers ended when we looked inside some of the caves carved into the side of the mesa. Back then, Santa Fe style really left a lot to be desired. The winters on the mesa had to have been bitterly cold, and as we crouched in the claustrophobic rooms, I noticed that the ceilings were blackened from decades of smoky fires.

The soot-encrusted ceilings of the Tsankawi caves reminded me of my first visit to Santa Fe with Michael during the Harmonic Convergence of 1987. Michael and I had wanted to see Santa Fe, because like many gay men in the 1980s we had developed a crush on Georgia O'Keeffe. I knew nothing of the Harmonic Convergence, the alignment of four planets that was supposed to mark the beginning of a new cosmic era, but Michael knew all about it, as he was already working on building up his soul just like he was building up his body. His goal was to have his chakras as clearly defined as his abs. In many ways, Michael is a very different person from me. He's keenly interested in spirituality and is someone who has lived in India for six months, chants daily, and has his own guru. Ordinarily just one of those interests would be enough for me to end the friendship.

When we arrived in Santa Fe, Michael and I made a deal. We would spend three days camping in the back-yard of a meditation center in La Cienega, a small town fifteen miles south of Santa Fe, then for the rest of the week we would be tourists and stay at a motel.

Our first night at the meditation center, we participated in a Native American sweat lodge ceremony that involved sitting in an excruciatingly hot tepee where fiery rocks were continually doused with water and bundles of sage were burned. It was a useful reminder that Roman Catholicism is not the only religion with an unhealthy appreciation for suffering. I've never understood

the rationale behind seeking God through self-inflicted pain. Although afterward I had a revelation. When you're in a sweat lodge, you're continually asking yourself, *God, why am I doing this?* Under such agonizing circumstances, whatever answer you come up with seems like a divine reply.

I think too many faiths make too big a deal about martyrs who suffered physically. The repertory of martyrdom needs to be expanded from physical torment to include mental anguish. Instead of saints torn apart by horses, I'd prefer a modern martyr, Saint Jimmy the Indecisive, the patron saint of the wishy-washy, who was not only tortured by doubts about God's existence but by doubts about his relationship, his job, and what shirt to wear.

As we descended the final leg of the trail, I wickedly said to Tom, "These mesas would make perfect landing sites for UFOs." He flashed me a forced smile that said, *That's-so-funny.* Last night, after Richard had gone to bed, we had stayed up late and listened to Michael as he told us about how New Mexico was overrun with UFOs and how he had actually seen a little glowing man in the courtyard of the very house where we were staying. I waited patiently for Michael to follow up his story with how he'd found the lost continent of Atlantis underneath the seat of his car, and how he had finally determined the hypotenuse of the Bermuda Triangle.

I think I have a reasonable tolerance for my friends' eccentricities. Some of my friends believe in vegetarianism. Some of my friends believe in reincarnation. Some of my friends believe in astrology. But Michael was the first friend of mine who claimed to have met one of the inhabitants of the Zodiac.

I wondered what Tom was thinking. I had once had the gall to mock one of his friends because of her habit of mentioning only first names whenever she talked about celebrities. At least she had never tried to impress us by dropping a name from another planet. Tom had

met Michael only a few times before, and having your best friend tell your boyfriend about his close encounter with an extraterrestrial was a situation that we hadn't adequately prepared for in couples counseling. When we were in bed, Tom asked me if I thought that Michael had really seen an alien. I said that I had no idea, but that Michael probably *was* an alien. There are times when you know immediately that you've said the wrong thing. A good indication of your error is having your boyfriend say, "Not everything is a joke!" Tom didn't want to learn after midnight that, after the town of Roswell, he was staying at the second most popular spot for alien visitations in New Mexico.

Michael lived on a dirt road in a remote area outside the city, and the next morning Tom claimed that he'd been sleepless all night. I sympathized with him, because when I was in the fifth grade, I had suffered from my own nightmares after reading UFO magazines that said strange men in black harassed people who knew too much about UFOs. After I woke up one night crying, my mother had said, "I don't want you reading any more UFO books!" When I look back upon it, my thinking that a fifth-grader could possess too much knowledge about UFOs was the earliest indication of my own inflated sense of self-importance.

The room we were staying in at Michael's house probably contributed to Tom's unease. This was the first time we had ever met Michael's new boyfriend, Richard, and we were relieved that we liked him, although I was horrified to see that Richard had hung on the walls of our bedroom his framed collections of dead beetles and butterflies. Entomology is a hobby that can appeal only to someone who has never lived in a New York City apartment. In Manhattan hanging dead bugs on your walls for decoration would be regarded as not only unhygienic but pretentious, since you could probably find a more varied and spectacular collection under your kitchen sink.

At some point in your life you have to stop trying to explain your friends, just as you have to stop explaining your family. All you can do is mock them and love them unconditionally. As we drove home from Tsankawi we passed a stable, and when the smell of manure wafted into the car Michael said, "You know, from working on farms when I was a teenager I can smell the difference between cowshit, horseshit, pigshit, sheepshit, and chickenshit." This struck us as an unusual talent to brag about, and we laughed loudly when Richard said, "Bullshit."

Before we left Tsankawi, I had put back the pottery shard. I didn't do this because I'm particularly noble; I put it back because my cowardice is stronger than my ruthlessness. I knew that if I kept the shard I would superstitiously start to think it was bad luck, and I really didn't need a possession that added to my personal failings when I was fully capable of doing the job myself.

Chimayo

On the way to Taos, Tom and I were planning to visit El Santuario de Chimayo, a chapel built in 1810 that is renowned as the Lourdes of the Southwest because of the reputed healing properties of its dirt. I had read that some of the people who come to seek help from the Holy Dirt of Chimayo rub it on their bodies or even mix it in water and drink it. I couldn't help but think if they mixed the dirt with wheatgrass juice it would be like drinking a lawn. The idea of Holy Dirt isn't far-fetched in Santa Fe, an entire city that violates my mother's housekeeping vow of never living in a dirty house. One reason I wanted to scoop up a handful of the soil at Chimayo was because it might be the only way Tom and I would ever acquire property in our price range.

I wanted Tom to see Chimayo because the one time I've ever had anything resembling a mystical experience

was during my first visit there. I know that trying to tell about a mystical experience is like trying to give an account of an orgasm. It's never as vivid or interesting to the hearer as it is to the person who experienced it. But Tom was trapped in the car with me, and the only way he could avoid my tale was by alien abduction.

On that first trip to Santa Fe with Michael, he and I had driven to Chimayo on a weekday, arriving early, around nine A.M. The chapel was already open but there were no other tourists. Michael and I walked in and admired the brightly colored, early nineteenth-century New Mexican religious artworks. Whenever I visit a church just to see the art or architecture, I always feel slightly guilty that I'm not there to attend mass or say a prayer.

For a stand-up comedian, saying an occasional prayer feels completely natural, because I have experience in saying monologues to an unresponsive audience. God is the ultimate tough crowd.

Whenever I pray, I always feel that I'm trying to get the attention of an overworked bartender. He knows that you're there and want to place an order, but you're just going to have to wait your turn because he's really busy right now. Then if I become impatient and rudely try to interrupt him, I'm always afraid that he'll get pissed off and completely ignore me.

I don't understand why the development of monotheism is always regarded by historians as such an achievement. One God doesn't seem enough, no matter how much they tell us he's capable of handling the workload. At least with many gods, people could ask another one for help if the first god they tried didn't answer their prayers. Exchanging many gods for one is an improvement only if you consider eternal loneliness to be a virtue. Most people don't think it's a good idea for a person to spend a lifetime alone, so I don't know why we think it's great that the Creator of the universe should have to endure the same thing for eternity.

One of my biggest problems with Christianity has always been the belief that we're still being punished for what Adam and Eve did. It makes God seem petty. "I asked them to do one thing for me. Was that too much to ask?" God needs to let go. If my father, who was a cop, could forgive me for smoking pot in the basement, I think God could have handled the apple business better.

Adjoining the nave of the church was a small room that had hanging on the walls the crutches of the healed and messages giving thanks for blessings received. At the end of a passage in the adjoining room was a smaller room that was about the size of a closet. I entered it and all I saw was a small shelf that was filled with candles. I said to Michael, "Where's the healing dirt?" Michael laughed and said, "You're standing in it." It was the first time I noticed the dirt floor that gently sloped into a shallow bowl. I felt sheepish, almost as if I had mistakenly started doing my laundry at Lourdes.

Then an elderly Hispanic man and his young son or grandson stepped through the doorway. As all four of us stood there, the elderly man, who moved with great difficulty, tried to reach down and touch the earthen floor. I saw that he couldn't bend over and, without thinking, I reached down and grabbed a handful of dirt and put it in his outstretched hands. At that moment, I had the experience that time and space stood still, and I felt such an overwhelming sense of love that, for a moment, the universe made sense. It was as if I had stuck my finger in a light socket, and instead of experiencing pain, I experienced illumination. When I left the room, I was speechless until we stepped outside the chapel into the fresh air. I said to Michael, "I think something just happened to me in that room." Michael surprised me by saying that he had felt it too.

But this story has an appropriately spooky ending. During our trip Michael and I had taken several rolls of film, and one of the ground rules for our photos was that

we always waited until other people moved out of the viewfinder as neither of us wanted snapshots of strangers. Our one exception being a woman whom I surreptitiously photographed standing in front of the Painted Desert because she was wearing a bright pink velour jogging outfit that exactly matched the scenery. But when I developed the photographs that I'd taken at Chimayo, I saw that in one of the pictures the old man was shown entering the chapel. I somehow must have taken the photo before I went in, but I don't remember taking it and I can't imagine why I didn't wait for him to get out of the picture. In five roles of film, he was the only person who was accidentally photographed.

When I finished relating my experience, Tom looked over at me with a smile on his face that said, *If-you-say-so.* Somehow, without changing my name to Storm or Squall, I had become another Sante Fe kook with a story.

Heart Failure

Tuesday, January 2

ONE **DISADVANTAGE** of digital clocks is that they allow you to remember precise moments that you would rather forget. It was 6:34 A.M. when I awoke to the sound of my sister's voice coming from the answering machine in the other room. As usual, I couldn't find the cordless phone. Every advance in technology creates new opportunities for aggravation; we now misplace appliances that had once been stationary.

"Bob, it's Carol. Pick up! Bob! Wake up, it's Carol. Pick up the phone . . ."

"Tom. Wake up. It's Carol. I can't find the phone!"

Tom threw off the covers and joined in my search, but by the time we found it, Carol had hung up saying,

"All right...well, call me back—right away!" I sat down at the kitchen table and punched in her phone number, both of us knowing that she would say exactly what she said: "Dad died this morning."

I've received too many telephone calls announcing the death of someone I care about. At times, I've thought of changing the outgoing message on my answering machine to, *"Hi. I'm not home right now. At the sound of the beep, please leave the name of the deceased and the time of the memorial service and I'll call you right back. ...but I won't know what to say."*

Carol and I talked calmly for a few minutes, going over the events leading up to Dad's death as if we were detectives trying to rule ourselves out as suspects. But of course, we weren't. My father was an alcoholic. Four years ago, he had come close to dying from congestive heart failure brought on by years of steady drinking. His recovery had been complicated by the fact that while hospitalized he also suffered from alcohol withdrawal. When we flew home to see him he was delirious and had to be kept in bed with restraints. When he dried out, his doctors told him that he was lucky to have survived. But if he didn't stop drinking, they said, he wouldn't be so lucky the next time. After he was released from the hospital, he joined AA, quit drinking for a while, then slowly started up again. This was the next time.

When I started going out with Tom seven years ago, I didn't spring my family on him all at once. Ideally, one should never reveal one's family's faults in less time than it took to acquire them. It's best to slowly reveal your family in the escalating order of human failings: odd ways, harmless foibles, annoying quirks, minor addictions, personality flaws, neurotic tendencies, major addictions, psychotic episodes, crimes against humanity. Talking to Tom about my family, I have felt at times like a magician pulling bad habits out of a hat.

After hanging up with my sister, I called to make

plane reservations for our flight to Buffalo. When they put me on hold, Tom came over and gave me a hug. I wanted Tom to come with me, but instead of just saying that I asked if *he* wanted to come. "Do *you* want me to come?" he asked. It was one of those small confusing moments in a gay relationship; even though Tom had visited my parents twice and had come to know my sister and one of my brothers fairly well, he was concerned that his presence might be unwelcome on such a sensitive occasion—one involving not only the immediate family but the extended family as well. (The terms "immediate" and "extended" are apt because my immediate family can cause instant mood swings and my extended family is better kept at a distance.)

We vacillated until common sense said this is our family and of course we want to be together not just for the baptisms, the birthdays, the weddings, but the funerals too. I made three reservations for a flight at one o'clock; for my sister, myself, and Tom.

We had only a few hours to get ready and Tom's ability to be decisive and get things done was remarkable. He made coffee, packed our luggage, and then called our friend Michael and arranged for him to drive us to the airport and take care of Grady. It's evil, but I thought maybe I could induce the same sense of urgency in Tom by waking him in the middle of the night to tell him, *"Someone died! Quit smoking and choose a career!"*

I called my mother. The telephone is the perfect means of communication with my family: We can attempt intimacy while remaining thousands of miles apart.

"Hel-lo . . ." My mother was crying.

"Hi, Mom. I'm so sorry about Dad."

"Oh, Bob. I wish I had been there. They told me that it was okay to go home. I wasn't there for Dad."

"Mom, there's no reason to feel guilty."

Of course, that observation had never helped me but

I felt compelled to say it. On her kitchen counter, my mother has a set of five canisters for the staples—Flour, Sugar, Salt, Coffee, and Tea. I pictured them behind her as she spoke, relabeled to hold the emotional staples with which I was raised—Guilt, Anxiety, Denial, Humor, and Love.

"Dad knows that you would've been there. No one expected this to happen."

"I know. You're right. I'm gonna miss him. It's the drinking that killed him. I don't know why he couldn't stop. Bob, why couldn't we get him to stop drinking?"

"Mom, only he could make himself stop drinking."

"Yeah, that's true."

"I wish you weren't all alone now."

"I'm okay. Ted's driving up. He'll be here in a few hours."

My oldest brother, Ted, lived in Syracuse.

"Mom, we're going to arrive tonight at ten-thirty. Our flight is United, number forty-nine from Chicago."

"Let me get a pen. Okay. Say it again."

"United, flight number forty-nine . . ."

"Oh, damn. This pen doesn't work. And I just got it as a gift from the dry cleaners. . . ."

"Mom, I'll call you later with—"

"I hate them anyway. They ruined my red blouse. Okay. I'm ready."

"United. Flight number forty-nine, at ten-thirty."

"All right, Bob. I'm gonna hang up now. I want to drive over to the hospital and see Dad."

At that moment, the thought of her going to see his body seemed the saddest thing I'd ever heard. Like most men, I have a heart like a carton of milk: I never know whether it's full or empty until someone or something shakes it.

"Are you sure you want to do that by yourself?"

"Yes. It will make me feel better."

"Okay, Mom. We'll see you tonight. I love you."

"I love you too. Bye."

"Dysfunctional" is an inadequate term for describing my family. My family's not on the blink. It's more precise to describe us as Fucked Up. Dysfunctional sounds like something that can be repaired by tinkering or by tightening a few loose screws. My family's like a broken computer. It would almost be cheaper to buy a new one than to pay to get the old one fixed, but I stick with the old one because I know how it operates.

That morning, I kept thinking about my father and wondering, *Could I have done more? Could we have done anything?* and then made a mental note to think about this later, knowing all too well that my mental notes always end up in a huge unexamined pile on my mental desk. Later, at an unexpected and inconvenient time, the note would fall to my mental floor, and after picking it up I'd try to decipher the illegible scrawl on the crumpled mental cocktail napkin. When I did, after a rush of feeling, I'd quickly put it back in the pile and restart the process once again.

I know the answers provided by Al-Anon, an organization that helps families of alcoholics. Al-Anon has always sounded to me like the name of a character in a W. C. Fields movie. "One can't stop an alcoholic from drinking. It's an illness." Should we have tried a last-minute intervention? Unfortunately, the practical difficulty in doing an intervention is that the families most in need of one would first need interventions to confront each member of the family with the need to plan and carry out an intervention.

Two hours later Carol arrived at our apartment with her husband, Mark. I was surprised to see him because he had recently had back surgery and his doctor wouldn't allow him to fly. Mark, who loved and respected my father, gave me his condolences in the traditional, masculine American style of expressing a strong emotion—he made his handshake grip firmer than usual and wore an extremely solemn facial expression.

Carol is two years younger than me, but in some

respects about ten years more mature. I turn to her when I need advice on anything, from auto repair to whether a joke works. She's the funniest person I know who doesn't do it for a living.

Carol was very close to my father—he had taught her how to repair cars—and when she walked in the door of our apartment, at first her eyes welled up with tears, but then she started laughing. "Oh—I didn't tell you what Mom told me on the phone. She said, 'Just because you're coming home for your father's funeral doesn't mean we can't have fun!' "

Have I mentioned that my mother had a nervous breakdown?

The fucked-up family is the foundation of the entire Judeo-Christian tradition, and trying to figure out why your family is fucked up has become one of the great quests of Western culture. As I've grown older, I've had to reconsider my dismissal of the story of Adam and Eve and the idea of original sin. Making one mistake and having it become a constant source of punishment and misery, retold over and over from one generation to the next, is a tradition of human nature that my family has always celebrated. My one modification of this idea would be that original sin isn't something that each child is born with—original sin is the chain of petty feuds, small misunderstandings, and resentments that every child is born into. It seems that if you pulled on a problem in my family it would unravel a strand of DNA going back thousands of generations.

The Chaos Theory has helped me to better understand my heritage. The classic example of Chaos Theory is the so-called Butterfly Effect, which proposes that the flapping of a butterfly's wings in China can start, by the minute ramifications of its action, a cascading chain of atmospheric changes that eventually can culminate in a tornado in Arkansas. Could a careless flapping of the tongue by one of my great-grandparents be responsible

for my mother's nervous breakdown, my father's alcoholism, my sister's divorce, and my biting my nails?

In my family, death never kills your appetite. While we waited at the Los Angeles airport to board our plane, we ate quarter-pound cheeseburgers. Out of consideration for the solemnity of the occasion, we split one large order of French fries among the three of us. Our flight stopped in Chicago, where we would meet my brother John, who was flying in from Phoenix. John, the second oldest, is a very successful MBA who is the vice president of a major liquor company; an ironic career choice for the son of a man who drank himself to death. According to the latest theories, alcoholism may possibly be genetic. Alcoholism definitely runs or staggers on my father's side of the family. When I mentioned to Tom my own fear that my blood type might be AA, he said, "Don't worry, you might just be a carrier—you'll only cause other people to drink."

When John met us in Chicago he was dressed in an expensive gray suit and a long camel hair coat and he was carrying a large briefcase. He's a classic overachiever. If John ever played Willy Loman in *Death of a Salesman*, he'd win Willy a raise and a promotion. Tom was curious about John; this was the first time they had ever met even though we had been together for seven years.

I found it difficult to describe my siblings accurately to Tom before he met them. The danger is to judge too harshly and find oneself wanting—a new family. But what verbal snapshot do you show? Baby, high school, wedding? What you think might consider to be a good likeness, your brother or sister might find to be terribly unflattering. It seems that even with the best intentions, all our family photos turn into mug shots.

John recently overcame a "little problem" with sleeping pills. I wasn't surprised to hear this. Our

mothe℞ has been taking tranquilizers for more than thirty years. When I take an inventory of the addictions in our family, it makes me wonder why no one has ever marketed a set of self-help encyclopedias? They could be sold at supermarkets and cover everything from Alcoholism to Zoophobia. Each week, my mother would buy a new volume, which would be apropos, because she also has a problem with compulsive shopping.

When we arrived in Buffalo my brother Ted was waiting at the gate to meet us. Ted, the oldest, is a paramedic for the Syracuse Fire Department—a perfect career choice, since he's the only child to live within driving distance of my parents and he's been responding to alarms, real and false, for his entire life.

Ted and John didn't greet each other. I turned to Tom and gave him my *Now-Do-You-See?* look. My brothers are in a fraternity where the hazing never ends. Ted, John, and I have drifted apart, a turn of phrase that suggests icebergs floating, although unlike icebergs, we're hidden even on the surface. While I feel completely confident that I could depend upon my brothers in an emergency, thinking of your brothers as a floatation device isn't exactly brimming with sentiment.

Ted and John ignored each other during the short ride to my parents' house in Kenmore, an older suburb north of of Buffalo. Tom didn't say a word while Carol and I made jokes to keep us from driving in silence. When we walked in the back door, my mother was standing at the top of the kitchen steps. She was smiling and teary-eyed as if she was confused as to what her reaction should be—having her children visit was always a pleasure but somehow my father's death was interfering with her enjoyment. After everyone, including Tom, kissed her on the cheek, she sighed sentimentally and said, "Oh, your dad would've liked this. . . ."

I said, "Mom, he would've liked us coming home— not coming home for his funeral."

She smiled. "Oh, you know what I mean."

Unfortunately, I did.

In the living room, sitting in a chair, was ninety-three-year-old Marie Cash, godmother to my mother and myself. Marie was wearing too much of her favorite perfume, Chanel No. 5^{500}. It was like being hit in the face by a three-hundred-pound rose petal. Marie is an extremely elegant woman who never goes out without gloves and a hat. Her tailored clothes are clearly of another era; at the end of the twentieth century she almost appears to be in costume. Marie was beginning to have problems with her short-term memory. She wasn't senile but she was starting to forget simple recent facts. Over the next few days, she would say to me several times, "Bob, do you like New York?" Then she would remember and say, "Oh, I forgot. You don't live in New York anymore." My mother handled Marie's loss of memory with admirable lightness. Of course it took a while for my father's death to register with Marie. "Sue, where's Matt?" she'd ask.

In a very loud direct voice, my mother would say as if she was talking to a child, "Marie, Matt's *dead*."

"Oh, that's right. I'm sorry . . ."

My mother would smile and say, "That's okay, Marie."

Marie's long-term memory was unimpaired, and it was a good thing: She was our only source of information about my mother and her family. She had married into our family by marrying a cousin of my grandfather.

"I married Wells's cousin, Phoebe's son, Bill Cash— of course, his name was ironic because he never had any. We split after six months. It was right after I graduated from D'Youville, which was a girl's prep school at that time. All it did was teach you how to get married."

Carol asked, "Who's Phoebe?"

"Phoebe was your great-grandmother's sister. Did you know that your great-grandmother Rose made book?"

"Our great-grandmother was a bookie?"

"No! She just took bets." Marie paused. "Well, yes. I guess that is a bookie. But she was nice. If someone lost but they needed the money, she paid them a little something."

I asked her, "What about our great-grandfather?"

"Everyone said that Fred loved Rose so much. He worshipped the ground she walked on. Of course, most people thought he was a simpleton. He always said, 'I work for the railroad.' We didn't know if that meant he put pennies on the track or what. He could've been pushing around toy trains for all we knew. Fred was a stupe. I never had much use for him."

For years, Marie had been a part of our family's Christmas and Thanksgiving celebrations, but after my mother's nervous breakdown she had disappeared from our lives. Marie explained that my grandmother Charlotte had forbidden her to have any contact with our family.

"After you were born, Carol, they never mentioned you. So I figured you were either retarded or handicapped. Charlotte used to pick me up and we'd drive out to Kenmore—to this house. And she'd say, 'Marie, I'm just going to run in for a minute.' And I'd sit there in the car like a stupe for an hour. Then when your mother had her nervous breakdown, Charlotte didn't want people knowing about that. She'd say that she thought it might hurt Wells's career at the bank. But we knew it was because she thought people would blame her. And we did. Charlotte could be a bitch. But she was always nice to me. Although she 'borrowed' my Tiffany lamp for a party and I never got it back.

"Then one day Charlotte told me that your mother couldn't see me anymore. Her nerves couldn't take it. And that's when Charlotte bought me my complete set of silver. I knew that she was buying me off. But what could I do?"

During a previous visit Marie had been told about Tom and me by my sister. Marie had nodded knowingly,

"I worked with many of 'them' downtown for years. I never had any problem with 'them.'"

Shortly after we arrived, Marie announced, "I'm losing my eyesight. I can still make out colors and I can see peripherally but that's it." It was then that Marie looked directly at Carol and said, "Carol, you've really gained a lot of weight. You're really heavy." Carol laughed because this wasn't said out of malice. It was as if she had momentarily come into focus. I said to Carol later, "That must make you feel great when a legally blind woman comments negatively on your appearance."

Carol has gained a lot of weight in the past few years, a fact that hasn't gone unnoticed by my mother. My mother thinks that belittling someone is a weight-reduction program. Carol and my mother have a mother-daughter relationship that parallels my mother's painful relationship with her mother—Mom always said that her mother was too critical of her. Carol and I have both tried to explain to my mother that her comments are hurtful, but my mother claims that she's only trying to help. She's a lifeguard who would throw an anchor to someone drowning.

At some point, every adult wonders about the psychological facts of life: Where do big babies come from? I have sought our family's history in an attempt to figure out my parents lives and marriage. I now have as many conflicting theories as there are about the Kennedy assassination. What happened on the grassy knolls of my parents' childhoods? Why was my mother always sent away every summer to stay with her grandparents? Was it to keep her away from my grandmother's verbal abuse, as Marie has reported? Is that what eventually led to her nervous breakdown? The single-parent theory has been discredited because my grandparents never divorced but conspiracy theories still abound. From the evidence, certainly, more than one shot was swallowed. Most of the witnesses have died and all we can do is ask the few survivors what they remember. I've been tempted to

watch our home movies in slow motion to see if I can't find some clue.

That night, my mother made an announcement: "Your father wanted to be cremated." After hearing this, I said, "Cremated? With all the scotch in him, he'll burn for seven days." As everyone laughed, my brother John said, "I hope that's not going in your act." Before I'm accused of being heartless, let me explain that the boundaries for expressing humor in my family are limitless. It's the expression of every other emotion where there are constraints.

My mother continued talking, as she's developed the ability to ignore my most outrageous remarks just as I've developed the ability to ignore her incessant commentary.

My mother then informed us that "he wanted to have his ashes thrown in the river near his boat."

We all commented on how surprising it was that my father, the law-enforcing state trooper, would ask us to do something illegal. Dumping your ashes is an ironic method of showing your appreciation for an area of natural beauty. It almost seems malevolent: If I can't enjoy it, then no one else will either. If this trend continues, someday, the heaped remains of environmentalists will give our redwood forests the same picturesque quality as steel mills. What if people who loved the indoors wanted to do the same thing? My father was also a hockey fan, but it would be considered unreasonable to throw his ashes on the ice during a Sabres game.

The Niagara River was the setting for much of my father's life. After he finished college in the early 1960s, his first job was as a construction worker on the Niagara Power Project in Lewiston. And after his retirement, his last job was working as a security guard at another power plant located on the river. He also kept his boat in a marina on the river. My father loved his boat and he would launch it in the spring as soon as the ice had melted and keep it in the water until as late as possible

in the autumn. Whenever any of us visited our parents, going out on the boat was mandatory. During the summer, our entire family enjoyed swimming in the river, and now my father will be going for one last swim. We'll have to put his ashes in slowly, though, in remembrance of how he always took forever getting used to the river's cold water.

Within two hours of our arriving home, my two brothers were arguing about the sleeping arrangements. Carol had sensibly suggested that John and Ted share the only bedroom with two single beds. But John made it clear that he wouldn't share a room with Ted. I sometimes think that if one of my brothers needed a kidney from the other, his body would reject the organ out of spite.

I thought about Tom having to listen to this, but while I was annoyed, I don't feel responsible for the embarrassing behavior of my family. In fact, I'm so well adjusted that there are times when I don't even feel responsible for my own embarrassing behavior. The first time my family lost all sense of shame and self-restraint in front of Tom, instead of becoming upset, I rejoiced. It was a moment of acceptance, tinged with malice, they were saying: *You're a member of the family now.*

Tom and I ended up sleeping in the room that my brothers refused to share. The two single beds were the old bunk beds that John and I slept in when we were children. The upstairs of our house is entirely different now than it was when we were growing up. All of our personal possessions were removed, after my mother made an effort to "fix up the upstairs," making the rooms now feel strange and yet familiar. The most fully furnished rooms in the house are the bathrooms. The two toilets are upholstered in pink fake fur, which in our drafty old house means that they're more comfortable than the inhabitants. My mother cherishes the belief that she's very ladylike and since real women no

longer conform to the gender roles she grew up with, she now assigns these outdated values to inanimate objects. Her latest interior decorating idea is to cover every small item in the house with flowery fabric and then tie a ribbon or bow around it. Wastepaper baskets, boxes of tissues, and spare rolls of toilet paper have all received this treatment. It makes everything seem like a really disappointing Christmas gift.

After Tom and I got into our two de-bunked beds, we talked over the events of the day. I apologized about my family's behavior and told him that even I thought that they were crazy. He reassured me that they are. After we turned out the light, Tom said, "I'm sorry about your father. I know how much you cared about him."

All I could say was "Thanks."

Wednesday, January 3

The next morning, I woke up before everyone and made coffee. Coffee in the morning allows me to go from feeling sleepy to feeling anxious, which is what I consider to be normalcy. When I entered the kitchen, my mother's new calico cat, Frisky, hissed at me. (My family's never been particularly gifted in the naming of our pets: Our two dogs were called Chips and Smitty.) Frisky is the first pet that my parents have owned that doesn't recognize any of their children. She treats us all like strangers who should be feared and mistrusted. It really makes a visit home uninviting when you have a strained relationship with the family pet.

My mother was the next person to wake up. While we each had a cup of coffee, she said, "Bob, they were selling some of those red AIDS ribbons here in Kenmore and I bought two. I bought one for Marie and when I put it on her coat she said, 'Sue, I don't want to wear one of those. I'm not for AIDS.' Then I wasn't sure. Bob, are the ribbons for AIDS or against AIDS? I always get

that mixed up." I laughed and then she asked me, "Bob, I forgot to tell you that yesterday the hospital called. Do I have to pick your father up and take him to the funeral home?" The image of her doing that made me laugh even more.

Today, Carol and I had to take care of the funeral arrangements. John was going to look through my father's papers, and Ted had offered to shop for food and make dinner. Since Ted works for the fire department, he frequently prepares meals for twenty men at a time—a food-to-consumption ratio that was perfect for our family of six.

The first thing John did after he woke up was to change the message on the answering machine because the current outgoing message was my father's voice. My mother sweetly and ludicrously asked John to save the tape because she might later want to listen to it. I'm not sure how much comfort it would be to hear a dead spouse saying, "Hi. We're not home right now." It would be like being haunted.

Since I'm the writer in the family, my first task was to write my father's obituary. As I had never written a death notice before, I used one from the *Buffalo News* as my literary template. The format of a death notice is almost as rigid as a limerick. Each death notice must include the use of terms of affection, such as "beloved," "loving," and "dear" before the names of each family member listed—confirming my long-held belief that men find it easier to express their true feelings when they're no longer capable of having any. I typed out a first draft:

Smith, Matthew C.

January 2, 1996, of Kenmore, N.Y., former First Sergeant of The New York State Police, beloved husband of Sue (Corey), loving father of Theodore, John, Robert, and Carol (Mark) Reifer, dear brother of Roger (Jane) Smith, Lorraine Brown, and the late

Ann Pace. Friends and Relatives may call Thursday from 7 to 9 P.M. at The Lester H. Tarnbauer Funeral Home, 3890 Elmwood Ave., Kenmore, 555-5500. Drinking Buddies are welcome at Happy Hour from 5 to 6. In lieu of flowers, please just send a bottle of Four Roses.

The death notice is like the list of ingredients on a package. The contents of a life are given but it certainly doesn't explain a life any more than potassium sorbate and partially hydrogenated soybean oil explain a cookie. My sister read it and after laughing she made a few deletions and faxed it to the newspaper. We needed to finish discussing the funeral arrangements with my mother. Since my father had left no written instructions, this meant that my mother, who couldn't make him happy during his life, was determined to try to make him happy in death. She claimed that my father didn't want a funeral, which was probably true but I wondered if that was healthy for her. I was afraid that after we left in a week that she would have second thoughts about not having a funeral. Second thoughts being my family's primary form of regret. But when I brought up that point, she maintained that she was certain. We decided not to have a funeral, just a short memorial service. My mother also insisted on having a closed casket.

"Who wants to look at you when you're dead?" she asked.

A point that, like many of my mother's assertions, was arguable.

Carol said, "Lots of people—I want to see him. And the boys probably do too."

"Okay. But no one else."

"Mom, what about Uncle Roger and Aunt Lorraine? They might want to see him. They're his brother and sister."

"No. Dad wouldn't have liked it."

"Mom, if we're going to see him. Then they should too."

"Hmmm. Well . . . if you think so. But no one else!"

"Mom, Paul will want to see him. He was his best friend."

"No!"

"Mom, funerals are for the living. Not for the dead."

Reluctantly, she agreed. "All right."

"Mom, should we have a time in the evening when friends and neighbors can come by the house?" my brother Ted suggested.

For a moment she cheered up, "Oh, yes. That would be nice. Remember all the people who came to Dad's retirement party? That was something. . . ."

When my father retired from the state police, his retirement party was attended by over three hundred guests and had even made the local 11 o'clock Eyewitness News. The videotape of that news story and the turnout for his party was a source of solace to my mother after my father's alcoholism became undeniable.

Carol asked, "Are we going to have a priest say a few prayers?"

My family's adherence to the Roman Catholic faith was once summed up by my mother when my father was first hospitalized for drinking. We were all in his room when a nun stopped by and cheerfully asked if Carol and I wanted to receive communion. The sister quickly excused herself when my mother threw cold holy water on her suggestion with her sour lament, "Oh, *please*. I'm the only one who goes to church."

After a prolonged consultation with my mother, we decided on a private viewing with only family members from three to five. From seven to nine friends would be welcome and there would be a short service conducted by a priest.

Carol asked Tom and me to help her pick out clothes for my father. Since my father's retirement, my parents

bought clothes in quantities normally purchased only by the despots of developing nations or the third wives of Las Vegas entertainers. Looking through his closet, I realized that my father owned more clothes than both Tom and I. Since my father was going to be cremated, we didn't have the added pressure of trying to choose something that he'd be wearing for eternity. We examined his four suits.

Having been raised with the Christian belief of bodily resurrection on Judgment Day, I wonder if the last outfits will also be resurrected? Imagine the embarrassment of people who were buried during the 1970s? I wouldn't want to meet my maker in a puka-shell necklace and platform shoes. We finally decided on a light gray suit with a blue shirt and red-and-blue tie. Carol then asked Tom and me if we wanted anything. The thought of wearing a dead person's clothes was repellent to Tom, somehow it made being dressed to kill morbid. On an impulse, I took my father's black satin bowling jacket, which had embroidered on the back THE BEVERLY LANES, NIAGARA FALLS, NY.

After Carol packed my father's suit and shoes in an old shopping bag, we departed for the Lester H. Tarnbauer Funeral Home. In the car, my sister informed us that Lester was also a heavy drinker who had known my father. Lester came out to greet us. He spoke in the dulcet tones of a man making an obscene phone call, murmuring condolences in a manner that bespoke years of practice. Lester had dark lifeless hair, a small decomposing mustache, and a waxy cadaverous complexion. He looked as if the hands on his watch were clammy. Why is it that so many morticians look cadaverous? My theory is that they spend so much time trying to make the deceased look good that they slowly start to think that looking like a corpse is looking good. It could be argued, though, that a fit, tanned funeral director might be too incongruous.

Lester then introduced us to his assistant Harold.

His face was as cheerful as Lester's was somber. Harold looked vaguely familiar to me. Carol later reminded me that he used to be a regular customer at Henry's, the hot dog stand where John, Carol, and I had worked during high school and college. "Remember? He used to drive the hearse up on his lunch break. And he always wore his stained work apron. That apron gave me the creeps. Henry used to make him park the hearse out back because he said it didn't look good for business."

Lester showed us the two viewing areas and he said that we were to be given the larger of the two. Most funeral homes have the dreariness of a well-ordered old-lady's apartment. The furniture is good, but it's also drab. I can't decide whether the atmosphere is depressing intentionally or incidentally. The setup of these places always reminds me of an auto dealer's, with the showrooms out in front and the service center in the back.

The first decision we had to make was to pick out a casket. Lester showed us the casket showroom, which bore an uncanny resemblance to a mattress store. The only difference being that comfort wasn't as important a consideration in this purchase. My mother was going to have a limited income and we didn't want to spend a huge amount of money on a casket. But we didn't want to be unseemly and put my father in the cheapest option—a plain pine box that looked exactly like the coffins in Westerns. Lester tactfully excused himself to give us an opportunity to discuss our choice. The most expensive models were made of bronze and other metals. They gave the impression that you weren't being buried but merely placed in storage. The other casket choices were oak, cherry, or walnut. Carol suddenly looked on the verge of tears.

"Let's get an oak one," I said. "Covered with drink rings and cigarette burns. We can set up a bar on it during the wake." Carol laughed, which is exactly what I wanted to hear.

Looking at the caskets, Tom said, "I want to be cremated."

I said, "Me too."

Carol then mentioned that our grandmother Smith once told her, "I think cremation is like you're already burning in hell. You might need your organs up in heaven. You don't know what you might need on the other side."

Did I mention that three of her four children became alcoholics?

We decided on a casket that was upholstered in a gray quilted fabric, oddly giving it the appearance of an oven mitt. For a casket, it was relatively inexpensive but it still cost more than any piece of furniture that my parents owned.

After we told Lester of our choice, he led us into his office to pick out a prayer card that would be printed with my father's name and date of death. Lester gave us a catalog to look through and then excused himself again. I never realized that death involved so much shopping. Each card had a small illustration and a spiritual message. Carol showed us a card that said, *God grant me the strength to accept the things I cannot change, courage to change the things I can, and the wisdom to know the difference.* She said, "When I read this one, I thought, This is perfect. Until I remembered that it's the prayer that they use in Alcoholics Anonymous."

I said, "Oh yeah, that would be really appropriate." Then I added, "Why don't we use this one with the chalice on top?"

We eventually chose a card that showed two hands held together in prayer. When we told Lester of our choice, his head nodded in sympathy for our plight. He ended his official consolation with an anecdote about my father. For years, my father had rebuilt car starters for extra money and recreation, and Lester said, "You know, your father rebuilt all the starters on our hearses and

ever since then we've never had a problem with any of them."

After Tom and I dropped Carol off at the house, we went to a florist's called Flowers By Michael because Tom's parents had asked him to pick out some flowers to send in their name.

After we told the middle-aged woman behind the counter our reason for being there, she kindly asked if we would like to see a catalog of funeral floral arrangements. It was filled with what the catalog called "Floral Tributes": red-and-white displays of carnations on easels, large floral crucifixes, and grand arrangements of flowers that could be draped over the casket. It occurred to me while we turned the pages that Tom and I had never sent flowers for a funeral. It's not that we've had such a limited experience with death. We've both buried more friends than some people twice our ages, but our friends have never had traditional funerals. Ralph insisted that his ashes be placed in a bright yellow cookie jar from his collection of Bauer pottery.

Tom took his time making a decision. While I appreciated the sentiment behind his wanting to buy the perfect flowers, I just wanted him to pick something quickly. But nothing in the catalog appealed to Tom. It's amazing that florists haven't increased the botanical possibilities for funerals. Cactuses or snapdragons could be sent in memory of really difficult relatives. Venus flytraps could be sent in memory of predatory businessmen or women who have been married more than three times. Sequoia and redwood saplings could be sent in remembrance of former hunks. A pitcher plant would have been appropriate for my father.

In the refrigerated display case there were several prepared floral arrangements. I tried to steer Tom into picking the one that had an unusual but attractive mixture of flowers, which included small yellow orchids. Finally, with trepidation commensurate to the purchase of

an automobile or house, Tom made his choice. He then had to write a card, but as he hesitated I snapped at him, "Just write, 'With deepest sympathy, The Lawrence Family.'" He did, and then after we gave instructions as to where the flowers should be delivered, the woman said, "That's the eighth order we've had for him. He must've been really well liked."

We went home to have lunch. As we made sandwiches, my mother mentioned that a loaf of banana bread had arrived from one of her neighbors, Marilyn. My mother had already filled us in about Marilyn.

"She makes all the money, while her husband stays home and takes care of the kids. And there's nothing wrong with that."

The loaf of banana bread was already almost finished. My sister claimed that John had practically sliced it while it was still in Marilyn's hands. The doorbell rang again. Another neighbor had brought over a large covered casserole dish. After my mother thanked her, we lifted the lid and peered inside. There was a repulsive congealed mass of chicken, pinto beans, sliced green beans, and pasta. One can always find forgiveness in one's heart but the stomach is implacable. Everyone let out a collective "Yuck."

"What the hell is that stuff?"

"She said it's stew."

"It looks more like, Chicken in a Casket."

"It's still warm from the oven."

"Yeah. Let it cool off before we throw it out. We don't want to start a fire."

Tom and I went upstairs to take a nap before dinner. We lapsed into my usual pattern whenever I visited: short bursts of interaction with my family followed by a nap or reading to pass the time.

When we came downstairs, John and Carol were going through my parents' bills and papers. My father kept

every important document stuffed in the top drawer of the buffet in the dining room. If the papers had been jammed in any tighter, the compression would have turned them back into lumber. My parents' filing system was that really important papers like their will and mortgage were bundled together in a large overstuffed envelope that was held together with rubber bands. Bills and other papers were loosely placed in a folder. The bookkeeping that we needed to do wasn't that complicated. We only had to figure out my parents' debts since we were already aware of their liabilities and our obligations.

So far, Carol had determined that they owed three huge credit card bills of more than ten thousand dollars each. Even though my father had a good pension, over the past few years they had spent more than they took in. From the evidence, my parents handled money like my father handled alcohol. No matter how much they had, it was never enough. They seemed to be researching a self-help book called *Spend What You Want and the Money Will Follow*.

They had even recently taken out a second mortgage on the house. My father had several confusing life insurance policies, but much of that money would be needed to pay off their bills. The most idiotic decision that they had made was to choose to have his state police pension end with his death because during his life it meant that they had received an extra few hundred dollars a month. My mother would now have to depend entirely on her meager social security check, which would be roughly a thousand dollars a month. One of my mother's favorite sayings whenever something bad or stupid happened was, "It's enough to make you drink." For the first time, I agreed. I was starting to think that the chaos in my family wasn't caused by the flapping of a mere butterfly's wings. It had to be caused by the flapping wings of Mothra, the giant monster moth of Japanese science-fiction movies.

My brother John informed my mother about her financial condition.

"How could you be so stupid? You're broke!"

"Oh, John. Let's not worry about that now. I'll be all right."

For my mother, the line between wishful thinking and delusion is like the border between Kansas and Nebraska: She crosses it without hesitation because she's never learned to distinguish between the two states.

"Well, someone has to worry about it."

"Oh, John, I forgot to tell you. Your boss called. He sounds nice. He said, 'If there's anything I can do. Please let me know.' "

"Yeah, there is. How about support you?"

We all laughed.

"Oh, you're quick." She then said to herself, "He sounded kind of nice. . . . Oh, shut up."

During our first visit, Tom had pointed out that my mother has a habit of making an assertion, questioning it, and then finally disagreeing with herself. As we drove through an older section of Buffalo, she would say, "The houses around here are nice. The people take good care of them. Well, not everyone does. I don't know. I guess it's not that nice. I don't like this area." Or she would say, "Your dad and I liked to eat out. We ate out all the time. Well, your father liked to eat at home too. So do I. I like to cook sometimes. There's nothing like a home-cooked meal. Oh, why cook? We eat too much anyway. I'm sick of eating." Her chains of thought are held together by missing links.

John continued for the rest of his stay to behave as if he was on a family business trip. He wanted to figure out what the financial figures were. Come up with a plan. Get it going. Then once everything's running smoothly, check on it occasionally to keep it running that way. Later, John said to me confidentially, almost as if he was giving me a tip on a good stock, "Now if you

and Ted send her a hundred fifty dollars a month each and I take care of her mortgage. She'll be fine."

While we were discussing my mother's destitution, the phone rang. It was Mr. Gardiner, our next-door neighbor, calling to ask if he could come to the earlier private viewing as he couldn't come to the later one because he had bowling. My mother agreed to this immediately because in Buffalo, even your own death isn't a valid excuse to miss bowling.

That night, Ted had prepared a hearty dinner of Chicken Parmesan and Baked Ziti, with Carrot Cake for dessert. Carol said to Ted, in a mock-sentimental tone, "Oh, Ted. You're making 'The Heart Attack Meal.'"

Ted smiled and said, "Oh, yeah. I forgot that. Well . . . eat up!"

Once before Ted had made this exact same meal at the fire hall and after dinner one of the firefighters had had a heart attack. Fortunately, the man lived, but from then on Ted's Chicken Parmesan and Carrot Cake was always called "The Heart Attack Meal." It lived up to its name. The carrot cake was made with three cups of oil and two pounds of cream cheese.

That night, my mother was in a sentimental mood. But my mother's remembrance of things past isn't a longing for lost happiness, she's more of a nostalgic Nostradamus who looks back with satisfaction about her previous predictions of doom. During the commercials, she would say, "I told your father that if he kept on drinking he'd kill himself. I said, 'Matthew, the drinking is going to kill you.' He wouldn't listen. Drinking's a sickness. I hope you kids don't drink. If you do, watch out."

After listening to her for the entire evening, when my mother went to bed, I said to her, "Lulu." Lulu was a nickname I had bestowed upon my mother when I was teenager, probably after reading a *New Yorker* profile about the actress Louise Brooks. "Remember, if *anyone* asks to marry you, you have our permission."

She said, "I'm not getting married again! Good night, Tom."

"Good night, Mrs. Smith."

"Don't stay up too late."

Thursday, January 4

Tom woke up the next morning and decided that he wanted to help my mother by cleaning out the basement. Our basement being the only mess in the house that could be cleaned up in one day. I couldn't decide if Tom just wanted some time away from my family or if he was going to attempt to tunnel his way out. When my mother was informed of his intention, she joked, "Never mind cleaning; just buy me a new place." Her response made us laugh because it was what she really thought. Carol decided to help Tom while I offered to get in their way.

During the late 1960s, my parents had remodeled our basement into a family recreation room, complete with a home bar. To create a tavernlike ambiance, a pool table was installed and the walls were hung with beer and liquor advertising signs. It's a look that allows alcoholics to feel that they're still having a night out even after their driver's licenses are revoked. One corner of the basement was also filled with my father's workbench, tools, and equipment for the boat. My sister sorted stuff in preparation for either giving it away or disposal. Ted had already asked for my father's complete set of wrenches. Carol took a digital volt meter, a battery tester, and a wood plane. Tom already had a complete set of tools, so we only took an official state police flashlight, a tiny rusty anvil splattered with old paint that I planned on using as a paperweight, and an old horseshoe that had belonged to my grandfather, who was raised on a farm. Carol warned us that according to superstition, the horseshoe had to be hung upright because otherwise all the luck would run out. She pointed out that my father

had had it hanging the wrong way for years and that he proved the truth of this folktale.

Sitting on a shelf was an objet d'art class that I had made when I was nine years old. It was originally a rectangular shaped liquor bottle. The reason why I had used that particular bottle for my project was because of the molded black-plastic cover that entirely hid the bottle's spout. It looked futuristic to me in 1968, an era when I imagined that by now we'd all be living in cities that looked like Brasília, the then new capital of Brazil.

Following the initial suggestions of our teacher, I had glued little squares of cardboard to the sides of the bottle in a random but what I thought was a very groovy pattern. Afterward, the entire bottle was covered with aluminum foil. Then black spray paint was applied to the bottle, but before the paint dried, I was instructed by the teacher to use a rag to quickly wipe off as much excess paint as possible, taking care not to tear the foil. The aluminum foil now looked burnished with the remaining black paint highlighting the cardboard cutouts. For years, the bottle sat on my dresser but at some point it had become a dispossession. Dispossessions are all the items that eventually end up in attics and basements where our sense of ownership has to fade before they can finally be thrown out.

After Tom and Carol had put the basement in order, we showered and changed into our clothes for the early viewing. As I stood in front of the mirror in our living room, fumbling with my necktie, I remembered that my father had taught me how to tie a necktie in front of the very same mirror. On Easter Sundays or other "dress-up" occasions, we three boys would take turns having our neckties tied by our father until we learned how to do it ourselves. He would first try to knot our ties while standing behind us, but he always became frustrated and then resorted to tying it on himself. He'd then slip the knotted tie over our heads like a lasso.

For the first time, I started to cry and Tom had to

help me finish knotting it. When everyone was finally ready, my mother commented on how nice everyone looked. "If only your father were here."

At the entrance to the funeral home, a large sign announced VIEWING ROOM A: THE SMITH FAMILY and VIEWING ROOM B: THE SMITH FAMILY. It made it seem as if my father could only be viewed in two separate caskets—the victim of some horrible accident. We peeked in Viewing Room A and saw an extremely elderly white-haired woman lying in a casket. My mother took one look at her and said in a loud whisper, "Oh, look at her. I don't want to be like that!" I wasn't sure if she meant being old or dead. I speculated on how the funeral home was going to distinguish between the two families. *"You're here for the Smiths? Alcoholism or Alzheimer's?"*

We had arrived early at the funeral home to make sure that we had time to see my father before anyone else. When we walked into the room we saw him lying in his casket. His face was heavily made up. It made him look like a tired old queen, which is not how most heterosexual men want to be remembered. His folded hands looked incredibly worn and wrinkled. When John knelt next to his casket, he immediately started crying. The only time I ever see men cry is at funerals. Men use their tears like windshield wiper fluid—sparingly and only when it's absolutely necessary. And afterward, we usually feel that instead of making things better, it just made things worse.

My father's friend Paul was the first person to arrive. I thanked him for coming and introduced him to Tom. Beforehand, I had already decided that I would introduce Tom to everyone and that my introduction would be, "I want you to meet a friend of mine, Tom." I was aware that this wasn't the most progressive position I could have taken, but I was feeling vulnerable and there are times when coming out to people starts to feel like a cuckoo coming out of a clock. I also rationalized that by

now, most people were capable of filling in the "boy" before "friend." Paul ran a collision shop. We had met only a few times previously, and before I had a chance to feel apprehensive as to what we were going to talk about, Paul mentioned the snow that had fallen the night before.

He said, "There's nothing like being a body man in Buffalo. The winter's my bread and butter. Every time it snows heavy, I know business is gonna be good. Now *you* drive carefully while you're here. But everyone else..." He chuckled as we both had visions of cars crashing.

He then asked me, "How's living in Los Angeles?"

My parents' friends know three facts about me: I'm a stand-up comic, I live in Los Angeles, and I'm gay. Which to most people in Buffalo is three deviant lifestyles. Paul also said, "You used to live in New York, right?" When I told him yes he continued, "My daughter lives in New York. She works at an art gallery." I've found from experience that many people regard the equation, New York + Art = Gay. So I took this to be an unspoken acknowledgment that he knew that I was gay and that he could handle the news without hostility. He confirmed this by saying, "You know, after you did your comedy special, your father scouted out every bar on Delaware Avenue trying to find the one with the largest big-screen TV. Well, he settled on Bob's Branch Office. Not his usual hangout, but a really big TV. He got all his buddies to watch your tape. And we even watched that lesbian too."

There were more than two dozen flower arrangements in the room. But instead of being an expression of grief, the flowers became a source of grief as Ted and John went around the room reading the cards in a competition as to who had the most flowers sent in his name. Ted was visibly distraught learning that John had more arrangements sent by his business acquaintances than Ted had received from his fellow firefighters. Carol saw

the flowers that Tom's family had sent and pointed them out to my mother. Tom still had doubts about the flowers though; "I should've picked something else," he told me.

My aunt Lorraine was the first of our relatives to arrive. She's my father's sister and I have a joke about her in my act: "My aunt Lorraine's a chain-smoker. She's always lighting up. True story. She once saved a man's life by giving him mouth-to-mouth resuscitation. Six months later, he was dead from emphysema." Aunt Lorraine was dressed in black slacks and a white-and-purple ski jacket. As she greeted everyone, I remembered that her oldest son, Neal, who was my sponsor at my confirmation, drank himself to death before he was thirty. He had literally collapsed in a bar and died. When I kissed Aunt Lorraine, I could smell liquor on her breath, which meant that she was relatively sober because normally you only caught a whiff of breath on her liquor. In my family, dying of alcoholism is dying of natural causes. I don't divide my family between optimists and pessimists who look at a glass and judge whether it's half full or half empty. My family is divided between alcoholics and co-dependents. The alcoholics are miserable because the glass is half empty while the co-dependents are miserable because the glass is half full.

When Aunt Lorraine walked up to the casket, she looked at my father and then said simply, "He looks better now than he has for the past eight months." A remark that my sister and I found hilarious, but we could only indicate this with a secretly exchanged look of amusement. It was also apparent that Aunt Lorraine was deeply pained by her brother's death.

My uncle Roger walked in while I was talking to Aunt Lorraine. Uncle Roger was my father's younger brother, and he started quietly crying when he saw my father. Uncle Roger had always been a very robust man, but he was gaunt now after having recently undergone triple bypass surgery. When Uncle Roger stood up from

my father's casket, he blew his nose violently and as he wiped it, he said to me, "Bob, do you know how many times your father bailed me out of Kenmore jail? Well, I used to go to The Bird to drink."

"The Bird" was the nickname of a well-known local bar called The Golden Pheasant. I assume that the nickname arose because it's easier to pronounce "The Bird" when you're drunk than "The Golden Pheasant."

"I could walk to The Bird. I didn't have to drive. That way, all I'd get arrested for was drunk and disorderly. Then your dad didn't have to pull too many strings because I wasn't driving while intoxicated. Now I don't drink at all. It almost killed me. It was hard to quit. I remember I had to stop eating Jane's chocolate-chip cookies for a while because the alcohol in the vanilla extract used to give me the shakes."

Tom listened to this story with a noncommittal expression rigidly imposed on his face to hide his dismay. While I was horrified to recall that The Bird was also the bar where I had my first underage drink with my high school buddies.

My aunt Jane and my cousins Betsy and Betty arrived in a separate car. Aunt Jane is very short and extremely heavy, but her most noticeable feature is that she shaves her eyebrows and then draws them back on in a startling manner. It looks like she has French accent marks over her èyés.

Betsy and Betty are identical twins. Betsy had lost weight and it was a relief to see that they had stopped dressing the same. When they were teenagers, Betsy (or was it Betty?) was much heavier than Betty, which had the unfortunate effect of making them appear to be Before and After models.

The big news in their family was that Uncle Roger had just received a paper shredder as a Christmas gift. For years, Uncle Roger had been concerned that it was conceivably possible for someone to go through his garbage and retrieve his personal papers. Uncle Roger is

slightly paranoid, although I don't regard him as a dangerous extremist because I once heard him say, "Goddamn hate groups. Goddamn hate groups. Kill 'em all, I say. Kill 'em all!" Knowing of their father's fears, his children had finally bought him a paper shredder and he claimed that it was the best gift that he had ever received. Aunt Jane was also enthusiastic about the shredder. She told me, "We use it all the time. I have two piles. Regular shred and double shred. Now when I see a story in the newspaper that I think will upset Roger, I can shred it before he reads it." When I inquired about double-shred, Uncle Roger said, "Bob, you can't be too careful. Someone's going to invent a machine to put the shreds back together."

As we discussed the far-fetched possibility of a paper-shred fuser, our next-door neighbor, Mr. Gardiner, and his son Mike arrived to express their condolences before they went bowling. Mr. Gardiner was a security guard and also drove a hearse part-time for another local funeral parlor. Being in the business, he complimented a competitor, "This is the first time I've ever seen Tarnbauer's work. They do a nice job. Your dad looks good. But I'm glad I'm not driving him. It's really sad when you know the person." When the Gardiners left, my mother said, "Oh, your father would rather have been buried in the basement than have Frank Gardiner drive him. He never cared for Frank Gardiner. I don't know why."

At 6:30, we returned for the evening viewing. The night didn't start off well because Ted had asked that we all stand in a receiving line near the casket when people started to come in. John, as usual, bristled at any suggestion that Ted made and instead he stood at the door greeting people. If it was possible to make a sad occasion even more miserable, my brothers seemed determined to do so. Maybe I'm old-fashioned, but I like funerals to be unpleasant because of the event, not the survivors. Carol was concerned that my father's honor guard from the state police hadn't arrived. Traditionally,

the state police send an honor guard to the funerals of all former members. Just as people started to arrive, two tall troopers in their full-dress uniforms arrived. They apologized profusely for being late. For the rest of the evening, they stood at either end of my father's closed casket, which was covered with an American flag and my father's state police hat.

The room was soon filled. The crowd was almost evenly divided among people my father worked with, people my father drank with, and people my father was related to. It was fairly easy to spot the people my father drank with: The men all had bright red faces that seemed to need beerblock, and the women were all "Attagirls"—hard blondes who momentarily softened when they offered their condolences.

Most of my father's friends were cops and auto mechanics. I was surprised by the number of men who said, "I recognized you because your father showed us your tape." I was proud of how my father had handled my being gay. He had never made me feel uncomfortable— I always did that to myself—and whenever I talked to him on the telephone he always asked about Tom.

For the entire night, Tom and I stood a pussyfoot apart from each other. A "pussyfoot" is the unit of measure that every gay couple learns to gage instinctively. It's the distance needed to indicate that you're together but far enough apart so as not to provoke comment.

When my cousin Darlene introduced us to her husband, he said, "Hey, I saw you on TV." To which I said, "Oh thanks" in reply, even though no compliment had been offered. I hadn't seen any of my cousins since moving to New York eleven years ago. Darlene also introduced us to her lovely teenage daughter, Nancy, whom I had never met. Later, Carol refreshed my memory about some aspects of our family's history that I had forgotten: "Remember, Darlene was married to that bigamist. Nancy's their daughter."

My cousin Jeremy said, "Hey, Bob howarya?" Jeremy

spoke in the flattest-sounding voice of my entire flat-sounding Buffalo-accented family. Measured on an oscilloscope, his voice would be straight line. He proudly announced that he had recently become engaged and apologized that his fiancée couldn't be here tonight because she couldn't get off work from the prison where she worked as a guard. Jeremy's engagement was a shock because everyone in our family had always assumed that he was gay. He was in his late thirties and, until recently, as far as anyone knew, he had never dated anyone of either sex. My family assumes that if a man has reached his late thirties and has never married, then he must be either gay or weird. I consider it a small social advance that they now consider homosexuality to be preferable to weirdness, whereas twenty years ago it would have been just the opposite.

A young woman in blue jeans and a denim jacket came up to me and said, "Your dad was a great guy. He's gonna be missed."

After I thanked her, Carol sidled over to me and whispered, "That was Janice from Fletcher's. She's the one who sent Dad the card when he was in the hospital." When my father was in the hospital for an enlarged heart due to alcoholism, a get-well card arrived that had a cartoon drawing of a patient in a hospital bed on the front and on the inside was written:

Here's a little riddle for you when you're not feeling well.
What's the difference between a bartender and a nurse?
A bartender puts a shot in your glass!
Get well soon.

The card was signed:

Janice & the gang at Fletcher's
P.S. You missed a good party at Don's house!

During their last visit to Buffalo, Carol and her husband, Mark, had been taken by my father to all his hangouts and she was now familiar with many of his friends and acquaintances.

"Carol, who's that woman in the red over there?" I discreetly indicated a big-boned woman whom I suspected of being a lesbian with the same degree of certainty that I suspected World War II was over.

"She's Melissa Darby, the bartender at Fletcher's. I went to school with her. *She's a lesbian.*" Carol said this as if she might have to explain the term to me.

"I know. That's why I asked."

"I met her when Dad took Mark and me up there. Her father was a cop. She's tough. She told us, 'Because my father was the head of the police, if anyone gets out of line, I can wrestle them to the ground.' Dad liked her. When she works nights, her girlfriend always sits at the end of the bar."

Then my mother tapped me on the shoulder. When I turned around she said, "Bob, these are some of the girls from Card Club. You know Mrs. Moreland, this is Mrs. Wooderowski, this is Ellie Bing . . ." Standing before me were five smiling women of my mother's age who had played cards with my mother for over thirty years. While talking to "the girls," the thought crossed my mind that I was having a good time at my father's funeral, which I guess was all right as long as I managed to feel guilty about it.

A priest arrived after we had been there for almost an hour. Father Ralph was in his early sixties and very businesslike. He said to Carol and me, "What was the deceased's name? And what was his rank?" I sympathized with his plight. He didn't know my father. He was like a stand-up who flies in to do a show and needs a local

reference to plug in for a punch line. He then asked who was going to speak the eulogy. I was momentarily flustered. The thought of a eulogy hadn't even occurred to me. I assumed that he would just say a prayer and give a blessing.

Carol asked if I wanted to give it. I didn't want to but I felt that it was easier for me to do it than anyone else in the family. I only wished that I had thought of this the day before. I didn't like the idea of trying to improvise a eulogy. Unlike stand-up comedy, eulogies have the same emotional motivation as a Billie Holiday song—the worse the audience felt, the better she was doing. My biggest fear was hecklers: *"He's dead but you're the one dying up there!"*

When the priest said, "Now we'll hear a few words about the man," I stood up and thanked everyone for coming and then said, "My father's rank in the state police was first sergeant but in our house he was the commissioner. . . ." To my surprise, it killed. I don't remember what else I said but I know that I mentioned that many of the values in my own life, such as my sense of humor and love of nature, were directly attributable to my father's influence. I closed by saying the obvious—that we would truly miss him.

Father Ralph ended the ceremony with a short prayer. As we prayed for my father's soul, I thought, *Death is like a blind date with God. We've heard all these great things about him, but we're not even sure if he's going to show up.*

What I should have talked about in my father's eulogy was a conversation that I'd just had with a black woman state trooper. Since she was the only African-American person in attendance, I asked her how she knew my father. She said that she had driven four hours to be there because she would never forget that when she had first joined the state police, after they were forced to admit women and minorities, my father had been the only trooper who was friendly toward her.

I was impressed when she told me this because I knew that my father disagreed with affirmative action. He thought that women weren't physically capable of handling the job and that it was unfair for someone to get in with a lower test score on the entrance exam. Her story illustrated something I clearly knew, that my father was kind and generous. My father's hostility was only directed against himself.

I also could have told another story about my father that I had only heard for the first time that afternoon from Uncle Roger. He told me that last year my parents had been to the Annual Policemen's Ball at the Knights of Columbus when some of the men at their table started talking about the "gays" and ended up talking about the "fags." My parents listened in embarrassed silence, waiting for them to finish. When they did, my father said, "You know, my son's gay. And it takes a lot more guts for him to deal with being gay than it does for jerks like you to sit there talking with your mouths full and your heads empty. And I don't have to listen to it. C'mon, Sue. Let's sit somewhere else." Uncle Roger laughed and added, "Your dad was still angry when he told me about it. And it took a lot to piss him off—I wish I had seen it."

People began to leave immediately after the ceremony. When the last person departed, Carol and John asked Lester if they could see my father one last time. Lester agreed to this but he asked if we would mind stepping out of the room for a minute because he would first like to "make sure that everything's all right." Lester's funereal manner made us imagine some ghoulish disfigurement that he would feverishly try to repair. When everything was found by Lester to be satisfactory, we came back in the room and then talked quietly about how many people had showed up and how it was nice to see everyone again. Finally, it was time to go and my mother and sister went up and kissed my father goodbye. Tears rolled down their faces as we left him. Even my mother was quiet as we drove back to the house.

259

* * *

When we arrived home, the first thing we did was have thick slices of the amaretto cheesecake that Ted had bought in case any people came back to the house. We ate in the living room and my mother became what she'd describe as "talkative." She changed the subject as the thought occurred to her. I sometimes feel that her brain works like a telephone. It doesn't process information, it only transmits it.

"We had a nice evening tonight," she said. "Why can't we have more times when we're all together like this?"

"Well, one reason is that you're too healthy."

"He didn't look very good," she said without missing a beat.

"Mom, you're not supposed to look good when you're dead. Unless you're a vampire."

After a moment, she continued. "People liked us. We were fun."

"Yeah, it's just your children who realized what assholes you were," I said, laughing.

"Hey, I want to tell all you kids. If you have any problems because of how we brought you up, get therapy. I don't want to be blamed for your problems. After this, blame yourself."

"Remember, Mom, you're alone," John said. "Not lonely. Alone. Not lonely." He had picked up this self-help mantra somewhere and had already told it to my mother several times.

"I know. I'll be okay. I put on Bob's tape when I want to see him. And if I want to be with Dad, I can put on the tape from his retirement party."

At one point Carol and John started reminiscing about some of the more notorious moments from our youth.

"Bob, remember when you got drunk with your friends from high school and totaled David's car in Mang Park?"

"John, remember when you got caught smoking pot by Dad? And remember the time when you and Patrick McCarthy put the cherry bomb in the Dusels' mailbox and the cops almost arrested you?"

"Carol, remember when you came home late from that party and Dad handcuffed you to the kitchen table?"

My mother smiled, looking off wistfully. "You kids had so much fun."

Monday, January 8

On Friday we sold my father's car and put my father's boat up for sale. Ted left early Saturday morning as he had to work at the fire department that evening. He offered to take more time off, but we all agreed that there was no reason for him to stay any longer. John left on Sunday, in order to make it back to work on Monday. His good-bye was, "Tom's nice. How the hell did he get stuck with you?"

This morning, I went to the funeral home to pick up ten notarized copies of my father's death certificate. We needed them for the life insurance claims, my mother's Social Security benefits, and to put the ownership of the cars in my mother's name. On the death certificate, listed under cause of death, was: CARDIAC ARREST DUE TO/OR AS A CONSEQUENCE OF: ALCOHOLIC CARDIO-MYOPOTHY AND CIRRHOSIS. It was one explanation.

We left on an afternoon flight, and by now Tom was ready to go. We had spent much more time with my family than we had on previous visits. When we brought our suitcases downstairs, Tom said, "It's going to be hard on your mother. Every day she's going to have to retell Marie over and over that your father died."

But I left feeling confident that my mother would be all right. I was also aware that I had left once before, thinking that my father had quit drinking. As we drove out to the airport, I said to my mother, "Well, Mom. It's been a lot of fun. I can't wait to come home for the next funeral."

It took her a moment to realize what I'd said before she laughed. "Oh, shut up! Tom, isn't he terrible? We're not having any more funerals." As we got out of the car, I reminded my mother, "If you feel lonely call us. You can always come out to visit." I believe Tom's body language stuttered on the word "visit."

As I leaned over and kissed her good-bye, a gray-haired woman approached us with a look of concern. "Hi, Sue. How are you doing?" She was one of my mother's friends from her card club, Mrs. Zarbo. I remembered seeing her at the funeral home. Before Tom and I could introduce ourselves, Mrs. Zarbo nodded her head in our direction. "Sue, are these your sons?"

My mother looked at Tom and smiled. "Yes, they are."

Acknowledgments

I **WANT** **TO** **THANK** my managers, Annie Albrecht and Bob Read, for their steadfast support and friendship, and my agent at Writers and Artists, Jim Stein.

I want to thank my wonderful editor and publisher, Rob Weisbach, for all of his enthusiasm and hard work. Thanks also to David Szanto and Gayatri Patnaik at Rob Weisbach Books.

Also thanks to the people who read parts of this book and offered advice and support: Carol and Mark Reifer, Marvin Bevins, Danny McWilliams, Lauren Dombrowski, Judy Gold, Glenn Rosenblum, Larry Hymes, Steve Kaplan, Michael Hart, Richard Dennis, Danny O'Donnell, and John Banta.

Then there are four people whose encouragement and assistance were invaluable: Suzy Berger, Jaffe Cohen, Elvira Kurt, and Tom Lasley.

And I want to thank my parents.